My
Learned
Friends

MY LEARNED FRIENDS

Adam Raphael

W H ALLEN

Copyright © Adam Raphael 1989

Printed and bound in Great Britain by
Mackays of Chatham Plc, Chatham, Kent
for the Publishers W. H. Allen & Co. Plc
Sekforde House, 175/9 St John Street,
London EC1V 4LL

ISBN 1 85227 094 2

CONTENTS

PREFACE

It is out of bad temper and ignorance that libel actions are born. Sir Patrick Hastings KC

This book should perhaps be dedicated to all the libel lawyers whose patience I have sorely tried over the years. My first encounter with the species came aged seven when I was walking with my barrister father one Sunday morning in Regents Park. I remember him greeting a whiskery man with sharp features who called back 'Who's that with you Geoffrey?' My father replied proudly 'That's my son.' 'Not much of a chap, is he?' joked Sir Patrick Hastings KC. I was furious, drew myself up to all of four feet and stomped off. If what I have written suggests a distrust of lawyers and the law of libel, it may be due to this early encounter with the most famous libel advocate of his generation.

I should also explain that much of this book was originally written when I was laid up in bed following a knee operation. As therapy it was splendid but more importantly it helped assuage the anger I felt on being described by the editor of the *Mail on Sunday*, Stewart Steven, as a betrayer of sources for giving evidence under subpoena in the Jeffrey Archer libel trial. That insult provided the spur to writing but what clinched the matter was the pressing need to finance my own libel action against the *Mail on Sunday*.

Though what follows cannot pretend to be dispassionate I hope I have been able to illustrate some of the dilemmas of ethics and the law that trouble the practising journalist. What

I have tried to give is an insider's view of libel from the perspective of a working reporter, who during a 30-year career in newspapers and television, has been a defendant, a witness, an honest broker, and finally a plaintiff.

The aim is to show through my own involvement in these cases backed by accounts of other notable recent actions why such an extraordinary poker game as libel has been permitted to continue unreformed for so long. Why do the costs frequently run into hundreds of thousands of pounds? Why are there such delays that it usually takes between two and four years for a case to come to court? Is there, in fact, any rhyme or reason to libel?

Or indeed anything resembling justice? The pianist Liberace was awarded £8,000 plus costs, a huge sum in 1959, for being described by Cassandra in the *Daily Mirror* as 'this deadly, winking, sniggering, chromium-plated, scent-impregnated, luminous, quavering, giggling, fruit-flavoured, mincing, ice-covered heap of Mother Love'. This, declared his Counsel, Gilbert Beyfus QC, carried the totally false innuendo that the pianist was a homosexual. A quarter of a century later Liberace died of AIDS after being sued for palimony by one of his many male lovers.

Is libel, in short, anything more than a cosy cartel for a handful of rich barristers, solicitors, and plaintiffs? Or is the truth perhaps simpler — that the British press has got what it deserves because the public, though it may love reading scandal, detests the ethics of Grub Street?

Damages in Britain have not yet reached the scale of the $26.5 million awarded to an all-American beauty queen for the distress caused to her by an article in *Penthouse* which claimed that her talent for oral sex was such that her lovers would levitate. But recent British awards of £300,000 to Miss Koo Stark, £500,000 to Jeffrey Archer, £600,000 to Sonia Sutcliffe, and the £1 million settlement out of court to Elton John suggest we are moving inexorably in that direction. In

King Alfred's time the slanderer had a choice of losing either a tongue or an ear. Today he has no such option. He merely pays through the nose; but in the end, as even successful plaintiffs find out, the only real victors of a libel action are the lawyers.

I should like to thank a large number of people who helped me in the writing of this book, in particular Malcolm Dean, Lloyd Turner, Derek Jameson, Charlotte Cornwell, Michael Meacher MP, Neil Hamilton MP, Alan Watkins, David Montgomery, Paul Foot, Laurence Marks, Ian Jack, Jonathan Mantle, David Hooper, Geoffrey Wansell, Andrew Neil, James Hogan, Michael Cockerell, Alastair Brett, Rupert Morris, Paul Halloran, Peter Preston, Andrew Roth, Julia Braybrook, Tom Crone and Geoffrey Bindman. I have also drawn on a large number of published sources — newspapers, magazines and books. A brief bibliography appears at the end.

I owe a considerable debt to those distinguished members of my profession — Lord Rees-Mogg, Alastair Hetherington, Andreas Whittam Smith, Lord Ardwick, Geoffrey Goodman, Bob Farmer, Louis Heren and Hugh Stephenson — who were willing to give evidence on my behalf in my libel action against the *Mail on Sunday*. My colleagues on *The Observer*, Adrian Hamilton, William Keegan, and Donald Trelford loyally stuck by me and patiently read sections of the manuscript. Not least I should like to pay tribute to my lawyers, Cyril Glasser, Andrew Nicol, David Mackie, Kate Buckley, James Price and David Eady QC for putting up with such a demanding client. Finally this book could not have been written without the encouragement and unerring eye for detail of my wife Caroline and the skill of my daughter Anna in digging out the relevant quotations.

AR, January 1989.

1

The Witness's Tale

Give your evidence,' said the King
'and don't be nervous, or I'll
have you executed on the spot.'

Lewis Carroll, Alice's Adventures in Wonderland

I was semi-comatose early one April morning when the doorbell rang. By the time I had stumbled out of bed and got downstairs Caroline, my wife, had let the caller in. He was a slightly built young man in a fawn mackintosh who looked like an insurance salesman. I was just about to say 'no thanks' when he thrust a subpoena in my hand accompanied by three £5 notes with the explanation this was my court appearance fee.

Still only half awake, I took the subpoena and spurned the money. As soon as he had left I cursed. The £15 would at least have bought a few drinks — and, as it turned out, it would not have made much of a dent in the £1 million that Jeffrey Archer's libel trial was eventually to cost.

The court summons, though unwelcome, wasn't totally unexpected. Through ill luck and a weakness for characters who make me laugh, I had got myself embroiled in 'the libel case of the century'. That, at least, was how it was described by the judge who eventually presided over Jeffrey Archer versus *The Star*. It began innocently enough one Saturday night in October 1986 when I was Political Editor of *The Observer*. Just before the first edition was printed around 7pm the News Editor, Angela Gordon, called me over. She said she had just received a tip that the *News of the World* would be running a story alleging that Jeffrey Archer had given a large sum of money to a prostitute to prevent her talking about their relationship. The report was regarded by the *News of the World* as so 'hot' that in a vain attempt to keep its exclusive to itself, it had printed a dummy first edition to try and throw its rivals off the scent.

The basis of the story was a series of tape-recorded telephone conversations between Archer and a Shepherd Market prostitute, Monica 'Debbie' Coghlan. The calls had been made by Monica on the orders of the *News of the World* in an attempt to confirm a story — being touted by an Asian solicitor Aziz Kurtha that Archer had been with a prostitute. After three weeks of telephone calls from Monica, Archer offered to give her money to go abroad. The Tory Deputy Chairman, it seemed, had been neatly trapped. That Sunday's *News of the World* was headlined, 'Tory Boss Archer pays off Vice Girl'. It quoted Archer as saying to Monica, 'Go as quickly as you can . . . you are being very brave, I admire you.'

In its inside pages, the paper carried an extensive account of this last call between Archer and Monica:

MONICA: I'm not trying to hassle you.

ARCHER: I realise you're not. What I'm saying is, would you go abroad if financially taken care of?

MONICA: Yes.

ARCHER: Would you be safe there?

MONICA: Yes.

ARCHER: And happy there?

MONICA: Yes.

ARCHER: How much money would that take?

MONICA: About three hundred for the flight, something like that, a bungalow and spending money while I was there. Look, I'm not after money. All I want you to do for me is just to let me go back to a normal life.

ARCHER: Well I'm trying very hard but it might help if

2

you were able to pop abroad again.

MONICA: You're sending me away for two weeks — what difference is that going to make? I want a normal life. What guarantee have I got of being left alone?

ARCHER: I can't guarantee that. You must understand. I'm trying everything I can think of.

MONICA: It's Kurtha that really worries me.

ARCHER: Well I will tell you that after today, he'll be a very frightened man . . . the longer period you can go abroad the better.

The 'phone call ended with Archer telling Monica that he would arrange for a friend — 'forty-five, grey hair, a little overweight' — to hand her a package of money at the entrance to platform three, Victoria Station the next day at 11am. This meeting, like the phone conversation, was monitored and taped by the *News of the World*.

With an election approaching it was clearly a story that I couldn't ignore. Archer was a very high profile character, not least because he was close to the Prime Minister who had insisted that he should be appointed Deputy Party Chairman. But I didn't approach writing about his alleged dalliance with a prostitute with much enthusiasm, having always taken the view that the sexual peccadilloes of politicians are their own concern. Nor was the *News of the World* report the first I had heard of the scandal.

Three weeks before, at the Conservative Party Conference in Brighton, I had had a brief conversation with the Prime Minister's favourite media adviser Sir Gordon Reece, who wanted to know why so many investigative reporters were around. 'Is there a sex scandal brewing?' he asked. I confessed ignorance but later I heard that a tale about a top Tory and a prostitute had begun to do its rounds. It was not the sort of thing that *The Observer* would touch so I thought no more about it. When I eventually learnt who the Tory was, I groaned.

Jeffrey Archer was a fringe figure, whom I knew and liked as a kind of political Walter Mitty. You couldn't take anything that he said very seriously but he was an amiable host, a perennial optimist, and above all he made me laugh. Jeffrey was a story teller and the fact that his stories often strayed into the realms of fantasy made them no worse for that. Politics can be a grey business and he lent a much needed dash of colour to the Tory Party.

But this time it looked as though the millionaire novelist had gone a bit too far in keeping up with his own larger-than-life reputation. I had three telephone numbers for him, his car, his London flat, and his home in Grantchester. I tried the last first as I thought at the weekend he was likely to be in the country. It was engaged; after a few minutes I tried again and the phone was answered by Archer.

Not surprisingly he sounded upset. When I asked him about the *News of the World*'s story he said that he had just been rung by the Editor of *The Sunday Times*, Andrew Neil, who had assured him that he was not going to run a single line about the story. Would I do the same? I replied that was not a decision for me but I would pass on his request to *The Observer*'s Editor, Donald Trelford. Archer then insisted that he must not be quoted directly, a tactic he frequently employed. But off the record — in other words for use unattributably — he told me he knew his political career was effectively at an end. 'Whatever I do, I won't let the party down,' he said.

When I asked him how on earth he had allowed himself to be trapped in this extraordinary way, I didn't get a coherent response. What happened next was to be the subject of a distinct difference of recollection between Archer and myself. When I pressed him, as the Court was to hear later from me, how long he had known Monica, he replied that he had met her only once 'very casually, six months ago'. At the time I thought little about this admission, not regarding it as particularly significant, which is why it was buried well down my story. I merely felt sorry that his resumed political career, by which he set so much store, might be destroyed because of one casual encounter with a prostitute. What interested me was not so much Archer's apparent acknowledgement that he had met Monica, but his recognition that he would have to resign his party post because of the resulting scandal.

In its next edition *The Observer* published my story which I wrote in haste after consulting the editor. The headline was 'Archer to Quit over Call Girl,' with my report predicting that the Tory Deputy Chairman would resign within 48 hours. The story made clear that I had spoken directly to Archer for it quoted him as saying that he had 'absolutely no comment' to make on the *News of the World* allegations. But *The Observer*'s front page report also quoted 'friends' of Archer as saying 'Whatever Jeffrey does, he won't let the party down,' and then further quoted the same 'friends' as claiming that he had met Monica 'Debbie' Coghlan only once 'very casually six months ago'.

The use of the ambiguous word 'friends' was a journalistic convention designed to hide the source of the information. However it was the thinnest of veils which would not have fooled any of my colleagues or for that matter many politicians at Westminster. The story in print, I went home looking forward to going on holiday the next day with my wife and two children.

On my return after a week in Mallorca, blissfully without newspapers, I was thus unaware that Archer had issued a statement categorically denying that he had ever met Monica, and had issued a writ for libel against the *News of the World*. Why, in the light of what he had told me, did he deny meeting Monica? I had never thought for a moment that Archer was telling me the whole story when I spoke to him that Saturday night. He was clearly very upset and determined so far as he could to limit the damage to his political career. But it was obviously compounding his problems to say two different things within 24 hours. When he told me that he had met Monica — 'very casually six months ago' — which was the evidence I was later to give to the court, what was in his mind? Could there have been a misunderstanding on the telephone as to what I had asked him? Was he so upset that he couldn't think straight that night? Certainly if Archer had told me that he had never met Monica, I would have pressed him very hard as to why he had paid her £2,000. I am still uncertain about the answers to these questions. All I am sure of is that I accurately reported what he said to me that night.

Many weeks later I learnt what happened in the hours after I spoke to Archer. Following a barrage of phone calls and a sleepless night, Archer had got up at dawn on Sunday and driven to London to see his lawyer, Lord Mishcon. The veteran Labour Peer asked his client only three questions. Did you sleep with this prostitute? Have you gone with any other prostitute? Do you still want to pursue a political career? Archer, who is still a prep school master at heart, replied briskly, 'No Sir,' to the first two and an emphatic 'Yes Sir,' to the last. That was enough for Mishcon, one of the shrewdest operators on the legal stage. Later that day, in a statement issued by his solicitor on his behalf, Archer flatly denied ever having set eyes on the prostitute let alone having slept with her: 'I have never — I repeat never — met Monica Coghlan nor have I ever had any association of any kind with a prostitute.'

Archer explained that some weeks before he had been telephoned by a woman calling herself 'Debbie' who said that she was a prostitute. A client of hers, she told him, was letting it be known that she and Archer had met in Shepherd's Market, Mayfair and had had 'an association'. He recounted that he had received several more phone calls from the prostitute. 'Foolishly, in my belief that this woman genuinely wanted to be out of the way of the Press and realising that for my part any publicity of this kind would be extremely harmful to me', he had offered to pay her money to go abroad for a short period until the heat had died down. 'For that lack of judgment and that alone, I have tendered my resignation to the Prime Minister as Deputy Chairman of the Conservative Party.'

This statement was regarded with scepticism in Fleet Street. Why should Archer have paid £2,000 to a girl he had never met merely on the basis of a few 'phone calls? Why hadn't he gone to the police and said he was being blackmailed? Why, when he had known that the tabloid papers were sniffing at the story, had he allowed himself to be trapped in this naive way? Why had he told *The Observer* that he had met Monica? Nowhere was the scepticism more rife than at *The Star*, then desperately fighting for its share of the ultra-competitive tabloid market.

The next day, Monday October 27, *The Star*'s Editor Lloyd Turner had a conference with his senior executives and told them he was determined to nail Archer. Turner ordered his staff to 'infiltrate' the *News of the World* and to carry out their own investigation into the scandal, to see if Archer was telling the truth. The story that 'Britain's Liveliest Daily', as *The Star* liked to describe itself, eventually came up with was largely based on the word of Monica Coghlan's nephew Tony Smith whom the paper had found in Manchester. The following Saturday *The Star*'s front page splash was 'Poor Jeffrey', with the sub-heading, 'Vice Girl Monica talks about Archer — the Man she Knew'. Basically it was a follow-up of the *News of the World*'s exclusive. But in one respect *The Star* went much further in suggesting that Archer had lied when he denied ever meeting Monica.

The Star's report, however, did not support its headline. It began confidently: 'Inter-City hooker yesterday told for the first time about her part in the downfall of Tory Party boss Jeffrey Archer.' But the second paragraph gave the game away, showing that the paper had not actually managed to speak to

Monica Coghlan who was being closely guarded by the *News of the World*. All *The Star* could write was: 'Speaking from a London hotel hideaway, she has told relatives: "I do feel sorry for Jeffrey . . . I didn't think he would have to resign. I didn't do this in order to lose him his job. Frankly, I didn't think it would cause so much fuss." '

The Star's report continued: 'Yesterday, Monica's nephew Tony Smith told of his conversations with the prostitute who was offered £2,000 by Archer to leave the country to avoid a possible scandal. Mr Smith said that Monica added: "The thing that angers me is that he keeps saying, 'I never, never, repeat never met this woman'." Lawyers acting for Mr Archer yesterday refused to discuss Monica's claim. "Mr Archer will have no comment", we were told.'

Apart from this conversation with Monica's nephew, *The Star* did not have much to report except to toss in the lurid claim that 90 per cent of Monica's clients were keen on various forms of sexual perversion, including one who liked dressing up as Little Red Riding Hood.

A second writ for libel was now issued by Archer. The first I knew of this was some weeks later. Shortly after Christmas I was telephoned at Lime Grove, where I had gone to work for the BBC current affairs programme Newsnight, by Lovell White and King, a firm of city solicitors who said they were acting for *The Star* against Archer. They asked where I had got the quotes used in *The Observer*'s front page article; in particular they wanted to know who were the 'friends' that I had quoted as saying that Archer had met Monica Coghlan once 'very casually six months ago'.

This information and its source was obviously crucial to *The Star*'s hopes of defending Archer's libel action because it appeared to contradict his claim that he had never met the prostitute. But I told *The Star*'s lawyers bluntly I was not prepared to help. They seemed unhappy as well they might have been. Unlike the *News of the World*, which had telephone

8

tapes and photographs to support its story of the pay-off, *The Star* had little to go on. Moreover the *News of the World* had published its original story in a deliberately ambiguous form which, unlike *The Star*'s report, left unclear whether Archer had ever actually been a client of Monica's.

The weakness of this second story explains why Archer chose to sue *The Star* first rather than the *News of the World* and why he was anxious to accelerate this action. A libel case normally takes at least two years to get to court but the Tory Deputy Chairman, claiming that his political career was in ruins, most unusually, succeeded in jumping the queue.

With the action set down for an early trial, I knew I was in serious trouble, not least because *The Star* clearly had more than a shrewd suspicion who my source was. An internal memorandum, written by its Editor Lloyd Turner on October 30, four days after the *News of the World* story, claimed that 'our political people said Raphael was telling other political editors that Archer had told him that he had met Coghlan.'

That, in fact, was wrong. Quite apart from being on holiday at the time I was alleged to have chatted to fellow lobby journalists, I had at that point told no one apart from my senior colleagues at *The Observer*. But in the light of the way the story had been written, and the fact that an almost identical story had appeared in another Sunday paper, *Sunday Today*, it was not surprising that *The Star* assumed Archer to be my source. It was not something, though, that I could admit publicly without breaching the confidence of my conversation with the Tory Deputy Chairman.

But once the subpoena was slapped on me I realised I would be pressed to disclose my source under threat of contempt proceedings. If I did so I knew I would be regarded by many in my profession as a betrayer of sources. If I didn't and refused to give evidence in defiance of the court, I would be liable to an unlimited fine or imprisonment. Neither option was attractive.

I was not the first journalist to be in such a dilemma. The most famous case was the Vassall Spy Tribunal in 1963 when two journalists, Brendan Mulholland of the *Daily Mail* and Reg Foster, a freelance, went to prison for six months for refusing to reveal their sources. In the case of Attorney General v Mulholland, Lord Denning said the interests of justice were paramount. 'The judge will not direct him to answer,' he said, 'unless it is not only relevant but also a proper and indeed necessary question in the course of justice to be put and answered.'

Partly as a result of the storm of protest that these sentences provoked, the law of contempt was modified in 1981 in an attempt to give journalists qualified protection from having to breach confidences. The key amendment, which became Section 10 of that act, provided that 'no court may require a person to disclose, nor is any person guilty of contempt for refusing to disclose, the source of information contained in a publication for which he is responsible, unless it is established to the satisfaction of the Court that disclosure is necessary in the interests of justice or national security, or for the prevention of disorder or crime.'

Section 10, however, proved to be of little help to journalists seeking to protect their sources as *The Guardian* found to its cost in the Sarah Tisdall case in 1983. She was a junior civil servant working in the Foreign Secretary's private office who anonymously sent the paper through the post confidential documents outlining the way the Government proposed to handle the deployment of Cruise missiles in Britain. On October 31st *The Guardian* published a story based on this secret windfall headlined, 'Heseltine's Briefing to Thatcher on Cruise'. This was such an obvious breach of security that the Treasury Solicitor demanded the return of the documents which the paper foolishly had failed to destroy. *The Guardian* realised it was now trapped. In an attempt to protect its anonymous informant the paper appealed in vain right up to the House of Lords against having to hand over the documents which it rightly feared would identify the source.

By a majority of three to two, the Law Lords decided against *The Guardian* — the Master of the Rolls, Lord Donaldson saying: 'The maintenance of national security requires that trustworthy servants in a position to mishandle highly classified documents passing from the Secretary of State for Defence to other Ministers shall be identified at the earlier possible moment and removed from their positions. This is blindingly obvious. Whether or not the Editor acted in the public interest in publishing the document was not the issue.'

This judgment forced *The Guardian* to hand over the documents to the Government with inevitable consequences. Miss Tisdall was traced, dismissed from her job, and eventually sentenced to six months' imprisonment much to the chagrin of Fleet Street which blamed *The Guardian* for not protecting her. A similar problem occurred in 1988 when *The Independent* was fined £20,000 after appealing in vain to the Law Lords in an attempt to protect one of its business reporters, Jeremy Warner, from having to disclose his source to a Department of Trade inquiry into insider trading. In effect Section 10 is a broken reed as far as journalists are concerned for when a court rules, as it invariably does, that the evidence is necessary in the interests of justice or national security the journalist has no protection.

These precedents were not encouraging but in the faint hope that I could find a legal loophole, I appealed to *The Observer* for help. Though I was no longer working for the paper, having defected to the BBC, I thought, rightly as it turned out, that they would do what they could for me. The initial advice from *The Observer*'s solicitor, David O'Callaghan of Turner Kenneth Brown, was bleak. He pointed out that Section 10 of the Contempt of Court Act 1981 only protected a journalist from having to reveal his source where the information was not regarded as essential in the interests of justice. He further noted that *The Star*'s solicitors had said that if I refused to reveal my source they would press for a disclosure order on the grounds that the information was vital to the defence's plea of justification. A further letter from Lovell White and King said they had been advised by leading counsel that Section 10 afforded me no protection in the circumstances of the case.

An even more discouraging opinion was now given by counsel whom *The Observer* had retained. At a meeting on June 24th, James Price advised in uncompromising terms that Section 10 gave me no immunity because what *The Star* was seeking from me was 'necessary in the interests of justice'. The issue was so clear cut, he said, that it was not even worth my being legally represented in court. In short, the legal advice was that if I refused to answer questions about my source I would be in contempt and would be liable to imprisonment and/or a fine until such time as I had purged my contempt. The only other option was to breach the confidence of my conversation with Archer but that I knew could potentially be very damaging because Ministers and other political sources who trusted me might cease to do so.

At this point I wasn't at all sure what I should do — just very worried. I should perhaps explain why betraying a source is regarded as about the worst offence that a journalist can commit. There is first the obvious pragmatic reason, that if a journalist gets a reputation as someone who does not protect those who give him information he will be mistrusted and be unable to get stories of any real importance. Second and more important is the moral issue. If, for instance, a civil servant had leaked a document to me during the Westland affair showing that the Prime Minister had lied to the House of Commons I would have been under an absolute obligation to keep secret his or her identity whatever the consequences, even if it meant going to prison for contempt.

It is not difficult, though, to think of circumstances when a journalist should place his duty as a citizen above that of a professional duty to protect his source. Say, for example, I was rung up by someone who said he wanted to tell me in confidence that he had learnt of a plot to blow up the Prime Minister at the Tory Party Conference but was too frightened to go to the police. I would have no hesitation in disclosing the identity of my source to Special Branch.

A journalist is not like a priest in a confessional or even a doctor who is obliged to protect his patient's confidence in all circumstances. What should determine a journalist's conduct is first of all the degree of trust that has been established between him and his source. But there are also other important issues: the public interest at stake, the interests of justice, the motives of the source in giving the information and the consequences if his identity was revealed. In the weeks before the Archer case came to trial I tried to apply this basic code of ethics to what I should do. It was not straightforward. My conversation with Archer that Saturday night, particularly the most sensitive bits of it, had clearly been 'off the record'. On the other hand if I refused to give evidence in his libel action on grounds that I was bound by confidence, the only result, apart from my going to prison for contempt of court, might be to pervert the course of justice.

Jeffrey Archer, moreover, had a reputation among journalists for darting on and off the record to suit his own purposes. In his conversation with me that night, whether or not he had told the truth, he was clearly trying to limit the damage. He was now bringing a libel action to clear his name and save his political career. The idea of going to prison for such a cause was not at all attractive either personally or professionally. But there appeared to be no alternative.

Archer knew of my dilemma because I was careful to keep him informed. But whenever I contacted him in the months leading up to the trial, he sounded confident that the case would be settled long before it got to court. Perhaps foolishly, I shared his view. I couldn't believe he would want to subject himself and his family to the ordeal of a trial of which the outcome must be uncertain. It struck me as a risk that not even the most hardened of gamblers would want to take. But as the trial drew near and there was no settlement, I became increasingly nervous. *The Star*'s subpoena began to look like a classic no-win situation and I started to joke that my address for the next year or so was likely to be Wormwood Scrubs, the insalubrious West London prison near my home.

It was, I thought ruefully, a ludicrous outcome to my relationship with Jeffrey Archer. I had first met him at a dinner given by the genial Conservative Party Treasurer, Alastair McAlpine in the late 1970s. All I remember of the evening was reeling home in amused disbelief at the stories he told. Archer's wife Mary takes a scientific view of her husband's story-telling. 'Jeffrey,' she once said in a burst of candour, 'has a gift for inaccurate precis.' An *Observer* profile written by that prince of profile writers Laurence Marks put it rather more sharply: 'All good raconteurs ornament the truth. Archer's technique is more radical. The facts of the story are usually true (more or less), but they have been dismantled, new roles allocated, details dramatised as dialogue, and then reassembled again. It is, so to speak, the Cubist school of table-talk; the effect is striking but somewhat lacking in verisimilitude.'

Archer, a generous host who cultivated journalists, used to invite me to parties at his penthouse overlooking the Thames. I usually accepted, not on account of the food — tepid shepherd's pie and warm champagne — but because they were among the best political gatherings in London, full of Cabinet Ministers at their most indiscreet.

Jeffrey liked to claim that only the Prime Minister and the Queen drew bigger audiences than he did around the country. There was something in this engaging boast for he went down wonderfully with blue-rinsed Tory matrons and there was no doubting his genuine passion for politics. He was hungry for political power, nakedly ambitious and almost touching in his egocentricity and longing to be praised. He fervently believed that one day he would work his way to the top of a Tory Cabinet.

Archer's dreams of a reborn brilliant political career had been fuelled by the Prime Minister's insistence that he should be given a key role in the 1987 election, to the horror of the party Chairman Norman Tebbit, who was only too well aware that he was the wildest of wild cards. But Mrs Thatcher would hear nothing against Jeffrey. She liked his bubbling optimism and the flattery he absorbed and laid on with a trowel. The Tory Deputy Chairman may have been a bit of a card but I certainly had no wish to injure him. His entrapment by the *News of the World*, whatever the truth of the story, had been sordid. I felt genuinely very sorry for him. But the idea of committing contempt and going to prison to rescue his political career had even less appeal.

I was trapped. After my counsel's advice that it was not even worth my being represented in court as there was no legal basis on which I could refuse to answer questions, it was clear that I was on my own. I hadn't yet made up my mind what to do but felt that initially I would have to refuse to disclose that Archer was my source. If I was then cited for contempt, I could ask for an adjournment which would at least give me an opportunity to talk to Archer in private and ask to be released from the confidence. If he refused, what then? I am not sure what I would have done. All I know is that I would have had some very harsh words to say to him about the position he had put me in.

In the event all this pre-trial agonising was unnecessary. A few days before the hearing began in the High Court, I was advised by *The Observer*'s solicitor, Julia Braybrook, that Archer would be going into the witness box at the start of the trial and was certain to give evidence about his conversation with me that night. *The Star*'s solicitors, Lovell White and King, had feared that Archer might not be produced as a witness. But as soon as I heard that he was going to give evidence, and that he would appear in the witness box before me, I realised with relief that I was off the hook.

From that moment I concluded, rightly or wrongly, that I had little to be worried about. Archer was bound to be questioned about his conversation with me that night; once he had given detailed evidence it would be he, not I, who breached the confidence of our talk. It was a view shared by my closest friends on *The Observer*, Adrian Hamilton, the Foreign Editor and William Keegan, the Economics Editor whom I had anxiously consulted. *The Observer*'s then Deputy Editor, Tony Howard, who is one of the shrewdest commentators on the media, also confirmed that I would be under no obligation if Archer first gave evidence about the conversation. But, to make doubly sure that Archer should be in no doubt about my position, I rang him two weeks before the trial and put the point directly to him.

'You realise Jeffrey, do you, that if you give evidence about our conversation I won't be bound by confidence and if I then give my version it is bound to be very damaging to you?' Archer did not reply directly but indicated that his recollection of our conversation that night was very different from mine. I replied I would have to tell the truth as I remembered it and urged him, 'For goodness sake, Jeffrey, please, please settle. The last thing I want to do is give evidence against you. This case can't do you any good.' The telephone call ended on reasonably good terms with Jeffrey assuring me, 'Don't worry, it will all be settled.'

Archer's optimism turned out not to be justified, although in retrospect *The Star* would have been well advised to have apologised handsomely and to have paid him substantial damages. There had already been one serious attempt at peace. In January Lord Mishcon, Archer's solicitor, telephoned *The*

Star's solicitors, Lovell White and King, and suggested a settlement on the lines of large but unspecified damages, all Archer's legal costs paid and a prominent front page apology. It was the last demand that stuck in the craw of *The Star*'s Editor, Lloyd Turner, and the offer was rejected.

Towards the end of June Lovell White and King warned me in a hand-delivered letter that I would be required to give evidence and that I should make myself available for the whole of the first week of July. Jeffrey Archer had, through Mishcon, engaged Robert Alexander QC to represent him. It was to prove a shrewd choice. Alexander, a tall, gangling, aloof figure, described by Lord Denning as the best advocate of his generation, had a formidable reputation. *The Guardian* once claimed he earned more than £1 million a year, which provoked an unanswered challenge from Alexander that if the paper would undertake to donate to charity the amount by which his earnings fell below seven figures, he would give precise details of his income.

Alexander's success was based on his knack of charming judges. But underneath his old world courtesy was a rapier intellect and an ice-cold cross-examiner. His view of the case in his first meeting with Archer was by no means optimistic. How the trial would go, he felt, was 'extremely open'; the odds were no better than evens. The payment of money to Monica, he warned, might prejudice the jury against him. He stressed to Archer that if he was to win, nothing unexpected must emerge during the trial. Archer's legal team were also understandably worried by the evidence that they knew I was likely to give.

The Star's defence team, for their part, were even gloomier about their prospects at trial. The assessment of Patrick Sherrington, a senior partner at Lovell White and King, was that the case would turn on the cross-examination of Archer. Was he telling the truth when he said he had never met Monica despite having paid her £2,000? Sherrington believed it was essential to have a really tough criminal advocate who was skilled at destroying defendants in the witness box. 'We are going to need someone who's really aggressive, who can break Archer,' he said.

That is why Michael Hill, a former chairman of the Criminal Bar Association, with a reputation 'for making murderers weep' was chosen. He had won a number of big headline criminal cases, among them the convictions of the Guildford IRA bombers. But defending a tabloid paper was an altogether different game from pursuing crooks at the Old Bailey. Right from the start Hill took a pessimistic view of *The Star*'s chances before a jury, warning its Editor at a meeting on April 22nd 'You won't win.'

At the next meeting on May 29th, Hill was slightly less pessimistic: 'If Kurtha proves a good witness, we might make it.' *The Star*'s final meeting with counsel took place in the week before the trial. By then Hill was taking a sunnier view saying that he thought Monica would get angry if her veracity was attacked. 'We are in with a chance,' he said.

Right up to the last moment both sides thought there might be a settlement. On Monday June 29th, just a week before the trial was due to begin, the Chairman of Express Newspapers, Lord Stevens, received a personal call from Archer whom he knew slightly but with little affection. 'What I want,' said Jeffrey, 'is £1 more than David Steel got, that's £100,001.' Stevens pointed out that *The Star* had in fact paid Steel only £10,000 for a crude pre-election libel suggesting falsely he was having an affair with a fellow politician's wife. But the real sticking point, as with the first attempt to settle in January, was not money but Archer's demand that 'most of the front page of *The Star*' should be devoted to a grovelling apology.

Stevens was not willing to do this. 'Why should we give in to that little shit?' he remarked to colleagues. The peace attempt thus ended inconclusively. 'You get your lawyers to get in touch with mine,' said Archer. 'No,' said Stevens, 'You get your lawyers to get in touch with ours.' For the publisher of Express Newspapers it was to prove an expensive piece of hubris.

2

In Court

Remember Mrs Archer in the witness box.
Your vision of her probably will never disappear.
Has she elegance? Has she fragrance?
Mr Justice Caulfield

Seven days later on July 26th, 1987, in the oak-panelled Number 13 court at the Royal Courts of Justice in the Strand, the case of Archer v *The Star* newspaper began before Mr Justice Caulfield. Aged 73, he was one of the most senior High Court judges but ominously for *The Star*, he had a reputation for having no love for Fleet Street. A northerner who had worked his way up from being a solicitor's clerk, 'Bernie,' as he was known to the advocates who appeared before him, was noted for his dry wit, colourful language and liking for jazz. As the jury were being sworn in, two of the twelve said they couldn't read the oath, one of them saying he had left his glasses behind, the other openly admitting to illiteracy.

It was not a promising start to what was to be a long drawn out struggle. The bare bones of the story were outlined by Archer's counsel Robert Alexander QC in his opening statement to the jury. *The Star*'s defence rested, he said, on the following account. On the night of the 8th September, Monica Coghlan was touting for business in Shepherd Market, a regular haunt for the oldest profession on earth. She was approached by a man whom she did not know at the time but later claimed was Jeffrey Archer who agreed to pay her £50 for intercourse. After the bargain had been struck the man went away to fetch his car. But by the time he came back some minutes later Monica had found a better prospect, the Asian solicitor Aziz Kurtha, and agreed to go with him.

Kurtha's Mercedes was then followed to Gillingham Street, Victoria, by the disappointed first punter who patiently waited outside the Albion Hotel in his car while Monica entertained Kurtha in room 6a. When she reappeared about fifteen minutes later, the still keen first client flashed his lights to attract Monica's attention and spoke to her discreetly through his car window though not before being recognised by Kurtha. The solicitor, excited by his apparent sighting of the Tory Deputy Chairman in such embarrassing surroundings, noted down the first three letters of his car registration and took the story of what he believed he had seen to *Private Eye* to whom he had given items of gossip in the past. But scenting the story was more trouble than it was worth, the *Eye*'s journalists promptly passed Kurtha on to the *News of the World*.

The heart of the case was the series of phone calls made to Archer by Monica Coghlan. On the face of it these seemed damning but Archer's contention that he was the innocent victim of a foul entrapment was powerfully put by his counsel. Robert Alexander QC, who at 6ft 6 inches towered over his client, said that Archer had taken the telephone calls from Monica because he was terrified that someone was attempting to ruin his reputation by smearing him with a scandal. 'False stories can damage reputations just as much as true ones because it takes time to nail the falsehood,' Alexander told the jury. As the conversations with Monica went on, Archer's counsel explained that his client had developed a genuine sympathy for Monica's claim that she was an ordinary working prostitute who was being hounded into a smear plot. That is the reason why Archer had agreed to pay her money to go abroad.

The plaintiff's examination-in-chief by his own counsel went smoothly. After taking Archer through his colourful career,

Alexander asked gently about the state of his marriage: 'It is our 21st wedding anniversary on Saturday, sir,' replied Archer. 'I say this without any reservation. Mary was the most remarkable woman I knew when I was young and she remains that way now, sir.' Archer went on to deny that he had been in Shepherd Market that night or that he had ever associated with a prostitute. The evening of September 8th, he had dined with his literary editor Richard Cohen and his wife Caroline at the Caprice and had later had a drink at the restaurant with his TV and film agent Terence Baker before driving him home around 1am.

Archer's cross-examination by Michael Hill QC proved to be much more uncomfortable. The Defence Counsel spent much of the first day questioning the Tory Deputy Chairman about when he had first learnt of the scandal circulating about him. Archer gave a series of conflicting answers, first saying he knew nothing about the story circulating about him until Monica's third phone call to him on October 23rd, six weeks after his alleged encounter with her in Shepherd Market. But later he modified this answer saying he might have learnt about the story 'just before the party conference' which began on October 7th.

Michael Hill QC for *The Star* pressed home these inconsistencies: 'Mr Archer, it would not be that it was your intention when you were giving your evidence in answer to Mr Alexander that you wanted to convey to my Lord and the jury that all these telephone calls came as surprises to you, took you by surprise and were unheralded by any other information that you had about this story?' Jeffrey Archer replied 'Certainly not, sir.'

Michael Hill also pressed Jeffrey Archer as to why he had lied to *News of the World* journalists when they rang him after they had monitored the pay-off at Victoria Station to check their story. Referring to a tape-recorded conversation with reporter John Lisners in which Archer had denied bluntly that he had paid Monica to go abroad, Hill said 'During which you lied and lied and lied, did you not?'

ARCHER: No, sir, and that is grotesquely unfair.

HILL: I suggest that that explanation was a piece of balderdash.

ARCHER: Well, I am sorry to disappoint you, sir, it was not.

HILL: Speaking on the record does not give you a licence to tell an untruth, does it, Mr Archer?

ARCHER: It gives you a licence not to go into details.

HILL: Would you answer my question, please, Mr Archer. Do you want me to ask it again? Do you?

ARCHER: Yes.

HILL: Speaking on the record does not give you a licence to tell untruths, does it?

There was a long pause, then Archer replied, 'No, sir, it does not.'

HILL: What you have been doing for the last ten minutes is wriggling off the hook . . .

ARCHER: I am innocent of this charge, and nothing you will say, however clever you are in the wording of out-of-context pieces, however clever you are in letting people know what on and off the record means, there is only one thing that matters in this court of law, sir: I have never met this girl. I have never had sexual intercourse with her and that is the truth!

This bruising encounter set the whole tone of the case. Occasionally Archer became emotional, accusing the *News of the World* of being 'a bunch of liars who had set me up'. But for 11 hours in the witness box he stood there, denying point after point put to him. Questioned about the reports that had

23

appeared in both *The Observer* and *Sunday Today* quoting 'friends' as saying that he had met Monica once 'casually six months ago', Archer denied he had said any such thing: 'Absolute bunkum and I will be happy to prove it.' The Tory Deputy Chairman went on to say that he had been rung up by 50 to 60 journalists that night and while he couldn't remember the details of every conversation, 'I made it clear to every one of them that I had never met this girl and that I had never had a sexual relationship with her. I said it again and again and again.' Asked by Michael Hill whether he had done anything to correct the reports in either *The Observer* or *Sunday Today*, Archer replied that he had not but there were so many errors in so many articles about him at the time that correcting them all would have been 'grotesque'.

Archer's alibi also provoked detailed questioning particularly as its details only became public at the trial. He told the court that on September 8th when he was alleged to have picked up Monica around midnight he had spent the evening dining at the Caprice with his literary editor Richard Cohen and his wife. This fact was not disputed because there were several witnesses to attest that Archer did indeed dine at the Caprice that evening. It was what happened after the meal ended that led to prolonged questioning. When the Cohens left him at around 10.30, Archer told the jury he began to table-hop before leaving around midnight with his theatrical agent, Terence Baker.

Baker in his evidence supported this, saying he was driven back to his home in Camberwell by Archer in his light grey Daimler, getting home at 1.15am. Under cross-examination, Baker was asked how he could be so sure that he had met Archer at the Caprice on that particular night as he had no record of a bill, no cheque stub, no diary entry or credit card voucher to prove it. He replied 'I just knew.' Michael Hill pressed him on this crucial point:

HILL: I must ask you again and I ask you to concentrate

on the question: Why did you accept that it was September 8th that you had seen Mr Archer? You have no basis for recalling it yourself so far as I can see.

BAKER: I had not seen him, as I say, for a very long time. I remember very clearly, he is a distinguished client of mine and if you don't see somebody for a long time you tend to remember very clearly when you do meet them.

HILL: When did you next see Mr Archer?

BAKER: I cannot honestly remember, sometime later, a few months later I think, a few weeks later.

HILL: Before or after this story broke?

BAKER: Well after . . . Yes, I had gone to America again.

HILL: What do you say to the suggestion that it was not the night of the 8th of September and the morning of the 9th September that you had been with Mr Archer in the Caprice?

BAKER: I would say it was bunkum.

If Baker's evidence was correct, it was impossible that Archer could have met Monica around midnight in Shepherd Market, Mayfair. But there was some dispute about when the alibi had been established. Archer claimed to the court that he first contacted Baker to see if he would confirm his presence two weeks after the *News of the World*'s story on his agent's return from holiday around about November 15th. Baker gave a different account telling the court that Archer had contacted him immediately after the *News of the World*'s story appeared on October 26th. This conflict in dates was developed by Michael Hill in cross-examination.

HILL: What would you say to the suggestion that it was not until mid-November that Mr Archer contacted you and asked you about this matter and if you would make a statement?

BAKER: I would say that was incorrect.

HILL: If I tell you that that is what Mr Archer has said himself, what do you say then?

BAKER: I'm sorry, that's not my memory of it.

HILL: Mr Baker, let me make it quite clear. I suggest that you were not in the restaurant with Mr Archer on the evening of September 8th, 1986, in circumstances where you went home with him from the restaurant at some time after 12.30 in the morning?

BAKER: Well, I was, sir.

This conflict in dates was further stressed by Michael Hill who sought to cast doubt on Archer's account by confronting him with different statements he made to reporters about his whereabouts that night. An article in the *Daily Express* written by Tony Dawe after an off-the-record conversation with Archer reported that the Tory Deputy Chairman had been at 'a function with 40 other people'. Nicholas Constable of *Today* reported him as having said that he had been at 'a meeting with 50 other people'. An almost identical story appeared in the *Mail on Sunday* saying that he was 'at a function attended by almost 50 people'.

HILL: These are different things: a meeting, a function and a private dinner for three people.

ARCHER: Mr Hill, we are playing with words.

HILL: No, we are not playing with words. I am suggesting that you were putting forward a different account from the one which you are giving under oath in this witness box.

The implication that Michael Hill repeatedly put to the jury was that Archer had had considerable difficulty in constructing an alibi and was unsure in the immediate aftermath of the *News of the World*'s story what to say about his whereabouts that night. On the essential issues the jury clearly felt that Archer and his agent were telling the truth.

In the course of my research for this book, I came across a diary entry kept by Archer's political secretary David Faber which indicated that the Tory Deputy Chairman had an arrangement to dine with his key alibi witness on Tuesday September 9th, the day after according to Archer's evidence he met Terence Baker by chance in the Caprice. Whether this dinner, at one of the author's favourite stamping grounds, an Italian restaurant called Sambuca just off Sloane Square, ever took place is not known. The restaurant no longer has a record.

But on the assumption it did happen, Jeffrey Archer was on two successive nights in the company of his theatrical agent a man whom he told the court he rarely saw. Why the existence of this diary entry did not emerge at the trial can only be guessed at. There is nothing to suggest that either Archer or his lawyers knew of it which explains why it was not disclosed to *The Star*. David Faber was never called as a witness nor was Angie Peppiatt, Archer's personal confidential secretary. But my own judgment is that, even had the jury known of the existence of this diary entry, it would not have altered the outcome of the case.

By the end of Archer's marathon three-day appearance in the witness box, *The Star*'s defence team knew it was fighting a desperate uphill battle. Concluding his cross-examination, Michael Hill put a series of pointed questions to Archer:

HILL: Do you accept that you have, in the course of the events since October, advanced differing stories from that which you now say is the truth?

ARCHER: No sir.

HILL: And saying to two reporters that you had met Monica Coghlan before when you had not?

ARCHER: No sir.

HILL: Do you accept, Mr Archer, that in relation to the events of 23rd – 24th October you have deliberately lied to this court as to the inception of the plan to get that woman out of the country by paying her money to do so?

ARCHER: No, sir.

HILL: Mr Archer, the truth of this matter is that you did solicit that woman on the night of the 8th/9th September.

ARCHER: No sir.

HILL: You did pay her for her sexual services.

ARCHER: No, sir.

HILL: You have maintained a dishonest front in order to avoid the consequences of that and your subsequent conduct coming into the public eye.

ARCHER: No, sir.

HILL: I have no further questions to ask.

Before the case, *The Star*'s counsel Michael Hill had boasted, 'I am going to stalk him till he cracks.' But his quarry proved to be extraordinarily elusive. Jeffrey Archer not only did not crack, he made such a good impression on at least one member of the jury, a middle aged woman sitting in the front who continually smiled in his direction, that *The Star*'s Editor Lloyd Turner turned to his counsel and said despondently, 'The best we can do is $11-1$.'

The Star's case took another serious reverse when Mary Archer stepped into the witness box wearing an immaculate blue and white summer dress. There was an immediate stir from the habitues of the High Court as she took the oath. She told Robert Alexander that she was dumbfounded when she learnt what the *News of the World* was publishing: 'The thought of my husband consorting with a prostitute is preposterous. Anyone who knows him well knows that far from Jeffrey accosting prostitutes, if one accosted him he would run several miles in the opposite direction very fast, it would terrify him.'

Asked by Robert Alexander to describe the state of her marriage, she replied firmly: 'We have a very happy marriage.' Alexander then asked somewhat euphemistically, 'Do you live a full life?' To which Mary Archer replied softly 'Yes, sir.' Towards the end of her examination-in-chief Mrs Archer was asked by counsel what had been the effect of the case on her husband. She whispered, her voice breaking down, 'I think he has withstood an outrageous barrage of events and comment with great fortitude.' At this point Mary wept and the hearing was adjourned.

The most significant part of Mary Archer's evidence on the second day was the explanation she gave for the blunt contradiction between her husband's denial that he had ever met Monica and his apparent admission to *The Observer* that he had casually met a prostitute.

ROBERT ALEXANDER: Do you know one way or the other whether he ever spoke to Mr Adam Raphael?

MARY ARCHER: Yes, that name I know, I know the journalist, he did indeed speak to him.

ALEXANDER: Did you hear Jeffrey's side of the conversation?

MARY ARCHER: I did.

ALEXANDER: Would you tell my Lord and the jury what, if anything, you can recollect about Jeffrey's side of that conversation.

MARY ARCHER: I can tell you, but before I do I would like to say that although it is my genuine recollection that this was the conversation with Mr Raphael, I can't say that that recollection is not overlaid by the wish that it was so. Jeffrey certainly repeated, as he had throughout every telephone conversation, that he had never met Debbie, never had a sexual liaison with her or with any other prostitute for that matter. But then in the middle of this particular conversation he said something that was so striking that I remember it very particularly. He said words to the effect: 'Well, if I did meet her, I don't know about it. If there is a photograph of me with her, I don't know about it.' I was fairly dumbfounded. I waited until the end of the conversation. I asked him who he had spoken to, that is when I think I recollect it was Adam Raphael but I won't say on oath that it was. I said, 'What on earth made you say that? How can you say you have never met her and then you have met her?' I think I said much in that tone of voice. Jeffrey said, 'Well, it's occurred to me that the *News of the World* may have contrived some kind of meeting at some kind of public function.' I should explain that very many people come up to Jeffrey, shake him by the hand, throw their arms round him, kiss him even, photos are taken. He doesn't know who these men are from Adam or these women from Eve but it happens.

The next day *The Star*'s counsel found Mary Archer a very difficult witness to cross-examine. The sympathy of the judge and jury were clearly with her. Getting nowhere, Michael Hill made the cardinal mistake of losing his temper. When Mrs Archer responded to a question about what she had said to a *Daily Express* reporter with the ironical comment: 'Very ingenious, Mr Hill,' he retorted: 'No, don't be rude, Madam.' Mrs Archer: 'Why not?' Hill: 'Well, if you think it necessary to do so then do so. Would you answer the question?' Mrs Archer: 'I said very ingenious, Mr Hill. You are putting to me a set of quotations, I am doing my best with them. I have not seen this article. I do not recall exactly what I said. I have told you in truth what I do remember.' When Robert Alexander intervened on behalf of Mrs Archer to protect her from Hill's questioning, Mr Justice Caulfield rightly told him not to worry: 'The jury may think Mrs Archer is looking after herself very well.'

The Defence Counsel's complicated style also appeared to lose the jury at times. At one point he went into such detail about dates, times and places that even the judge lost his patience. 'There is no dispute about the lunch at the Royal Bath, come on!' said Mr Justice Caulfield.

Michael Hill fared no better in testing Mary Archer's explanation of how the misunderstanding occurred which led *The Observer* to report that Archer had met Monica casually on one occasion. Asked by the Defence Counsel how it was that she remembered her husband's conversation with Adam Raphael, Mrs Archer replied, 'Jeffrey said to me in Grantchester "How can that have got about? It is just not possible I could have said there was a chance meeting six months ago." I said to him, "I know what that is, that's that ridiculous or injudicious answer I heard you give that very night about the possibly contrived photo opportunity," and I might have added in respect of that phone conversation, by which I was so struck, that when the phone had been put down I said, "Who was that? What on earth made you say that?" I said, "Well, for God's sake don't say it again," to my husband. So I remembered all this very precisely.'

Pressed by Michael Hill on her admission that she was not sure whether her genuine recollection of the conversation was not overlaid by a wish that it were so, Mrs Archer replied that she was certain that she had recalled the conversation accurately. But she admitted she could not be totally sure that it had been with Adam Raphael.

With the Archers undented, the case now turned on the evidence given by Monica Coghlan and her client, the Asian solicitor Aziz Kurtha who had tipped off *Private Eye* about the scandal. Neither was to be a satisfactory witness from *The Star*'s point of view. The 35-year-old prostitute was firm in identifying Archer as the client who had approached her in Shepherd Market; she later confirmed that she had not met Archer previously. But she owed the paper no favours and certainly gave none.

Monica was furious with it on two counts. *The Star*'s charge that she hoped to make £50,000 from the *News of the World* had put her whole 'arrangement' with that paper at risk for it appeared to taint her evidence. But worse from Monica's viewpoint was *The Star*'s claim that she specialised in 'kinky sex'. Prostitutes have their pride. 'I enjoy my job — if a man's all right with me, I am all right with him,' she indignantly told the jury. *The Star*'s defence team realised that she was bound to disown part of its story in court. What the paper didn't know was that in court she would lash out and denounce their story as largely a 'fantasy'.

If Monica was less than helpful to *The Star*'s case, Aziz Kurtha was a disaster. The solicitor was a crucial witness because it was his identification of Archer as Monica's client that had set the whole story in motion. He knew long before he got up in the witness box that he was cast in a villain's role and would get no sympathy for the way he had been done over by the *News of the World*. 'If you live with dogs,' he told the jury, 'you can't complain if you have fleas.'

Kurtha was, as my colleague Laurence Marks noted, an unlikely figure to be scrabbling in the undergrowth of tabloid journalism. Born into a comfortably off family in Bombay, he came to Britain at the age of nine. He read law at the London School of Economics, was called to the Bar in 1966, qualifying later as a solicitor before returning to Pakistan as one of the New Dawn socialists. From there he moved to Dubai where he built up a lucrative legal practice before returning to London. Charming, good looking, a gambler and a bit of a playboy, he drifted into the fringes of journalism. Having been a presenter on Channel 4's Eastern Eye programme, Kurtha liked to think of himself as a man about town. But in Court 13 he was lost in a totally alien world.

Under Robert Alexander's tough cross-examination, he came over as a malicious schemer whose evidence could not be relied upon. That was fatal because *The Star*'s case depended on his identification of Archer as Monica's client. But by the end Kurtha was reduced to claiming that he was colour-blind to explain why he had wrongly described Archer's Daimler as green when it was in fact light grey.

Aziz Kurtha's evidence was treated with such distaste even by *The Star*'s counsel that that night Robert Alexander wrote himself a note: 'Archer will win and will receive £500,000.' Three days later Alexander, suspecting that pride might come before a fall, tore up his forecast. *The Star*'s Editor Lloyd Turner, however, had reached a similar conclusion. After Kurtha's evidence he wrote in his diary: 'We've lost the case.' Michael Hill was equally gloomy. He found Kurtha's appearance in the witness box such an ordeal that during each interval, he had to go to the cloakroom to wash his hands and wipe the sweat off his brow.

Even before this disaster, *The Star*'s defence appeared to be in serious trouble. When I was called to give evidence on the eighth day of the trial, both the judge, who later in his summing up described me as 'a thorn in Archer's side,' and the jury, who looked at me with puzzled frowns, appeared to regard me as an unhelpful distraction. Michael Hill, probably because he was uncertain as to what I was going to say, seemed unsure how to extract my story to *The Star*'s best advantage. After noting that I appeared under subpoena, he went straight to the point by asking the source of the quote in *The Observer*'s story that Archer had met Monica Coghlan only once 'very casually six months ago.'

I had decided before the case began that if Archer gave evidence about my conversation with him I could not remain silent. Nor in the light of the unequivocal legal advice I had received that Section 10 of the Contempt of Court Act gave me no protection did I see any point in making a song and dance about confidentiality of sources. To make a token show of resistance and then give in when threatened with contempt would merely undermine the principle of confidentiality. No doubt in the light of what subsequently happened, it might have been wiser if I had agonised publicly at having to break a confidence. But the truth was that I was certain that I was acting not only correctly but honourably. With the Archers having already given detailed evidence of the conversation with me, the idea of offering myself up as a martyr and going to prison for contempt on the grounds that my professional code required me to be silent struck me as so absurd that I didn't believe anyone would seriously entertain it.

During Jeffrey and Mary Archer's evidence, though I was not allowed to be present in court, I had been receiving nightly reports about what they had said. I wanted to know precisely how far the Archers had gone in discussing my conversation with Jeffrey. It was quite clear from these, as well as from the detailed reports of the case in all the national daily newspapers that both Jeffrey and Mary had not only given their versions of his conversation with me that night but that their accounts did not accord with what I remembered of the conversation.

On several counts I felt I had no further obligation to Archer. First he had given the court his version of the conversation. Second this account was, according to my recollection, incorrect. Finally if I let his version stand unchallenged, it would reflect on my professional competence and might prejudice the course of justice. Therefore when I stepped into the witness box just vacated by a sobbing Monica Coghlan I was in no doubt as to what I was going to say. When Michael Hill put the direct question to me: who was my source? I confirmed it was Jeffrey Archer. In answer to further questions I explained that the story was written from notes immediately after I had spoken to Archer that night. Sitting in the well of the court as I gave evidence were Jeffrey and Mary Archer. They did not look up, appearing to be engrossed in writing furiously.

Robert Alexander began his cross-examination by seeking my views on the way that Archer had been trapped by the *News of the World*. I said I detested that form of journalism. But he reached stonier ground when he asked me to comment on Mary Archer's claim in her evidence that she had listened to Jeffrey's telephone conversation with me that night.

ALEXANDER: Mrs Archer said that Jeffrey certainly repeated, as he had throughout every telephone conversation, that he had never met Debbie, never had a sexual liaison with her, or with any other prostitute for that matter. Could you indicate what parts of that, if any, of Mrs Archer's recollection on that matter you share?

RAPHAEL: None.

ALEXANDER: None at all? She remembers him saying in one conversation, which she thinks is with you, 'Well, if I did meet her, I don't know about it. If there is a photograph of me with her, I don't know about it. I was fairly dumbfounded.'

RAPHAEL: I am fairly certain those words were not spoken to me.

ALEXANDER: Mr Raphael, I suggest to you that the conversation that Mrs Archer recollects did, in fact, take place.

RAPHAEL: That Mrs Archer recollects?

ALEXANDER: Mrs Archer recollects her conversation with Mr Archer, who also recollects making it quite clear that he had never had any form of liaison with this woman.

RAPHAEL: I'm afraid that can't be the case because if he'd said to me 'I have never met this woman,' the sort of questions I would have asked would have been of a totally different kind. If that had been said to me, I would have then asked a number of questions — 'Why on earth, if you've never met this woman, did you pay her off?' But that was not the question I asked.

At the end of his cross-examination, having failed to get me to admit doubt about what Archer had said to me that night,

Alexander asked silkily, 'Journalists sometimes make mistakes, don't they?' to which I meekly responded, 'Yes,' suppressing the retort that so, on occasions, do lawyers.

It proved to be an effective performance by Alexander, for the judge in his summing up seized on my admission under cross-examination that Archer had been very upset in his conversation with me. He advised the jury that therefore not too much reliance should be placed on my version. The jury, who appeared to regard the whole case as a media nightmare, were clearly not impressed by the fact that *The Star*'s Editor, Lloyd Turner though present in court throughout the trial, had chosen not to give evidence. That the paper was not apparently willing to stand up for its own story, after it had been described by one of its own principal witnesses — Monica Coghlan — as a tissue of lies, made its chances of winning remote.

At the start of the case Lloyd Turner had expected to be the last witness for the paper to take the stand. But towards the end of the second week, he was told by the defence lawyers that there had been a change of tack and he would not be required to give evidence. It was an opening seized on by Robert Alexander, Archer's counsel. He sarcastically asked the *News of the World* Editor David Montgomery whether Lloyd Turner, who had been present in court throughout the trial was able to speak. 'He has the power of speech,' replied Mr Montgomery. To which Mr Alexander riposted, 'Does he have any physical infirmity which prevents him giving evidence in this court?' At this sally the jury smiled.

Libel actions are battlegrounds for the minds of juries. What Robert Alexander succeeded in doing brilliantly was to turn the case from being a test of whether or not Archer had slept with Monica into a trial of the ethics of the popular press. The methods used by the *News of the World* to entrap the Tory Deputy Chairman were held up for the court's examination and found seriously wanting. Archer may have behaved foolishly but the catalogue of lies and deception used to ensnare him by the *News of the World* left a bitter taste. The millions who read tabloid papers may like their daily dose of scandal but when confronted with the methods used to obtain it, they turn away in disgust.

The tactic of putting Fleet Street in the dock was shrewd in relation to the jury but as far as the judge was concerned it worked almost too well. When the details of the Archer case are forgotten, the extraordinary over-the-top summing up by Mr Justice Caulfield will be remembered, in particular his tribute to Mary Archer: 'Remember Mrs Archer in the witness box. Your vision of her probably will never disappear. Has she elegance? Has she fragrance?' The judge clearly had no doubts. Living with such an elegant, fragrant vision, how could Archer possibly be 'in need of cold, unloving, rubber-insulated sex in a seedy hotel?'

This partisan summing up was so riddled with errors that *The Star*'s Counsel had to ask Judge Caulfield to correct nine mis-statements of fact before the jury retired to consider its verdict. Michael Hill began by saying that the jury should have been directed on the importance of 'the lies told by Mr Archer to Mr Adam Raphael' — a statement which produced a furious objection from Archer's counsel, Robert Alexander. As the jury withdrew, a heated row broke out between Alexander and Hill. 'That remark was absolutely disgraceful,' said Alexander, threatening to report Hill to the Bar Council with Hill responding in kind. Learned Counsel do not usually brawl publicly in this way. It was a sign of the explosive tensions generated by the case.

Relations between the Defence and the Bench were hardly warmer. When Michael Hill sought corrections of the numerous errors in the judge's summing up, Mr Justice Caulfield seemed to have difficulty in following the argument let alone remembering the material facts. Hill pointed out the judge in his summing up had given a misleading impression of Mrs Archer's evidence when she claimed to have recalled her husband's telephone conversation with Adam Raphael. This intervention produced the following dialogue of the deaf:

JUDGE: I was right about the relation of Mrs Archer's evidence, was I not?

HILL: No, my Lord, your Lordship was not. Your Lordship related her as saying that her husband had said 'Well, I don't know, I suppose I could have met her some months ago or six months.' My Lord, that is not her evidence.

JUDGE: That is Mr Archer's evidence, is it?

HILL: No, my Lord, that is neither evidence. Mrs Archer's evidence, which was the passage to which I was inviting your Lordship's attention just now, day five, page one, and I will read what she said was the conversation: 'Well, if I did meet her, I don't know about it. If there is a photograph of me with her, I don't know about it.'

JUDGE: This is Mr Archer.

HILL: This is Mrs Archer describing Mr Archer on the telephone.

JUDGE: What page is that again?

HILL: Day five, page one.

JUDGE: That is Mrs Archer's evidence.

HILL: That is right, my Lord.

JUDGE: That is the evidence you wish me to include in the . . .

HILL: Yes, my Lord, and to correct that, if you would be so kind, which your Lordship gave yesterday.

JUDGE: Yes.

Despite this lengthy passage at arms, the judge still failed to remember to correct his summing up when the jury returned and had to be reminded once again by Michael Hill. If Mr Justice Caulfield was tired, it was only to be expected. Nor was it surprising if the jury at the end of a long three-week bitterly contested case also found the complicated evidence hard to follow. But juries, at least, have a way of sorting out the wheat from the chaff.

It thus took only four hours before the bow-tied foreman came back to deliver the jury's verdict: £500,000 for Archer. There were gasps in court at the huge size of the damages, a record for a British libel trial. Michael Hill and Lloyd Turner shook their heads in dismay. A statement from *The Star* said that immediate consideration would be given to an appeal.

Why did *The Star*, in view of the judge's conduct of the case, not go to the Court of Appeal? A draft appeal prepared by the defence described the summing up as 'biased, unfair, and unjudicial'. Michael Hill, who was furious at the way the case had gone, urged his clients that they had a very good chance of securing a retrial. Lloyd Turner agreed. But in the end the view taken by the Board of Express Newspapers, after a tough argument, was that even if the appeal were allowed and a new trial ordered, the risks were too great. The problems of keeping Monica Coghlan and Aziz Kurtha under wraps while a new trial was prepared would be horrendous; the additional expense would be considerable; and a new jury, given Fleet Street's dubious standing, would probably reach the same verdict.

For Archer the result of the case must have been deeply satisfying. The following weekend a celebration party was held at his Grantchester home attended by a glittering array of celebrities, headed by the Lord Chancellor Lord Havers, the Foreign Office Minister David Mellor (a former personal assistant of Archer's), and the Treasury Minister Norman Lamont. Also drinking the celebration champagne was Dr David Owen, whose wife Debbie is Archer's literary agent, and Stewart Steven, the Editor of the *Mail on Sunday*.

Financially too, Archer had come out of the case very well. In addition to getting a record £500,000 in damages he had his costs of £230,000 paid by *The Star*. Top libel counsel like Robert Alexander do not come cheap, though on the strength of his performance in this case, he was worth every penny of his fee. Many of the newspapers the following day estimated his brief fee at £150,000. The Garrick Club rumour mill put it at £75,000 — sizeable but probably nearer the mark. As for Archer, having been awarded his £500,000 damages, he declared that he would give it all away to charity. And there was more to come. For soon after the conclusion of *The Star*'s case, the *News of the World*, which had defiantly said despite the record libel damages 'We stick by our report. Nothing more, nothing less. For us it is a matter of honour,' also decided that discretion was the better part of valour and settled to the tune of £50,000 plus costs.

But for Jeffrey Archer money, not even loads of it, can help rebuild his political career. Members of the Cabinet and national newspaper editors continue to flock to his dining table but they know and he must know that his chances of climbing up once again the greasy pole of politics are non-existent. As one his colleagues remarked, 'The trouble with Jeffrey is that he is an accident waiting to happen.'

A month before the case came to court, Lovell White and King had told *The Star* that if it lost the case, which it estimated, would last four days, it faced a possible maximum bill of £290,000 including damages for Archer of £100,000. This turned out to be a serious under-estimate. Hill's thorough style and the numerous lengthy legal arguments meant that the case dragged on and on. *The Star*'s final bill, including the damages and costs, was just over £1 million.

Perhaps the final irony of the Archer case is what happened to the *Daily Star* in its aftermath. Some have speculated that the reason the judge summed up in such a bizarre fashion was that he saw it as a way of striking a blow against the ethics of Grub Street. But the immediate result was to drive *The Star* even further downmarket into association with the multi-nippled *Sunday Sport* owned by the convicted pornographer David Sullivan.

After less than three months of falling sales and defections by major advertisers, Lord Stevens decided to restore *The Star*'s independence. H.L. Mencken's boast that no one has ever gone broke in underestimating the taste of the public had, for once been proved wrong. The Archer case also showed the distaste of juries for the ethics of modern tabloid journalism. The scale of damages awarded was out of all proportion to the actual libel, let alone the damage alleged to have been caused by it. The judge's summing up was regarded in the legal profession as a disgrace but the verdict would probably have been the same even if he had been more impartial. For Fleet Street, particularly its seamier end, the Archer trial had been an expensive but on the whole a salutary lesson.

3

The Plaintiff's Tale

Very few people have ever embarked on a libel action without bitterly regretting their adventure before the case comes to trial.

Sir Patrick Hastings KC

If the case was a triumph for Archer, it was less happy for me. The initial reporting of my evidence was damaging because it seemed as though I had voluntarily betrayed a source. As I came out into the Strand after my stint in the witness box, a battery of photographers flashed their cameras in my eyes. I felt like a felon and learnt a doubtless salutary lesson of what it is like to be on the wrong side of the media fence. That evening both the BBC and ITV early news bulletins failed to make clear that I had been forced to give evidence under subpoena despite this having been clearly stated in court.

The first I learnt of this was at a dinner that night at the Institute of Directors. Anne Lapping, editor of the Channel 4 political programme, A Week in Politics, and an old friend, came up to me and asked, 'Why on earth did you give evidence against Archer?' When I explained that I had only given evidence about the conversation after Jeffrey Archer had given his version of it to the court, Anne stressed that it was vital to correct the impression that I had voluntarily betrayed a political contact.

Borrowing a mobile phone from one of the other guests I rang both ITN's and the BBC's news desks and urged them to put the record straight in their later news bulletins. The next day my photograph was blazoned across the front page of *The Sun* topped by the splash headline, 'TOP TV JOURNALIST IN ARCHER SHOCKER'. Apart from the sensational headlines in the popular tabloids, highlighting that my evidence might lose Archer his case, the coverage was fair, noting that I had appeared under subpoena. So when I went on holiday that night for a week in Brittany with my family, I felt reasonably confident that I would not be criticised, damaging though my evidence had been to Archer.

I was wrong. Driving back from La Baule, I heard the staggering size of the damages received by Archer. When I got home there were 17 messages on the telephone answering machine. Most were from friends but two, from the *Mail on Sunday*, sounded ominous. Its news desk said it wanted to speak to me urgently. The paper had also tried to get hold of me at the BBC and, as I later learnt, had sent a reporter round to my home. Finding me away they had asked the neighbours where I was. As all the messages were a week old there was nothing I could do so I shrugged and thought no more about them. The papers next day were full of the sensational conclusion to the trial and I settled down to a happy time with them. But when I read *The Independent*, which has a justifiable reputation for being accurate and fair, my enjoyment abruptly ceased.

Its report under the headline, '£500,000 Archer Libel Award Sets New Damages Record' noted that no one came out of a libel trial smelling of roses but then went on to say, 'There was concern among some people when Adam Raphael, the television journalist highly regarded by both sides, who gave evidence under subpoena, breached his confidential conversations with Mr Archer.'

Who was *The Independent* reflecting when it reported this concern that I had betrayed Archer? William Keegan, *The Observer*'s Economics Editor and one of my oldest friends soon told me. Had I seen the *Mail on Sunday*? When I got hold of the July 19th edition, I was first amazed, then hurt, and finally explosively angry. The third leader, which I later learnt was written by the *Mail on Sunday*'s Editor Stewart Steven, had had this to say about me under the headline, 'A Question of Honour':

> Welcome Adam Raphael to the Peter Preston school of journalism. After a most deplorable incident, *The Guardian* edited by Preston has been dubbed the newspaper which betrays its sources.* Now along comes Adam Raphael, late of *The Observer*, who in a witness box in the High Court, relates in great detail his own version of remarks, which, whether reported accurately or not, were indubitably given to him off the record. Funny isn't it that, how it's the journalists who come from the so-called quality papers which claim to uphold journalistic standards who time after time fail to understand where honour and integrity lie?

After consulting friends with cooler heads than mine, I decided that as far as *The Independent* was concerned, I would have to get a letter of correction in fast. So I sent a letter to the Editor by dispatch rider, putting my reasons for giving evidence; it was published in *The Independent*'s next edition.

Dear Sir,

Your report of the Archer libel trial concludes that few people come out of such an event smelling of roses. That is surely right but your comment that there was concern that

---

*Sarah Tisdall, a foreign office clerk in the Foreign Secretary Sir Geoffrey Howe's private office was sentenced to six months prison in March, 1984. She was traced as the leaker of documents to *The Guardian* after the paper had complied with a court order and surrendered the confidential papers which dealt with the Government's tactics in deploying Cruise missiles in Britain.

I 'breached confidential conversations' with Mr Archer is less than fair. You note that I was forced to give evidence under subpoena but you do not point out the much more significant fact that I only revealed the source of the conversation after both Mr and Mrs Archer had given a detailed account of it to the court naming me as the journalist.

If I had refused to answer questions, claiming confidentiality, despite their evidence, it would have been absurd and treated as so by the Court. It would have done nothing to uphold what I regard as an important obligation, the duty of a journalist to protect his sources. In this case, the source had put the conversation plainly on the public record.

As far as the *Mail on Sunday* was concerned, a polite exchange of civilities was going to achieve nothing. The Editor, Stewart Steven, with access to the best legal brains in Fleet Street, had evidently decided I was a ripe target for a head-on attack. A defensive letter from me buried away on an inside page many weeks later, even if he was prepared to publish it, would be no remedy. What was interesting about the *Mail on Sunday*'s leader was that not only was it defamatory but it also appeared to be a contempt of court. Criticising a key witness in mid-trial before the judge has summed up is likely to prejudice a jury.

Stewart Steven had obviously thought this risk worth taking. Nor did I believe it an accident that his paper had gone for me so boldly. Fleet Street tabloids carefully calculate the odds of attracting a writ before engaging in such a direct attack. Thus litigious millionaires and politicians are treated with kid gloves unless the evidence against them is cast iron. The small, the insignificant, and above all those whose resources are unlikely to make them serious litigants, are dealt with much more cavalierly.

Though I clearly fell into the latter category, the only option I had if I was going to get a retraction was to consult 'my learned friends'. As a general rule, I don't believe it is a good idea for journalists to be too thin-skinned. We are, after all, in the business of dishing it out. Thus it ill becomes us to scream too loudly if occasionally we get a dose of our own medicine. Over the years, I had had one or two wounding brushes with *Private Eye*. On one occasion they dubbed me 'Keyhole Kate' after I had had a series of exclusives during the Chrysler crisis in 1975 which they claimed had been garnered by unorthodox methods. But these attacks I accepted as par for the political course. More recently the television critic of the *Financial Times*, Chris Dunkley described my new career at the BBC as a presenter as 'an embarrassment' which I had to shrug off ruefully as fair comment.

The *Mail on Sunday*'s attack was, however, of a different nature. To write of a political journalist that he is a betrayer of sources without honour or integrity is to engage in character assassination. It was also very damaging professionally, a point that was soon brought home to me in conversation with Ministers. Unless I was prepared to lie down and forget it, I had to fight. The *Mail on Sunday* had not just got its facts wrong, its comments were to my mind grossly unfair. I determined then and there that, whatever the cost, the paper's editor, Stewart Steven, should be made to apologise.

I had never met Steven but I knew he had a mixed reputation in Fleet Street. The protégé of the Editor-in-Chief of Mail Newspapers, Sir David English, he had had considerable success editing the *Mail on Sunday* — at least in terms of circulation. But in his rise to the editor's suite, Steven had become known as a risk-taker. Three of his 'exclusives' were notorious in Fleet Street.

On November 25th, 1972, the *Daily Express* carried a sensational exclusive story under Stewart Steven's by-line: 'BORMANN IS ALIVE'. Proudly the paper announced on its front page 'Martin Bormann, Hitler's deputy and once one of the most powerful and feared men in Nazi Germany, is today living the life of a prosperous businessman in Latin America. All speculation concerning his fate can at last be swept aside following an astonishing, dramatic, and sometimes dangerous nine months' search through six South American countries for Bormann, now the world's most wanted man.

'Today the *Daily Express* can reveal that the search—led by the author Ladislas Farago and in which I took part—has turned up incontrovertible evidence that, far from having died during his frantic escape from Hitler's bunker, Bormann succeeded in reaching safe haven thanks to the protection of the Vatican, former Argentine President Juan Peron and some of the most powerful politicians and financiers in South America.'

Unfortunately for Steven he had been tricked. The *Daily Express*' 'Bormann', the 17th to have been arrested in South America since 1945, turned out to be a 54-year-old Argentinian high school teacher, Nicolas Siri. Nor was that the end of Steven's 'exclusives'. On May 18th, 1977, the *Daily Mail*, his new employer, carried another sensational story under Steven's by-line: 'WORLD-WIDE BRIBERY WEB BY LEYLAND'. . . 'British Leyland, the nationalised car manufacturer, is paying bribes and conspiring to defraud foreign governments on a massive scale in a desperate attempt to win overseas orders.' The crucial evidence for this remarkable tale was a letter allegedly written by Lord Ryder, chairman of the National Enterprise Board, to Alex Park, the Chief Executive of British Leyland, informing him that the 'special account arrangements' had been nodded through by the Secretary of State. Sadly for Steven, the document on which he based his story was a blatant forgery complete with elementary spelling mistakes. The story cost the *Daily Mail* more than £200,000 in libel damages and costs.

The last story for which Steven will always be remembered

in Fleet Street is perhaps the funniest. One evening three unlikely characters turned up at London Heathrow Airport in safari suits and pith helmets and convinced the *Daily Mail* that they had found the Lost City of the Aztecs, the fabulous city of gold in Central America. Unfortunately for connoisseurs of tabloid journalism, this epic only ran for one edition because the Editor, David English, spotted it and ordered his then night editor, Stewart Steven, to replate the paper at considerable expense.

Whatever his merits as a journalist, Steven evidently revelled in being a risk-taker. In the only interview in which he set out his editorial philosophy, he expressed it as follows to the readers of *Woman* magazine: 'I believe passionately that you can take one of two courses: either you never take risks or get involved in controversy and lead a reasonable, sensible existence. I have many friends like that, for whom I have the greatest respect, but that is not what I am. I take risks, put my head above the parapet and do adventurous things. Sometimes this has got me into immense trouble; sometimes it has given me the most extraordinary rewards. I know of no one who is a great success — and I am only a medium success — in any field who has not at one time or another been involved in scandal or terrible trouble.'

As someone who was also about to take a huge risk, my first problem was to find a firm of solicitors to represent me. I knew it would be foolish to economise because the potential costs of losing were enormous. But I rapidly found out that many of the bigger firms had been engaged in the Archer libel trial and thus ruled themselves out on grounds of possible conflicts of interest. Others were less than keen to take on a private client with limited resources. My friends, meanwhile, were telling me I was mad to gamble in such a treacherous and expensive field of the law; sensible advice to which I turned a deaf ear. Caroline, my wife, and daughter of one of the last editors of the *Rand Daily Mail*, also counselled caution at the outset but soon gave her full hearted support without which I could not have continued.

Eventually through Geoffrey Grimes, a senior partner at Lovell White and King, whom I had got to know when I was at *The Guardian*, I rang David Mackie, the senior litigation partner at Allen and Overy. Their offices in Cheapside were disturbingly plush and I began to appreciate why top city solicitors charge £100−£150 a hour. My interview with him was short and to the point. Mackie made it clear that his firm didn't encourage private clients to launch themselves into the lottery of a libel action. He was cautious, and business-like, but when he saw I was determined, he drafted the following letter which was hand delivered to Stewart Steven demanding an apology:

Dear Sir,

We act for Mr Adam Raphael, whose attention has been drawn, on his return from a week's holiday, to the third item in the leader column of your issue for Sunday, 19th July. This item refers to the evidence recently given by our client in the High Court and suggests that he has betrayed his sources and has failed to understand where honour and integrity lie.

It is difficult to conceive of a more serious attack on the professional reputation of a journalist than to imply, as you have, that he has betrayed a confidential source. Your article ignores the truth, omitting as it does any reference to the facts that our client:

a. gave evidence only under compulsion having been served with a subpoena;
b. did so unwillingly after refusing to provide a statement or to offer any co-operation to the Defendants' solicitors and after obtaining advice of solicitors and counsel as to

his right to decline to answer questions;

c. and did so only after Mr and Mrs Archer had given a detailed account of the previously confidential conversation in the Court naming our client as the journalist.

Our client is a self-employed journalist whose livelihood is critically dependent upon his reputation, which as the parties to the litigation were at pains to make clear is of the very highest. Your malicious attack can have had no purpose other than to damage that reputation. Our client has also been deeply angered by these allegations which have provoked wide-spread misunderstanding of the circumstances in which he gave evidence and as a result, have given rise to hurtful and misplaced criticism. Your attack is also apparently intended to deter potential witnesses from complying with the law by criticising our client so severely for doing so.

We have advised our client that, if he were to issue proceedings, he could expect very substantial damages. Our client has no wish as a journalist, to take High Court proceedings unnecessarily against a newspaper. His concern is to have the record put straight swiftly and clearly before further damage is done. For this reason our client is prepared to take the matter no further provided that you:

a. publish, in this Sunday's edition of your newspaper, an apology substantially in the terms of the enclosed draft in the same type and position as the item of which our client complains;

b. undertake not to publish again the same or any similar libels of our client;

c. make a payment (of a sum to be agreed) to a newspaper charity to mark your regret.

d. pay our client's legal costs.

Unless you have accepted and implemented these proposals within seven days of the date of this letter our client will institute High Court proceedings against you without further notice.

Stewart Steven's response to this missive was, as I had expected, procrastination. The *Mail on Sunday*'s lawyers telephoned mine and had a series of inconclusive, off-the-record conversations. It soon became apparent that Steven was not prepared to apologise, though the *Mail*'s lawyers would have preferred to ward off a potentially expensive writ.

Further evidence, meanwhile, was beginning to trickle in about the damage done by the *Mail on Sunday* article. The Granada TV programme What the Papers Say presented by Richard Ingrams, the former Editor of *Private Eye*, had repeated the libel, although in a slightly less offensive form. My attempt to get a correction drew only a pompous response from Granada's solicitors, Goodman Derrick, saying, 'it would be wrong as a matter of principle for any apology or retraction to be published . . . when they (the programme) had done no more than report faithfully and in a balanced fashion what was said in the newspapers the preceding week'. More serious from my point of view was what Ministers were saying about me in private.

The first indication I had of this was when I rang up David Mellor, then Minister of State at the Foreign Office, and asked his private secretary if I could speak to him privately about the Gulf War as I was due to interview him that night on Newsnight. I had known him for several years on a friendly basis. But when he came on the line that day, Mellor indicated that my evidence in the Archer trial had not gone down well and that Westminster was abuzz with damaging gossip about me. 'Is this conversation going to end on the front page of the tabloids?' he asked apparently only half in jest. I was so disturbed by what had been said that I wrote Mellor a personal letter the following day enclosing the letter that Allen and Overy had written to the *Mail on Sunday* on my behalf and urging him to do what he could to 'nail the lies' that were going round about me.

To my dismay I soon discovered that the gossip was circulating at a much higher level. A few days later I was told by a mutual acquaintance that the Lord Chancellor, Michael Havers, had been holding forth in the Garrick Club about my conduct, saying that he would never trust me to keep a confidence in view of the way I had treated Archer. For Havers to gossip in this way about a case still subject to an appeal struck me as extraordinary even though, as was well known, he was a personal friend of Archer's. No less odd I thought was it for the Lord Chancellor to criticise a journalist for obeying the orders of a court and giving evidence under subpoena.

Michael Havers, however, had never been renowned for his discretion. A splendidly unstuffy politician, he loved holding court at the Garrick with his legal and journalistic cronies. Indeed such was Havers' liking for high and low gossip that I, like many other political journalists, had found him a very useful source over the years. On one occasion when I rang him up about some political scandal, I half expected to get a flea in my ear. Instead he boomed 'Do you read *Private Eye*?' When I replied, 'Yes,' Havers, then the Attorney General, said he couldn't tell me anything except to say that 99 per cent of what it had printed was correct.

This time I found the Lord Chancellor's taste for gossip less amusing. As soon as I heard what he had been telling his chums at the Garrick, I wrote to him explaining why I had felt obliged to give evidence, noting that Archer had been warned by me in advance what I proposed to say and pointing out somewhat pompously that my main concern had been to help the course of justice. My letter ended with a polite sting in its tail: 'I hope you will understand why I feel so upset at the criticisms that have been levelled at me, why I felt it important that I should write to you immediately and trust you will be able to reassure me that I have your confidence as a journalist who does not welch on his obligation to protect his sources.'

When Michael Havers finally replied, his response was distinctly cool though he noted his reported remarks about me had got 'rather fiercer in the re-telling'. Saying that he was writing 'simply as a member of the Garrick in no official capacity', the Lord Chancellor indicated that he was still not satisfied with my explanation. What still made him 'anxious', he said, was that counsel for the defence would not have been able to cross-examine Archer in such detail about his conversation with me that night if I hadn't co-operated in advance with *The Star*'s lawyers or at least gossiped to others about what he had said.

'As a (sadly no longer) cross-examiner,' Havers wrote, 'I would never dare put such a question without the firmest possible instructions so the inference I drew, rightly or wrongly, was that you must have told *The Star*'s lawyers about this conversation . . . Hill acted on instructions and my anxiety is the instructions could only have derived from you which again, rightly or wrongly, means that you must have told someone. That is my anxiety, it is nothing to do with you answering a subpoena and saying, quite rightly in those circumstances, I must tell the truth; I think that is quite right and I am not sure that I approve of journalists who like to be martyrs rather than helping the course of justice.'

The Lord Chancellor was clearly suggesting that, even if I was right in claiming that I had acted properly in public, I had not done so in private. There was a further damaging implication in that his letter suggested that I had deliberately sheltered behind Archer's evidence in court about our conversation as an excuse for disclosing him as my source.

This letter, which failed to give the assurance to which I felt entitled, so angered me that I immediately dashed off a rude reply. Fortunately, before I posted it I sent a copy to David Mackie at Allen and Overy who counselled a cooler response. I therefore contented myself with explaining how it was that *The Star*'s defence team had been able to cross-examine Archer so directly without any help from me. What Havers hadn't appreciated, I pointed out, was that I was not the only witness who revealed Archer as his source for the information of his relationship with Monica Coghlan. The other journalist was Rupert Morris of *Sunday Today* who had written in terms almost identical to my story that 'Archer has told friends that he did meet the woman once but denies sleeping with her'.

Rupert Morris had got this information from Archer just as I had on the Saturday night. But whereas I had refused to co-operate, he had thought it his duty, despite considerable personal misgivings, to confirm to *The Star*'s lawyers in advance of the trial that Archer was his source. When Morris rang me up two months before the trial and said he was concerned that he might have let Archer down, I advised him to contact Archer and tell him what he had done. When he did so, Archer, according to Morris, 'huffed and puffed' and said he would have sued both of us for libel if he had thought we were going to stick by our stories.

As I pointed out in my letter to Michael Havers, armed with this information from Rupert Morris and my use of the identical, not very opaque code of 'friends of Jeffrey Archer', it did not require much courage on Michael Hill's part to cross-examine Archer on the basis that he was the sole source of my story. I ended the letter with a distinctly cheeky postscript: 'I welcome your assurance that you were merely expressing anxiety as a private individual about my conduct . . . but I fear you don't appreciate how comments which you make in the privacy of the Garrick are retold around Westminster in a way which is damaging to me. You are, after all the Lord Chancellor, not just an ordinary Minister.'

This letter produced the response I was hoping for. Michael Havers now wrote that he 'accepted totally' my explanation, that I had his 'complete confidence' and that he was reassured that 'my belief that you are an honourable man is confirmed'. I learnt later that before writing this letter, the Lord Chancellor had approached *The Star*'s counsel, Michael Hill, who told him that I had given the defence absolutely no help before the trial.

Meanwhile the preparations for my libel writ against the *Mail on Sunday* were proceeding. As I had expected, Stewart Steven was unwilling to apologise, leaving his lawyers with the task of playing for time. The *Mail*'s legal department twice telephoned my solicitor to explain there was 'a difference of view' between the *Mail*'s lawyers and its editor. In the second call the *Mail*'s lawyer claimed he wanted to be briefed more fully so that he could persuade the editor to make a decent apology but that clearly was the last thing Stewart Steven had in mind.

James Price, the barrister whom *The Observer* had earlier briefed on my behalf to advise me about my rights as a witness at the Archer trial, was now called in to help. He pointed out that the *Mail on Sunday* would almost certainly seek to defend any action on the basis that its criticisms of me had been fair comment. Unlike justification, the other main defence to a libel action, a defendant who pleads fair comment does not have to prove the truth of his attack, only that it had been honestly made. The law rightly gives the widest licence to comment on matters of public interest, a category under which the Archer trial certainly fell.

The three crucial questions, Price explained, which would determine whether the *Mail on Sunday* had overstepped the mark were: Was its comment based on facts that were truly stated? Was it 'fair'? And finally was it made maliciously? This last hurdle, which in non-legal terms meant having an improper motive, was undoubtedly the most important, because if it could be proved it would defeat any defence of fair comment.

My counsel's initial advice was that it would be 'uncomfortable' to have a trial which depended solely on malice. But James Price was more hopeful about the other two questions. He believed the comment was not on 'facts truly stated'. The *Mail on Sunday* had not indicated that I had been subpoenaed, nor that I had been given legal advice that I was obliged to give evidence about my source because it was 'essential in the interests of justice'. Furthermore its attack had made no mention of the fact that Archer had already given evidence about the conversation and that I had warned him in advance of the trial that if he did so I would have to answer questions about it.

This led Price to conclude: 'I do not believe there is a defence of fair comment on facts misleadingly stated by reason of the omission of other material facts which strongly colour the stated facts.' On the other issue, was the comment 'fair'? Price said that he doubted that a jury would hold that it was having heard all the facts. The traditional legal test of fairness was: 'could any fair-minded man (prejudiced though he may be) honestly express that opinion?' It was not relevant that the *Mail on Sunday* might not have known the full facts. 'If you are going to make defamatory comments about someone it's up to you to establish the facts first,' he pointed out. Overall James Price's written conclusion was fairly confident: 'Though this action cannot be described as free from risk, there are in my view sufficient grounds to justify proceeding with it. My own view is that a jury would come down on Mr Raphael's side.'

This was very much what I wanted to hear. On August 12th, three weeks after the *Mail on Sunday*'s attack, my writ for libel was served on Mail Newspapers plc. It alleged that the editorial published in the *Mail on Sunday* meant that 'by voluntarily giving evidence in the High Court the Plaintiff betrayed the confidence owed to him to his source, and therefore, although claiming to uphold journalistic standards, in fact lacks honour and is without integrity.' It then went on in time-honoured fashion: 'By reason of the foregoing the Plaintiff's professional reputation has been seriously damaged and he has been gravely defamed.'

The initial response of the *Mail on Sunday*'s Editor to this missive was defiance. When *UK Press Gazette*, the journalist's weekly trade paper, asked his reaction to the writ, Stewart Steven said the action would be 'vigorously defended'. He went on: 'It will be one of the great *causes célèbres* of Fleet Street. This is a grave and important issue and I shall welcome having it tested in the High Court. I think I will find in the witness box coming to assist me in this matter will be some of the more distinguished journalists in Fleet Street, members of Parliament and members of the American Press. This matter won't be allowed to go away.'

Bluster it may have been, but Steven's remarks clearly indicated I was in for a fight. My first problem was the potentially horrendous costs. I knew if I lost I could be facing a bill as high as £250,000. In a libel action it is double or quits; the loser has to pay not only his own costs but also those of the defendant. If I lost I would be bust — and possibly would have to sell my house. But, perhaps foolishly, I was confident that this would not happen. Few journalists — and I certainly do not include myself in that category — can look back on their whole career and say they have never done or written anything that they don't profoundly regret. But in the Archer trial I had considered my conduct very carefully, consulted trusted colleagues and taken legal advice before giving evidence. I was certain that I had nothing to reproach myself with and believed that a jury would sympathise with the bitter resentment I felt about the accusation of dishonourable conduct levelled against me.

Nevertheless, right or wrong, I needed to be able to finance the action. Even if I won I would not be able to recover all the costs involved. Whether I was in or out of pocket would depend on the amount of damages, a lottery to be decided by a jury's whim. My initial money-raising idea was to write about the Archer trial. But that notion was clearly a non-runner, at least in advance of my own action. There is nothing lawyers like more than to cross-examine journalists about incautiously worded articles. Whatever I wrote was bound to give serious hostages to fortune. Moreover, I would not be able to write anything resembling the truth before the trial. And I soon learnt from Hilary Rubinstein, a leading literary agent (and founder of the Good Hotel Guide, for which my wife works), that non-fiction books don't yield serious advances of the scale I needed.

My next money-raising idea was equally far-fetched. I knew that Sir James Goldsmith had set up a libel fund under which he guaranteed the costs of worthy plaintiffs. A number of litigants had been helped, including the Tory MPs Neil Hamilton and Gerald Howarth in their libel action against the BBC over the programme Maggie's Militant Tendency. But somehow I doubted whether in Sir James' eyes I fell into the same meritorious category. The only time I had met him was when I volunteered to settle a libel action he had brought against *The Observer*. In what passed for a scoop in those days, Ms Polly Toynbee, then a feature writer on the paper, had incautiously quoted some medical research allegedly proving that the high salt content in Marmite was bad for babies. This infuriated Sir James, who on behalf of his leading British food company, Cavenham, brought a multi-million suit against the paper.

When I arrived at the great man's headquarters in Leadenhall Street, I found him pacing up and down like a caged tiger. Sir James sat me down but I found trying to talk to him as he strode around his huge office such a strain that I sought permission to accompany him in his perambulation. This did the trick. After 30 minutes and several thousands of yards, we reached agreement that *The Observer* had behaved disgracefully and would publish an apology. The resulting retraction was of the crawling variety. Not only did *The Observer* acknowledge that Marmite was good for babies, but we felt obliged to point out that the more that babies were stuffed with Marmite, the bonnier they became. Humiliating perhaps, but in libel actions wounded pride is, as I was rapidly learning, a dubiously expensive asset.

My only other contact with Sir James had been when he approached me in 1979 to write a political column for his new weekly news magazine *Now*. In the end I refused but I used the offer to good advantage, persuading *The Observer* that I was such a valuable commodity that I deserved an office car. I still have it, a very small VW Polo, a bit battered, a bit rusty, but still a runner. However none of this, I realised, was likely to endear me as a worthy plaintiff. A meeting with the administrator of the Goldsmith libel fund, the veteran solicitor Peter Carter-Ruck, soon confirmed this: he indicated that I was not the sort of person Sir James had in mind. I had to agree.

My last hope of serious money lay in another tycoon, Tiny Rowland, the chief executive of Lonrho and the owner of my old paper *The Observer*. Unfortunately I had also had my brushes with him. I had given evidence to the Monopolies Commission opposing Lonrho's take-over of the paper on the grounds that its world-wide commercial operations were bound to conflict with the interests of an independent paper. There had also been a spectacular shouting match between Tiny and me (he did most of the shouting) at what was intended to be an enjoyable lunch at *The Observer* to welcome the new proprietor and his board. I had been included as a mollifying and soothing presence. It was a serious miscalculation. When I objected to Rowland's demand that *The Observer* should play a more overt role in helping him get Harrods there was a tremendous display of proprietorial temper. Tiny turned puce at my presumption, his board turned white with terror and I reckoned my future at *The Observer* was likely to be short.

But over the years I had reached a wary accommodation with Tiny. Despite my reputation for being difficult or perhaps even because of it, he appeared to welcome my continued presence on the paper. So I thought it was just possible that, though I had by then left the paper for the BBC, Tiny would back me, particularly as the story that had landed me in trouble had been written when I was still its Political Editor. The *Mail on Sunday*'s attack was clearly aimed not just at my reputation but also at *The Observer*'s.

So when I telephoned Donald Trelford, *The Observer*'s editor, and put the case for support to him, I thought there was a sporting chance. Donald was cautious on the 'phone but promised to get back in touch. That night I wrote to him to confirm our conversation: 'Clearly whatever support, moral, financial, or otherwise *The Observer* can give me will be of enormous help because the *Mail on Sunday* know they have a much deeper pocket than mine and believe they can outface me. I hope you may feel it is not just my reputation but also the paper's which is involved.'

Two weeks later Donald rang me back. He sounded a bit embarrassed. He was afraid that Lonrho hadn't offered as much help as he would have liked. When I heard what the problem was I had to laugh. Through chance rather than choice, I had hit on the one firm of solicitors in London calculated to enrage Tiny. When he heard that Allen and Overy, the representatives of his sworn enemies, the Fayeds, were representing me, he went off the handle. In the circumstances Donald pointed out that I should count myself lucky: because of Tiny's liking for me Lonrho was prepared to offer £1,000 towards my costs. I thanked him but as such an amount was meaningless in the light of what might be needed, I decided not to take up Lonrho's offer.

I now knew that financially at least I was on my own. I thought of pursuing a 'do-it-yourself' action, dispensing with solicitors and representing myself in court. But libel is such a technical and treacherous field of the law that I realised this course would only increase my chances of losing and of having to pay the *Mail*'s costs which were bound to be considerable.

With few exceptions my friends in journalism thought I was mad to continue and did their best to dissuade me. They pointed out with some force that there would be no loss of face if I pulled out because I could not afford to sustain a lengthy action. But it was not just face that I was worried about. The *Mail on Sunday*'s attack had been widely read though no doubt it would eventually be forgotten by all but a handful. More worrying was the effect it was having on my relationships in Whitehall and Westminster.

The attitude of my new BBC bosses was also disturbing. With the gossip columns and the trade papers humming with news of my writ, I thought it sensible to write a short note to Ron Neil, head of BBC News and Current Affairs, telling him that I had reluctantly decided to sue. He didn't have the courtesy to acknowledge my letter, and from that point on I detected a distinct note of chill in the attitude of the BBC's apparatchiks. They clearly didn't like one of their current affairs presenters being caught up in a case involving the Deputy Chairman of the Conservative Party.

So why did I go on? I am not by nature a gambler. I am far too cautious and, I would like to think, streetwise for that. There is, however, a pig-headed legal streak in me, inherited from my father who was a barrister at the criminal bar before becoming a Metropolitan Magistrate. I was also confident that if I could sustain the action as far as a trial I would have a very good chance before a jury and that damages could be substantial. Whatever my motives — and frankly they were mixed — I never wavered in my determination to make Stewart Steven apologise and I decided very early on that I would not withdraw unless my lawyers told me I had a less than even chance of winning. With the odds, as I fondly believed, still in my favour I decided to carry on.

4

In Search of Evidence

*I have lost my reputation. I have lost the immortal part
of myself and what remains is bestial.*

Cassio, Othello.

I realised that if I was going to win against the *Mail on Sunday*,
I would have to do much of the work myself. However able
the lawyer, it is the plaintiff in a libel action who has the
knowledge and the contacts to be able to do the vital
background research. Even the most brilliant libel QC will not
be able to convince a jury if he doesn't have the facts. In my
action there were several areas where I knew I must get as much
information as I could.

The first and crucial point was to find out as much as I could
about why Stewart Steven had written the leader criticising me.
It was on the face of it a strange editorial judgment to attack
the integrity of a key witness in the middle of a trial. Did he
genuinely believe that I had breached journalistic ethics by
revealing Archer as my source and that this 'betrayal' was so
serious that it merited a head-on attack?

My writ and statement of claim was sent to the *Mail on
Sunday* on August 12th. It took another two months for the
paper to file its formal reply. Its defence acknowledged that
its editorial meant that I 'had not acted honourably in
elaborating on remarks' given to me off the record while giving
evidence in court. And, as expected, the *Mail on Sunday*
pleaded fair comment on a matter of public interest, 'namely
the nature and extent of a journalist's obligation not to disclose

the detail and sources of conversations which are off the record'.

The *Mail's* defence was fairly bland: it relied on the fact that I had failed to seek the protection of Section 10 of the Contempt of Court Act 1981 in order not to give evidence about my source. It ignored the fact that I had sought counsel's advice on Section 10 and had been told it was not even worth being represented in court as the issue was so clear cut. Even I, as a layman, could appreciate that the evidence I was in a position to give about what Archer had said to me about Monica Coghlan was 'essential in the interests of justice'. The *Mail*'s reply also skirted round the fact that Jeffrey and Mary Archer had given their version of his conversation with me to the court before I was called to give evidence. But the paper's defence was not entirely without force. The bounds of fair comment are rightly drawn very wide. If a jury concluded that Stewart Steven was genuinely expressing an honest opinion, they could, I realised, well find for him even if they concluded that the comment was 'unfair'. All this made it vital that I should find out as much as I could about how the leader came to be written.

From my contacts in Fleet Street I knew that there had been some dissension on the *Mail on Sunday* over the editorial. At least one senior journalist on the paper thought that Steven was 'fatally prone to bees in his bonnet', and had gone over the top. This information gathered by a good deal of painstaking digging over many weeks, encouraged me but didn't cast any light on the motive.

All that my contacts would say about this was vague. It was common knowledge in Fleet Street that Steven and Archer had an extremely close relationship. That they should get on well was not surprising: both were ambitious; both liked to play for high stakes; both came from humble backgrounds. Steven was brought to England as a child, as a refugee from Nazi Germany. Archer's early days are so uncertain that no one including his biographer is quite sure what the truth is. In Who's Who, he lists his education as 'by my wife since leaving Wellington School, Somerset', but his lack of formal academic qualifications did not stop his being accepted for a post-degree course at Oxford and running for the university and getting a blue. On the verge of bankruptcy in July 1973, 'the millionaire' gave a remarkable interview to Terry Coleman of *The Guardian* in which he claimed that he had made so much money from his fund-raising work that he need never work again. Steven is not in the same Walter Mitty league but colleagues say he has a similar romantic vision of himself.

Archer and Steven also had a common bond in that both had suffered from repeated attacks by *Private Eye*. Archer for years was hounded by the *Eye* over charges that he had submitted bogus expense claims to the charity he was working for in the late 1960s, the United Nations Association.* Steven came under fire for the way he edited his paper.

Whether it was misfortune or mutual regard that brought the two together, both had a lot to gain from their friendship. Archer's obsession with personal publicity was matched by Steven's interest in Archer's wide circle of political contacts. Archer courted journalists indiscriminately but his friendship with the editor of the *Mail on Sunday* was by far the closest. I learnt from sources close to Archer and Steven that they telephoned each other at least two or three times a week, lunched frequently and drank at a club called Jaks, just off the Tottenham Court Road.

The relationship was cemented in 1984 when the *Mail on Sunday* paid Archer £90,000 to print his latest novel, *First Among Equals*, in its entirety in four massive instalments with

---

*Archer sued Humphrey Berkeley, his boss at the UNA, over a letter that Berkeley wrote to Louth Conservative Association warning that their newly adopted parliamentary candidate was unfit to be an MP because he had falsified his expenses. The libel action was settled out of court in 1973 with Archer paying Berkeley's £18,000 costs.

another £500,000 pledged on a TV advertising campaign. Archer, a member of the Somerset Cricket Committee, also used his friendship with Botham to help settle a libel action that the England Test cricketer had brought against the *Mail on Sunday* over allegations that he had taken drugs on the New Zealand tour.

All this information was useful. But it did not prove there had been an improper motive on Steven's part for attacking me. Yet this was a crucial issue for unless there was sufficient evidence of malice the difficulty of defeating a defence of fair comment would be considerable. Malice in a legal sense is not the same as common usage. If you allege malice in a libel action the burden of proof is on the plaintiff. That meant I would have to establish to the satisfaction of the jury that Stewart Steven did not honestly hold the view that I had acted 'dishonourably'.

My lawyers were not initially very confident that there was such evidence. Nor were trusted colleagues convinced that Steven had acted improperly. But I knew my chances of winning would be increased if I could find out more about Steven's motives. Proving a state of mind is no easy task but the snide terms in which the *Mail on Sunday*'s leader was written struck me as a promising beginning. The last paragraph in particular suggested that its editor had a chip on his shoulder about papers like *The Observer*: 'Funny isn't it how it's the journalists who come from the so-called quality papers which claim to uphold journalistic standards who time after time fail to understand where honour and integrity lie.' The timing of the leader was also curious; for an editor to attack a witness in the middle of a trial, before the judge has summed up, is obviously dangerous. What had led Steven to take the risk of a prosecution for contempt?

A trawl through the BBC's newspaper cuttings library at Lime Grove and the Press Association's library in Fleet Street shed some light. The *Mail on Sunday*'s coverage of the Archer affair was, even by the standards of tabloid journalism, partisan. The first story the *Mail on Sunday* published on its front page on October 26th, 1986, the day of Archer's resignation, was an odd mixture of fact and comment. Describing the *News of the World*'s story as 'a disgrace', it went on: 'Mr Archer has been appallingly set up and appears to have been foolish enough to have walked into a trap carefully laid by the *News of the World*.'

The following week the *Mail on Sunday* returned to the fray with another front page story headlined, 'Archer's Alibi Diary': 'Fresh independent evidence has convinced Mrs Thatcher and Norman Tebbit that former Tory Deputy Chairman Jeffrey Archer never met vice girl Monica Coghlan.' Inside the *Mail on Sunday* had an 'analysis' headlined, 'Set up of Shame', which predicted: 'If the matter ever reaches court, it will take a QC less than five minutes to demolish the witnesses ranged against former Tory Party Deputy Chairman Jeffrey Archer.' After several hundred words of similar comment, the article ended in style: 'But if all his prosecutors can rely on is a prostitute, a pimp — and a newspaper like the *News of the World* — he (Archer) should at least be given the benefit of the doubt.'

Stewart Steven opened up his flank to another libel action as a result of this second article. Andrew Neil, editor of the *Sunday Times*, decided on the night the Archer scandal story was carried in his fellow Murdoch-owned paper, the *News of the World*, not to print a word about it on the grounds that 'it was not the sort of story I wish to see in the *Sunday Times*'. This explanation irritated Steven, who saw it as an attack on the morals of all the papers including his own which had followed it up.

The *Sunday Times*' editor, meanwhile, was understandably feeling rather sensitive about why his paper had failed to write a single line about one of the most sensational stories of the year. He was not amused to see it alleged by the *Mail on Sunday* the following week that he had suppressed it for improper reasons. 'All I am prepared to admit is that perhaps I made an editorial misjudgment,' said Neil. 'Any suggestion that I am a close friend of Archer's is ridiculous. I had to ask one of my reporters for his phone number.'

The *Mail on Sunday* was having none of such excuses. Its article said that 'the real reason why the *Sunday Times* didn't carry a word of the story was that Archer 'phoned Neil on Saturday night and pleaded: "Norman Tebbit has said I might survive if the story is confined to the *News of the World*. Please leave it out." ' The *Mail on Sunday*'s article then went on incautiously: 'Neil, whose staff believe that his links with Tory Central Office are too cosy, agreed.'

Whatever one makes of the *Sunday Times*' decision that night, the idea that Andrew Neil suppressed the Archer story because of his close links with Tory Central Office was laughable. Andrew Neil later told *UK Press Gazette* that he decided to withhold the story for three reasons. He was not happy about the elaborate subterfuge used in obtaining it; when Archer spoke to him he would not go on the record about either his resignation or the story; and finally Neil left it out because he was not sure how other papers would react. 'I was in a no win situation,' said Neil. 'If the *Sunday Times* had followed it up we would have been accused of being down in the gutter and because we didn't I have been accused of making a deal with Archer.'

Neil now wrote to Stewart Steven asking for a retraction and an apology. The answer from the *Mail on Sunday*'s Editor baffled him: 'We didn't attack you, you attacked us,' wrote Steven. 'I despair of British journalism and I am not going to let this one go,' retorted Andrew Neil. 'It will look very silly to have editors fighting each other in the High Court,' warned Steven who explained that Neil's excuse for not running the Archer story amounted to 'an attack on all those papers who did carry the story implying our moral standards are beneath those of the *Sunday Times*.' This encounter had all the signs of a promising battle of the Fleet Street giants. But in the end sense prevailed. After a sharp 12-month legal joust, Steven agreed to withdraw 'unreservedly' the allegations made by his paper against Andrew Neil and apologised for making them. In addition 'suitable damages' were paid which, with costs, *The Times* estimated, amounted to £10,000.

My old paper *The Observer* also had an article on November 2nd in which Laurence Marks commented on the way the Archer story had been shaped by the incestuous friendships and rivalries that exist in Fleet Street. Noting that the *News of the World*'s reporting team, which had monitored the final pay-off between Monica and Archer's friend Michael Stacpoole, had been exceptionally nervous, Marks drew attention to the Archer–Steven axis: 'The *News of the World* team had been worried that Archer might collude with his friend Stewart Steven, editor of the *Mail on Sunday*, to catch them red-handed in an unsavoury deal and expose them.'

The *Mail on Sunday*'s coverage of the actual trial was also revealing. On the first Sunday of the trial May 12th, the paper contented itself with a caption to a picture showing Jeffrey in a straw hat and his wife Mary in summer dress, relaxing in their garden in preparation for a charity performance in aid of the local church: 'Yesterday it was time to relax, far from the maddening crowd, at their country home, a converted 17th-century vicarage on the banks of the River Cam at Grantchester, deep in the Cambridgeshire countryside.' The other Sunday papers by contrast had long 'colour' articles about the trial itself. *The Observer*'s Tim Walker described it as 'a long and bloody war of attrition', while to the *Sunday Telegraph* it was 'the liveliest court drama of the year'. Not a word of the evidence was to appear in the *Mail on Sunday* throughout the three weeks of the trial.

The next Sunday, May 19th, the *Mail on Sunday* again ignored the Archer case. No mention appeared anywhere in the paper with the exception of the short editorial on the leader page accusing me of dishonourable conduct. Again the comparison with the other Sunday papers is revealing; nearly all of them devoted acres of space to the evidence of the Asian solicitor Aziz Kurtha and the other defence witnesses.

On the final Sunday, May 26th, after the verdict had been delivered and Archer had been awarded his £500,000 damages, the *Mail on Sunday* went to town. A front page exclusive interview by Susan Douglas with Mary Archer was headlined: 'My Worst Moment'. It began: 'She could talk now, for it was all over. Yet the strain of the last nine months was telling on Mary Archer. The world — and recently it has been an ugly world indeed — was now safely locked outside.' Perhaps it was the strain or maybe it was the interviewer but the only faintly interesting thing the fragrant heroine of Grantchester had to say when asked if she felt great now that it was all over, 'I feel nothing, nothing at all. When something cataclysmic happens I think you feel like that afterwards.'

Someone who was none too amused to read this interview when the first editions arrived in Wapping that night, was the editor of the *Sunday Times*. Jeffrey Archer had promised, so Andrew Neil believed, that the *Sunday Times* could have the first exclusive interview with his wife after the trial was over. When Neil telephoned Archer after the verdict and reminded him of this, he was told that neither Mary nor he were giving any interviews that weekend. To rub salt into Neil's wounds, the *Mail on Sunday* also carried a brief interview with Jeffrey on its inside page in which the author claimed, 'The verdict speaks for itself,' and said he planned to continue his legal action against the *News of the World*.

My trawl through the cuttings had provided some of the ammunition that I needed. The Steven–Archer axis was clearly demonstrated. But was there more to it than journalistic self-interest? I now turned my attention to the transcript of the trial. Unfortunately the copy I finally managed to borrow had its drawbacks. In what passed for a Fleet Street joke someone had attached a very old kipper to its binding leaving me with a very smelly research task. However buried away in thousands of pages of evidence there were clues suggesting that Stewart Steven had been more than a mere journalistic observer of the Archer–Coghlan story.

In particular the Editor of the *Mail on Sunday* appeared in the transcript to have played a role in warning Archer about the developing scandal. This was important because one of the most hotly contested issues at the trial was when Archer first learnt that a damaging story about him and a prostitute was circulating. In his evidence Archer gave a series of conflicting answers about this in order, it seemed, to try and reconcile his claim that the first call from Monica on September 25th had come as a total shock. He first said that he knew nothing about a scandal circulating about him before October 23rd but under cross-examination said he couldn't remember the precise date when he first heard the allegation about his relationship with a prostitute. There followed this exchange between the counsel for the defence and the plaintiff:

HILL: You are aware, are you not, that it has been said that you were told at the Tory Party Conference by a particular editor of a particular newspaper about the story?

ARCHER: Yes, I vaguely remember, sir.

HILL: You vaguely remember. Well who is Stewart Steven?

ARCHER: He is the Editor of the *Mail on Sunday*.

HILL: A friend of yours?

ARCHER: Yes, indeed.

HILL: Did he tell you at the Tory Party Conference about the story?

ARCHER: I'm not sure that he went into great detail on it, no, sir.

HILL: I did not ask you whether he went into great detail.

Will you answer my question, Mr Archer, please?

ARCHER: Well, you say will I answer your question, Mr Hill, as if I can remember an exact sentence. I'm sorry, sir. I'm sure — if he says that he mentioned it on that day, but I can't say to you hand on heart I remember the exact place, time and the person who said it first.

HILL: Now I will ask the question again. Did Mr Stewart Steven tell you at the Conservative Party Conference that there was a story about a sex scandal going the rounds about you?

ARCHER: I cannot remember, sir.

Stewart Steven was not called to give evidence at the trial. But he had acknowledged publicly that he warned Archer about the rumours circulating about him. According to the *Mail on Sunday*'s front page story of October 26th, 'Mr Archer was warned during the party conference by the paper's editor that this kind of story was being touted around Fleet Street for varying amounts of money.' The *Mail on Sunday*'s follow-up article a week later on November 2nd suggests, however, that Archer had been warned some time before the Tory Party Conference which began on October 7th. Archer, it said, was 'first told of the allegations by the *Mail on Sunday* six weeks ago'. That puts the warning on or around September 20th.

The timing is significant because of Archer's claim at the trial that he had no knowledge of any scandal involving him before the first telephone call to him by Monica Coghlan on September 25th. Did Steven tip off Archer before this date? To understand why the timing is important, it is necessary to go back to almost the beginning of the Archer story.

The alleged sex tryst between Archer and Monica was in the early hours of September 9th in the seedy Albion Hotel in Victoria. The next morning the Asian solicitor Aziz Kurtha excitedly told Paul Halloran, a freelance journalist working for *Private Eye*, that he had seen Archer with a prostitute. That same evening Halloran, who was also on a £400 a month 'retainer' from the *Mail on Sunday*, arranged to have a drink at Groucho's, a Soho club much frequented by journalists, with Sue Douglas, then features editor of the *Mail on Sunday*. Halloran told her about Kurtha's tale knowing that the *Mail on Sunday* would probably not be very interested because of Steven's close friendship with Archer. In view of the relationships that existed the story was also likely to get back to Archer very quickly indeed. So by the time the *News of the World* learnt of Monica's tale as a result of what Halloran claims was a chance meeting in a pub between its chief investigative reporter and Aziz Kurtha, Jeffrey Archer almost certainly knew of the plot against him through his friend at the *Mail on Sunday*, Stewart Steven.

All this is consistent with the evidence given by the editor of the *News of the World*, David Montgomery, at the Archer trial. He told the jury that he had had two telephone conversations with Archer before September 25th in which Archer had indicated that he knew stories were circulating about himself and a prostitute.

All this points to the probability that Stewart Steven tipped off Archer about the scandal very soon after Aziz Kurtha had touted it to *Private Eye*. Feeling, perhaps foolishly, that I had nothing to lose, I attempted to confirm Steven's role in giving this early warning to Archer by approaching Sue Douglas. It was a long shot. Sue, an attractive slim girl, accepted my invitation to lunch with alacrity but I learnt nothing and she spent most of the time seeking to persuade me to drop my libel action against the *Mail on Sunday*.

The transcripts provided one other revealing detail. In Monica's first two calls to Archer on September 25th and October 2nd, she stalled and refused to give him the name or telephone number of the man she claimed was pestering her and spreading rumours about her relationship with Archer. But in her third phone call on October 23rd, she finally told

Archer it was Aziz Kurtha. Archer's solicitor Lord Mishcon then wrote to Kurtha warning him off and saying he had 'unimpeachable sources' for the charge that he was spreading rumours about his client. Who was this unimpeachable source? The transcript of Archer's examination-in-chief by his counsel gave the answer:

> ROBERT ALEXANDER QC: By now Miss Coghlan had given you Mr Kurtha as the person who was spreading the story about you which you were concerned about. Did you seek to check with anyone else — and just for the moment answer the question 'yes' or 'no' — whether or not such a story was being put around by Mr Kurtha?
>
> JEFFREY ARCHER: Yes.
>
> ALEXANDER: Could you simply give the identity of the person with whom you sought to check that?
>
> ARCHER: The Editor of the *Mail on Sunday*, Stewart Steven.

I believed a jury would feel that an editor who acted in this way, though it was quite proper, was not a wholly disinterested spectator of the events that followed.

Around this time I made another significant discovery. The *Mail on Sunday*'s defence was based on the claim that Stewart Steven felt passionately about journalistic ethics and had been genuinely outraged by my conduct in disclosing Archer as my source. A jury wouldn't have to agree with his criticisms of me to find for the paper; they would only have to accept, provided that the facts on which Steven based his opinion were accurate, that it was honestly expressed. But did the editor of the *Mail on Sunday* really feel so keenly about the protection of journalistic sources?

His leading article attacking me had started with a mention of the only other major case in recent years involving confidentiality of journalistic sources: 'Welcome Adam

Raphael to the Peter Preston school of journalism. After a most deplorable incident, *The Guardian*, edited by Preston has been dubbed the newspaper which betrays its sources . . .' This was a reference to the case of the Foreign Office secretary Sarah Tisdall who was prosecuted under the Official Secrets Act in 1984.

Whether the *Mail on Sunday*'s readers understood any of this is, however, doubtful. Sarah Tisdall was sentenced to six months on Friday March 23rd, 1984 but the news came too late for the Saturday morning papers to write much about it except to print straight news stories. The first papers, therefore, to comment about the sentence and the background to it were the Sunday papers.

All of them, with one notable exception, seized on what was, in Fleet Street terms, a big story and commented about it extensively. *The Observer*, after remarking that no one came out of the case with credit, commented that 'protecting sources is the most sacred of all journalistic principles'. The *Sunday Express* accused *The Guardian* of 'shopping' Sarah Tisdall by surrendering the evidence against her. The *Sunday Times* said the error of *The Guardian* in failing to destroy the incriminating document was 'an error for which the Editor will privately suffer for many a long year'.

The following day the *Daily Mirror* joined in labelling the six months sentence 'a disgrace to the government which prosecuted her and a disgrace to *The Guardian* newspaper which indirectly put her in the dock'. These were not opinions that I personally shared. *The Guardian* had been guilty of a professional error in not destroying the documents before it was forced to by the courts. But to accuse the paper of betrayal when it didn't even know who its source was struck me as overly harsh.

The one paper that studiously ignored the whole Tisdall affair both that week and in future weeks was the *Mail on Sunday*. The paper did not write a word about it at the time unlike almost all its rivals in Fleet Street. That Stewart Steven should have rediscovered an interest in it three-and-half years later in the middle of the Archer case struck me as revealing. When another case of journalistic confidence involving Jeremy Warner, a financial journalist on *The Independent*, arose three months after my writ for libel had been served, the *Mail on Sunday*'s leader column waxed lyrical: 'If we value a free and vigorous Press independent of Government, we must allow journalists — save in the most extreme of cases — to be allowed to keep their sources of information sacrosanct. For the moment and not for the first time in our history, the conscience of one man must stand sentry duty for us all.'

This research as to Steven's motives was to prove invaluable at a conference with my counsel which took place on October 27th. It was my first meeting with James Price; his initial opinion had been delivered in writing. Just as policemen look younger and younger as one gets older, so do lawyers. Slight, dark haired with an attractive smile, he seemed deceptively meek behind his spectacles. Illusions of grandeur were also quickly dispelled. In contrast to the palatial reception rooms at Allen and Overy, Price's room at 10 South Square in Gray's Inn was so small that I seriously doubted whether all five of us — David Mackie and his assistant Tim House from Allen and Overy, myself, Price and his pupil — could squeeze in.

The conference began with Price saying that his view of the case had not changed since he gave his opinion three months ago. It was, in his view, 'a serious libel'. The leader had been written in vituperative terms. 'If the jury like you and they don't like Mr Steven, they might give very heavy damages — but not in the Archer class.' He explained that an oddity of the defence was that the *Mail on Sunday* were not seeking to claim that it was an established convention that journalists did not reveal their sources, merely that it was Stewart Steven's view that I should not have done so. He judged on the evidence submitted to him that we should now file a reply to the *Mail*'s defence, alleging malice. Price said that with the material I had dug up on Steven, it was 'a solid action, though of course, there were risks attached to it.'

As we came out of the dark chambers into the sunshine of Gray's Inn, my solicitor, David Mackie, the senior litigation partner at Allen and Overy said to me, 'I hope you were encouraged by that.' He obviously saw doubt on my face for he added, 'Price is acting for us in another private client case and his judgments have been very shrewd.' Mackie, who clearly thought my morale needed bolstering, went on to say that he hoped to get a settlement out of the *Mail* fairly soon by using 'his old boy network to put the frighteners on them.' I said nothing, but remembered others saying that the *Mail* tended to run their cases very long and that therefore the chances of a settlement until just before the case came for trial were probably slim.

The most important decision to come out of this first conference was that there was enough evidence to justify filing a Reply to the *Mail on Sunday*'s Defence, alleging malice.

The Reply, a formal but crucial stage in a libel action, set out five arguments why the *Mail on Sunday*'s editorial attacking me had not been 'fairly' written. First, the harsh language of the attack had been clearly designed to damage my professional reputation. Second, the Reply noted that Stewart Steven had failed to contact me in advance of publishing his attack to hear what I had to say. His leader had made no mention that I had sought legal advice and had been advised that Section 10 of the Contempt of Court Act gave me no protection. Nor did his editorial note the fact that I had appeared under subpoena and had given evidence about my conversation with Archer only *after* he and his wife had given their account to the court.

Third, he had neglected to point out that I had taken legal advice and had expressly warned Archer in advance of the trial about what I proposed to do. Fourth, the *Mail on Sunday* had failed to make any mention of the fact that I was not the only journalist who disclosed Archer as his source. It had also omitted any mention of Rupert Morris who had told defence lawyers before the trial that his story had been written after speaking to Archer. Finally, the Reply pointed out that Stewart Steven was a long-standing friend of Jeffrey Archer's and that Steven had made no attempt to correct, or apologise for, what he had said about me despite having been told the facts many months ago.

The reaction to this missive was an approach from Swepstone Walsh, the *Mail*'s solicitors, offering me a letter in the *Mail on Sunday* to put my side of the case. As a sign that the paper was none too confident about its position, I welcomed it. But otherwise it was clearly a trap aimed at mitigating any damages and seeking to establish that the *Mail on Sunday* had acted in good faith throughout. A tough response was drafted by Allen and Overy saying the offer completely ignored the nature of the dispute and the damage caused by the attack. 'If your clients now recognise the damage they have caused our client's professional reputation, they should put forward appropriate terms for settlement to include an apology, damages, and costs.'

Shortly before Christmas an important step was reached when a date was fixed in the New Year for a hearing before a Master at which a Summons for Directions establishing the procedural ground rules and timing of the action would be decided. At this point, I was advised it might be valuable to see if I could get expert witnesses to support my claim that I had not breached journalistic ethics in naming Archer as my source. From the start I was confident that the overwhelming majority of my colleagues, if they knew the full facts, would not be critical of my conduct in giving evidence in the way I had done.

I therefore wrote to a dozen of the leading members of my profession asking whether they would be prepared to give evidence on my behalf. The first to respond was Charles Wintour, former editor of the *Evening Standard*, whose reply was as equivocal as it was sobering. 'I think you are in a difficulty,' he wrote, 'because there are two views about whether you were right in your judgment about coming clean and some quite impartial journalists feel genuinely uncomfortable about your decision. Others would agree with you. But the *Mail on Sunday* might argue that their criticism, though harshly made, was fair comment.' Wintour's view expressed in his detailed letter was that the ties of confidentiality still existed even if the source disclosed that a conversation had taken place. Only if a serious crime was about to be committed did he believe that a journalist was entitled to break a confidence. 'In my view,' he concluded, 'it is impossible to come down flatly in your favour but I do think the *Mail on Sunday* went too far.'

This reply depressed me considerably. If one of Fleet Street's most knowledgeable editors thought my behaviour dubious, was it worth carrying on with my action? Fortunately for my morale the other experts were more supportive. Three of the twelve declined to get involved on grounds ranging from old age to conflicts of interest. But the other eight all said they were prepared to give evidence on my behalf.

Lord Rees-Mogg (then Sir William), the former Editor of *The Times*, counselled caution: 'The case could be a disaster for you financially and a disaster for you in the terms of personal anxiety that it would cause.' But he said he believed my conduct was 'perfectly proper in difficult circumstances and that the *Mail on Sunday*'s leader was most unjust'. He explained: 'Once the source has disclosed the nature of a confidential conversation, the journalist's obligation of confidentiality has been waived. If a source says, "I said X," and the journalist knows that he said Y, then the journalist is not under an obligation to assent by his silence to the public maintenance of a lie.' Rees-Mogg said he believed there were instances where a journalist's duty as a citizen overrode his duty to protect his source. 'A journalist who was told by Guy Fawkes that he intended to blow up the Houses of Parliament would have the duty of any citizen to report Guy Fawkes to the appropriate authorities. Nevertheless a journalist must put the duty of confidentiality very high and the social duty which might lead him to break confidentiality has to be of an absolutely compelling nature.'

The Editor of *The Independent*, Andreas Whittam Smith, whose paper was fined £20,000 after appealing right up to the House of Lords to protect one of his reporters from having to reveal his sources to an official inquiry into insider dealing, also took the view that I had acted correctly. 'As for the *Mail on Sunday*'s comments on your behaviour, I think the criticism was misplaced and very damaging to your reputation. Once a source has voluntarily admitted supplying a journalist with information, a journalist has a right to insist the transaction is accurately reported.'

To the specific question whether a journalist is still bound by confidence if the source disclosed in court his version of a confidential conversation, he replied: 'My answer is that in those circumstances, the source having voluntarily revealed his or her identity, then a journalist may have a duty to correct a misleading impression. Journalists are trusted to report accurately on events.'

The former Editor of *The Guardian*, Alastair Hetherington, said that while it must be exceptional for a journalist to breach confidence by identifying a source, it was sometimes necessary. 'Such cases come when a journalist's duty as a citizen has to override his duties as a journalist.' To the question, had I acted properly? Hetherington, my first editor in Fleet Street who is now Professor of Communications at Stirling University replied, 'As far as I can see, you were fully justified in disclosing the source . . . generally if the source has already identified itself, that relieves the journalist of the need to remain silent.'

Professor Hugh Stephenson, Professor of Journalism at City University and former Editor of *The New Statesman*, responded with a lengthy memorandum setting out his view of confidentiality: 'You will see that in this case my view is that you were justified in saying what you did in court . . . the justification for what you did was that Archer by his behaviour had in effect released you from a duty of silence even with the thumb screws on.'

To the specific question, was I entitled to break confidence once Archer had given his version of the conversation to the court? he answered, 'Certainly, as a working journalist I would have felt myself released from the moral obligation if my source subsequently gave on the record what I regarded as an inaccurate or tendentious account of a conversation.' He concluded, 'A journalist's obligation to protect a source cannot be simply defined. The general accusation, however, that a journalist is unable to keep a confidence, is highly damaging from a professional point of view.'

Lord Ardwick, former Editor of the *Daily Herald*, who sent me a detailed historical survey of journalistic confidentiality, was equally clear. He first posed the question: 'Can a journalist whose evidence is so central to the case that it will affect the verdict stand by and refuse to testify simply because it goes against the professional ethic? Can he stand by and allow an injustice to be done?' Lord Ardwick had no doubts: 'I think it would be very hard for a journalist who is directed by a judge to answer a question in such a case to refuse to do so and he would not have the sympathy of public opinion if he refused.' He concluded: 'Mr Raphael was not only free to speak, but justified in expanding the information he had printed, in an effort to rebut the reflection made on his professional competence as a reporter . . . Nobody has ever suggested that a journalist whose source has voluntarily come forward should refuse to confirm that this was the source. That would be carrying professionalism into theology.'

The former General Secretary of the Institute of Journalists Mr Bob Farmer, wrote: 'In the Archer case I do not think Raphael's decision was hard to take or that he took it wrongly.' A similar stance was taken by Louis Heren, former Deputy Editor of *The Times*: 'If a source reveals the basis of a confidential conversation, the journalist is no longer bound to protect him.' Finally Geoffrey Goodman, former Industrial Editor of the *Daily Mirror*, stressed that he took the strictest view of the need for journalists to respect the confidence of their sources: 'Your case is different chiefly because Archer had already disclosed to the Court that you were the journalist concerned and therefore the issue of violating a confidence did not arise.'

I was heartened by these replies. Eight of the most distinguished and respected members of my profession took the view that I had acted honourably and were prepared to appear as expert witnesses on my behalf. The views expressed also cast considerable doubt on Stewart Steven's boast in *UK Press Gazette* on receipt of my writ: 'It will be one of the great *causes célèbres* in Fleet Street . . . I think I will find in the witness box coming to assist me in this matter will be some of the more distinguished journalists in Fleet Street, Members of Parliament, and members of the American press.'

All this was very encouraging to me but it was to have less effect on the actual action. When the Summons for Direction was held in the High Court on January 5th, 1988, the Master ruled that he was not prepared to allow expert evidence at this stage on the grounds that this was unnecessary despite the fact that the *Mail on Sunday* also wanted to introduce it. David Mackie advised me that it was open to us to restore the summons at a later date and that it was extremely unlikely the court would refuse to make an order for expert evidence if both sides persisted in asking for it.

Two other points emerged from the hearing before the Master: he ordered that both sides should produce their lists of documents for inspection and required the *Mail* to reply to our request for further and better particulars of the defence. In my case neither of these steps was particularly important. But often the outcome of libel actions is determined in such procedural manoeuvrings. In particular the process of Discovery under which each side is allowed to inspect any correspondence or documents relating to the action, which are not privileged (e.g. are not written between the plaintiff/defendant and his legal advisers) can be decisive. But in my case these steps were merely formalities. Neither I nor the *Mail on Sunday* had many documents apart from newspaper cuttings and all we received from them, as they did in turn from us, were bland answers in response to the demand for further and better particulars.

Meanwhile I was continuing to inquire into the Steven–Archer relationship. Most of the those who helped me would, no doubt, want to stay anonymous so I can't go into any detail. But one contact proved absolutely vital. Through Archer's acquaintances, I tried to reach his confidential secretary Angie Peppiatt who organised Jeffrey's working life and who used to ring me up when he wanted to get in touch. For some months she refused to respond to my calls. Then one day out of the blue she rang me saying she had just left Archer's employment and wanted to come and see me.

When she arrived at my house just off Holland Park, Angie, a dashing middle 40s blonde divorcee was in a highly dramatic state. Her milieu is powerful, very rich men, which is perhaps why she has an exaggerated idea of what they can do. The main reason she had come, she said, was to warn me that Archer would go to any lengths to destroy me. When I laughed and asked what he could do apart from having my dustbins searched, she shook her head impatiently as if dealing with a small boy. She kept on asking whether I realised what I was taking on and claimed that Archer would do anything and say anything if it would help either himself or Steven. 'He will stop at nothing,' she claimed.

I took all this with a pinch of salt but Angie with her inside knowledge was helpful about the Archer–Steven friendship. The two, she said, were hand in glove, spoke to each other four or five times a week on the 'phone and frequently met for lunch or dinner. Archer, she said, had been in close touch with Steven during the trial.

When she left, I speculated about her reasons for telling me all this. It was possible that she had been sent by Archer or Steven to sound me out, but the more straightforward explanation, I thought, was that she had fallen out with her employer. Later I heard that Archer had refused to pay her a salary increase and they had had a row over money which she claimed was owed to her. But so far as I could tell Angie had useful information even if her motives were mixed.

Unfortunately it was clear that Angie was not willing to tell me all she knew. I had told her that if she wanted money for her story, I was the wrong person to come to. She must have known that already — there were many well-heeled suitors for the story she had to tell. Subsequently I heard that someone, without her permission, had been touting her exclusive story around Fleet Street for £100,000.

Angie Peppiatt's inside version of the Archer ménage prompted me to dig a little deeper into that world. The man whom Archer had employed to pay off Monica for him at Victoria Station with a bundle of £2,000 in fifty-pound notes was a long-time associate, Michael Stacpoole. Stacpoole is one of those characters who hang around the fringes of Fleet Street, with no visible means of employment or income but always ready for a drink and a gossip. If one was being kind, one might describe him as a high-class fixer. Archer, however, found him helpful and used him for a variety of tasks, apparently paying him some sort of retainer. It was thus with few illusions that I tried to get in touch with him. If Stacpoole had a fixed abode and a telephone number, no one knew them.

The way to reach him, I was told, was by leaving a message at the Solo Press Agency just off Fleet Street run by a former *Express* journalist turned impresario called Don Short.

Within hours Stacpoole returned my call and appeared only too keen to come and talk. When he arrived in crumpled pin-striped suit, discreetly smelling of gin, he too had an intriguing story to tell about Archer's world, but he made clear from the start that he wanted large sums of money for it.

For my purposes of wanting to find out details of the Steven–Archer relationship, he was useless. But after seeing Stacpoole I at least knew the sort of people I was dealing with. As to why he had come so readily, I had little doubt he soon reported back to Archer and possibly also Steven about what I was up to. But I didn't particularly mind them knowing. It was inevitable, in view of the extensive inquiries I had been making, that some of the details should filter back to them.

It appeared that someone was also making inquiries about me. Towards the end of January, Caroline, my wife, received a 'phone call at home from a man who described himself as a freelance journalist saying he wanted to know whether I had written anything about the Archer case. When I rang him back, he claimed he was proposing to write about the trial, saying he thought it had not been properly reported. After a good deal of waffle, he asked me whether I had written anything about the case. I referred him to my letter in *The Independent* and confirmed that I was suing the *Mail on Sunday*. But though he pretended to be interested that was clearly not what he had rung me about.

He began to ask me a series of detailed and sensitive questions about my evidence at the trial, in particular why I had decided to reveal Archer as my source. I skirted around these obvious traps for a couple of minutes before finally telling him he was a fool if he thought I would answer those sort of questions on the 'phone from someone I had never heard of. With that parting shot, I hung up.

The next odd episode was mostly my own fault. Pursuing my researches, I telephoned Aziz Kurtha and asked him to have lunch with me to discuss the Archer case. When he accepted, I suggested in a moment of bravado the RAC Club in Pall Mall, though I knew it was a less than discreet venue. A few days later I waited for my guest in the club foyer, chatting to *The Sun*'s Political Editor Trevor Kavanagh who was also waiting for a lunch guest. A minute later Jeffrey Archer strode through the swing doors and headed straight for Trevor, who, it suddenly dawned on me, was his host. I stared boldly at Jeffrey for a moment before he swerved and I stepped aside. By the time Kurtha arrived a few moments later, my nerve had cracked and I took him to lunch around the corner. The idea of Archer, Kurtha, and myself eating in the same restaurant would have been bad for all our digestions.

5

Victory

The defence of a just cause is easy.
Cicero

Another call which came out of the blue at this time was rather more welcome. Early in March 1988, an intermediary from the *Mail on Sunday* rang me at home. It was clear from this approach that the paper's lawyers, if not its editor, were anxious to get out of what was threatening to become a very expensive action. The outcome of this informal contact was a suggestion that I should write an article in the *Mail on Sunday* explaining why I had given evidence against Archer, to which Stewart Steven would be entitled to reply. I immediately made it clear that this would not be acceptable and that I wanted an apology in open court for an attack which had done me serious damage. I also said I would want substantial damages, all my costs paid and the freedom to write about the settlement. These terms were clearly too tough for the *Mail on Sunday* to swallow for I heard no more. It was a distinct fillip to my morale to know that the paper was sufficiently worried to consider a settlement.

This initial peace attempt was discussed at a second meeting with my counsel the following month. James Price felt it raised his hopes of an early settlement, that the *Mail on Sunday* was clearly worried about my action. The libel list (the queue of actions waiting to be heard) was collapsing, he noted, because in the light of the huge damages awarded to Archer and others newspapers were terrified of fighting actions. Perhaps made over-confident by this, I brashly said that I must have the word 'substantial' spelled out in any reference to damages. Price laughed and said that could be as little as £5,000. I demurred and said surely 'substantial' meant something above £10,000. Price said his view still remained that a jury was likely to be sympathetic to my argument, but he warned that in a fair comment defence nothing was certain.

The main purpose of the conference was a detailed discussion as to whether we should call expert evidence. My counsel clearly had decided against. Thinking of all the work I had put into this (and had put others to), I argued strongly that a jury would be influenced by the quality of those who had agreed to give evidence for me. Price said the danger was the case would turn into a trial of opinion, noting that the *Mail on Sunday* also wanted to call experts and therefore Stewart Steven must have got someone to back up his view. I said I couldn't believe it was anyone of much repute, but after putting up a show of resistance, yielded. It is no good hiring professionals in such a treacherous field as libel if you then reject their advice. Price did, however, accept my urging that we should use the *Mail on Sunday*'s failure to report the Sarah Tisdall case. Thus, when the further and better particulars of the Reply were served on the *Mail on Sunday*, this point was specifically pleaded.

The summer was spent in the interminable detailed pleadings of a libel action. The further and better particulars of our Reply was followed by the further and better particulars of the Defence. A year had gone by since the Archer trial and the *Mail on Sunday*'s attack, and I felt we were not all that much further forward. I knew it was going to be a long slog but I had not realised quite how slowly the wheels of a libel action grind. My action, I was told, was at least a year away from trial. Around this time I doubted whether it was all worth it. The action had taken up an enormous amount of my time and emotional energy; costs on both sides were mounting fast, but I was in too deep to retreat.

One welcome development was that I had rejoined *The Observer* as an Assistant Editor in charge of its investigative/consumer affairs column, Open File. I was glad to see the back of television on two counts. I had never mastered the seemingly easy, but to me fiendishly difficult, art of being a presenter and the BBC was also a very unhappy place as it was in the midst of John Birt's current affairs revolution. Returning to the world I knew and understood in Fleet Street – even though *The Observer* had by now moved to south of Chelsea Bridge – meant that I was back among supportive friends. I breathed a sigh of relief as, no doubt, did all those *Newsnight* viewers who had watched me struggling to read the autocue with my contact lenses going in and out of focus like a merry-go-round.

At the beginning of October, I received another call at home from the *Mail*'s intermediary who said that he would like to settle my libel action if at all possible. At first I was puzzled as to why I had been rung out of the blue after a six month interval, but then I heard that the *Mail on Sunday* was on the point of settling the *Sunday Times* action. Stewart Steven clearly wanted to get my action out of the way before the details of his settlement with Andrew Neil were announced in open court.

I gave the *Mail on Sunday* no indication that I knew about this but I deliberately took a tough line. I said I was still very angry, that I believed that Stewart Steven had acted disgracefully towards me and that, if necessary, I was prepared to go trial. All this was designed to convince the *Mail on Sunday* that I really was determined to risk everything to clear my reputation. It seemed to achieve that effect for it was then made clear that the paper wanted to know my conditions for a settlement. I listed four things: a statement in open court, an apology to be printed in a prominent position in the *Mail on Sunday*, my full legal costs, and substantial damages. When I was asked what I meant by 'substantial', I replied £30,000, a figure which I picked out of the blue but which I thought bore some relation to the amount of time, worry and energy that I had invested fighting the action. Pressed further as to whether the £30,000 was open to negotiation, I said yes but made it clear that a *much* lower amount would not be acceptable and that I was confident that a jury would award me a great deal more.

I also made clear that the statement in open court would have to acknowledge that I had not betrayed a source, nor acted dishonourably, and that Stewart Steven would have to apologise for writing what he did. These conditions did not appear to disturb the intermediary. I later wrote to my lawyer David Mackie: 'My gut impression is that the *Mail on Sunday*, if not Steven, would be prepared to settle on roughly my terms but will now try and haggle about the details. If nothing else, I think he (Steven) will be under no illusion about my determination to clear my reputation.'

A libel action is like a game of poker played for very high stakes. I knew the end play was now in progress and that it was vital to keep my nerve, but it was not easy. I was both worried and impatient; the strain on my family, in particular, was considerable. Allen and Overy had gone out of their way to help by not submitting a bill for over 18 months – a signal act of faith – but I knew my costs must already be well over five figures. I waited some weeks for the *Mail on Sunday* to come back to me but heard no more. Stewart Steven was still clearly hoping that I would back down.

At the beginning of December, I learnt that my case would reach the 'warned list' – the actions at the head of the queue for trial – on January 11th and could come on at very short notice any day thereafter. Around the same time, Donald Trelford told me that *The Observer* had been asked by Richard Hartley QC if I would object if he represented the *Mail on Sunday* against me. As Hartley had represented *The Observer* in a number of recent libel cases, including Michael Meacher's

which he won for us and Roger Scruton's, which cost us
£75,000 in damages, the answer went back to his clerk that
I would not be happy for him to take the brief.

With the *Mail on Sunday* gearing up for a trial, it was clearly
time for us to make our dispositions. Up to this point, I had
not consulted a senior counsel, having been very satisfied with
the advice given by James Price. But if the *Mail* was going
to be represented by a silk, I did not want to be outgunned.
I had also been impressed by the salutary lesson of Michael
Meacher's disaster against *The Observer*. He had not been
helped, so I thought, by the way his case had been fought.
The initial view of David Mackie was that the best counsel to
approach would be Charles Gray QC who was 'coming into
his prime'.

I knew very little about Gray but had heard he was good
at charming both judges and juries, though he was not thought
to be a particularly tough cross-examiner. In my action that
was not what was needed so I gladly endorsed the suggestion.
However, when Charles Gray's clerk was telephoned, the
unwelcome news came back that he had already been briefed
by the *Mail on Sunday* to act against me. Ironically it seemed
that by denying the *Mail* its first choice, I had in turn been
blocked from mine. David Mackie now recommended that we
should approach David Eady QC, a suggestion that I welcomed
for in my limited dealings with him I had found him both acute
and direct. Eady's clerk confirmed that he was available and
it was arranged that I should see him early in the New Year.

Stewart Steven must have heard of these arrangements – the
libel Bar is a very small place – because, a week before
Christmas, I received yet another call saying the *Mail* now
wanted to settle the action and 'wrap it all up before
Christmas'. It was obvious that the advice the paper had
received from Charles Gray was that it should get out from
my action as quickly and as cheaply as it could.

I was not very surprised, but was slightly taken aback, when

I was told that Stewart Steven was willing to apologise in the terms set out in my original demand for an apology. I responded to this peace offer by saying that though that original statement was broadly acceptable, it was written more than 18 months ago and that I would want any statement in open court and any apology printed in the paper to be more specific, in particular it would have to mention the fact that 'substantial damages' had been paid. I also said that I would require the apology to be printed on page 3 or page 5 of the *Mail on Sunday* in the top right hand column. But the sticking point as far as the paper was concerned was clearly the amount of damages. The *Mail on Sunday* put forward an initial offer of £15,000. I pointed out that I had already specified £30,000 as well as my full costs. A counter-offer of £20,000 was then suggested. At this point, feeling like a rug merchant in an Eastern bazaar, I replied that I did not want to get into detailed negotiations on damages but would want to take advice before either accepting or rejecting the offer.

With Christmas and the New Year intervening, there was no time to consult my lawyers before I heard, somewhat to my surprise, that the *Mail on Sunday* had paid £20,000 into court. This tactic set the meter ticking. I now had 21 days to take the money and run. If not, and the case came to court, I would be at risk of having to pay the costs of the trial if the jury awarded me damages of £20,000 or less. It was, I thought, in view of the peace overtures made to me only two weeks before, a less than friendly gesture. But David Mackie, at Allen and Overy, saw it as a normal defensive tactic by the paper. So did David Eady, whom I saw for the first time on January 5th in his chambers at 1 Brick Court. 'What we are principally talking about in this case is damages. I would regard the payment in not as a take-it or leave-it payment but as a sign that they want to settle,' he said.

With James Price sitting alongside, Eady said he believed that the most likely figure a jury would award me was in the

£50,000–£75,000 range. But he warned that juries were not well disposed to journalists. 'The view that they might take is that a dog should expect a few bites from a fellow dog but you ought to win on the merits.' He added though that he regarded the *Mail on Sunday*'s libel as a serious one. On the question of whether Steven had committed a contempt by attacking a witness in mid-trial, he thought that this by itself would not defeat a defence of fair comment, but it would make the jury less sympathetic to the *Mail on Sunday*'s case.

Eady also counselled a soft approach on the issue of malice. The best way, he said, of exploring the Archer–Steven relationship was by gentle cross-examination. If we produced witnesses such as Angela Peppiatt there was a danger of relitigating the Archer case and juries 'seem to like Archer'. James Price agreed and said that it would also be dangerous for us if we turned the case into an attack on Stewart Steven's journalistic record. We needed to keep the case simple and straightforward – it was about my reputation, no one else's. Though much of the conference was taken up in a discussion of how we would fight a trial, it was clear that Eady, Price, and Mackie were confident that this was a case that would settle.

Towards the end of the meeting tactics were agreed. We would go back to the *Mail on Sunday* saying that I required £30,000 plus my costs and an apology and that we were confident that I would get 'sensationally more' if it went to a jury. Eady said this settlement was the least unattractive option as far as Steven was concerned. If the action went to trial, he pointed out, the result would be very bad publicity and the real possibility of huge damages being awarded against his paper.

Following the conference, I faxed the text of a draft apology to David Mackie. It was headed, 'Adam Raphael – An Apology':

. . . In our leader column of the 19th July, 1987 we attacked Mr Adam Raphael, Executive Editor of *The Observer*, for betraying his source when giving evidence in the Archer libel trial. At that time we were unaware of the full circumstances in which Mr Raphael had been compelled to give evidence and that he had done so only after both Mr and Mrs Archer had given their version of the conversation to the court.

We were also unaware that Mr Raphael had specifically warned Mr Archer in advance of the trial that he would have to give evidence about the conversation if he (Archer) first disclosed details about it to the court. We now recognise that Mr Raphael felt obliged to give evidence in the way he did in the interests of justice. In the circumstances we are, therefore, happy to set the record straight, to apologise to Mr Raphael and to pay him substantial damages for this unjustified attack which we profoundly regret.

I had deliberately pitched the draft on the tough side to give Allen and Overy room to negotiate. Sure enough when Swepstone Walsh eventually responded on behalf of the *Mail on Sunday*, it was to offer considerably less than I had asked. The *Mail*'s solicitors proposed the following apology: 'In our leader column of 19th July 1987 we attacked Mr Adam Raphael, Executive Editor of *The Observer* for betraying his source when giving evidence in the Archer libel trial. At that time we were unaware of the full circumstances in which Mr Raphael had been compelled to give evidence and that he had only done so after both Mr and Mrs Archer had given their version of the conversation to the court. We now recognise that acting on legal advice Mr Raphael felt obliged to give evidence in the way he did. In the circumstances we are, therefore, happy to set the record straight and to apologise to Mr Raphael.'

From my viewpoint this apology was unsatisfactory because it failed to mention that the paper had been obliged to pay 'substantial damages', and it also omitted all mention of my pre-trial warning to Jeffrey Archer, as well as any expression of genuine regret. Most important of all, no undertaking was made as to where in the paper the apology was to be printed. The *Mail on Sunday* had also failed to meet my demand for £30,000 damages plus costs. Allen and Overy estimated my costs to date at £20,125, but Swepstone Walsh said they had been instructed to offer an 'all in' figure of £41,000 to cover both costs and damages.

However this first formal offer proved to be so much hot air because, in the event, it was too much for Stewart Steven to swallow. Quite what happened can only be guessed at. But clearly the editor of the *Mail on Sunday* was living up to his reputation for being difficult as far as lawyers were concerned. Swepstone Walsh now had the embarrassing task of returning to the fray with a completely new brief. Their next communication two weeks later withdrew their first offer of an apology and instead substituted an even queasier form of words which left open the question whether I had behaved properly: 'At that time we were unaware of the full circumstances under which Mr Raphael believed he had been compelled to give evidence. Mr and Mrs Archer had both given evidence in Court of an off-the-record conversation Mr Archer had had with Mr Raphael. Accordingly, Mr Raphael felt that he had been released from his obligation to the off-the-record nature of his conversation and felt it right to give his version of what had been said in evidence.'

I told Kate Buckley and David Mackie that I would prefer to go to trial rather than accept this half-baked retraction. There then followed days of telephone negotiation between the lawyers on either side in a vain attempt to find a form of words which would satisfy both Steven and myself. He was unwilling to concede that I had acted properly even if I believed I had. I was not prepared to accept anything less than a full apology. With my case rapidly approaching the head of the 'warned list', it looked as though this brinkmanship would carry us all over the edge into a trial.

As far as I was concerned I was less nervous than impatient.

After more than 18 months of waiting for a hearing I was fed up. The sooner it was all over I thought, somewhat rashly, the better. If I lost I would have to pay up but I hadn't gone this far merely to compromise. I was confident that so long as I called Steven's bluff, he would collapse. In the middle of February, Kate Buckley rang me and suggested that I come into her office for one final discussion before she put an ultimatum to Swepstone Walsh. When I arrived at midday, she said she had been on the telephone all morning to the *Mail*'s solicitor Mr Roderick Dadak. Stewart Steven was still insisting that any statement should say that I 'believed' I had been compelled to give evidence. He was not prepared to go an inch beyond this.

When I told Kate Buckley that I would not accept any statement that contained the word 'believed', she replied quietly, 'I want you to know that that word may cost you £100,000.' She was right to warn me. If I lost at trial the combined costs would be, at least £100,000, probably nearer £150,000. She also warned me that even if I won there must be some doubt whether the jury would award more than the *Mail*'s payment into court. If I got £20,000 or less in damages, I would have to pay the whole cost of the trial which was likely to be in excess of £60,000.

These huge sums should have sobered me but they didn't. I asked Kate Buckley to stand firm and insist on a proper apology. The next day she wrote to Swepstone Walsh: 'We state categorically for the record that our client will not accept any statement or apology which suggests that he simply believed he was released from this duty or believed he was compelled to give evidence. We remain of the view that the enclosed apology and statement are a fair means of disposing of this matter. However, it seems that your clients are not prepared to accept this and we have no choice but to go to trial.'

This tough letter did the trick. Two days later Kate telephoned me at *The Observer* with the news that Stewart Steven had backed down and was now willing to publish an apology in the terms I had originally demanded, leaving out only the last sentence which referred to substantial damages. The *Mail*'s lawyers still wanted me, however, to agree to include the phrase 'in good faith' in the statement to be made by its solicitor in open court: 'The article was published in good faith about a matter of fundamental importance to journalists, namely their duty to protect their sources.'

I refused bluntly to accept this. I was not prepared to have those words read out in court. But I accepted Kate Buckley's suggestion that we should compromise on a total 'all in' payment of £45,000 to cover both my costs and damages and that we should not insist on the precise placing of the apology.

Three hours later Kate Buckley rang me back to say the other side had agreed. We had a deal. The statement would be made in the High Court on Tuesday 28th Feburary and the *Mail on Sunday* would carry the agreed apology in 'a prominent position' on page 5 above the fold in its next edition. I had got 95 per cent of what I wanted but there was a perverse element in me that regretted that I had not got the financial means – and the nerve – to fight it out in court. A jury, I speculated, might have given me a huge sum. It would also have been satisfying to see Stewart Steven being cross-examined on the basis of the information I had so laboriously researched. I did not believe he would have emerged with credit. By chance, I met Arthur Davidson, the *Mail*'s chief in-house lawyer, in our local swimming baths the next day. Dripping under the showers, we exchanged pleasantries.

There was one last passage at arms between the lawyers. Four days before the statement in open court, Swepstone Walsh wrote to my solicitors attempting to put conditions on the agreement reached: 'We confirm the terms of settlement agreed between us on the strict understanding that the terms are in the normal way confidential to the parties.' Kate Buckley knew even without telephoning me that I wouldn't accept this and replied bluntly, 'It was not a term of the settlement that the terms should be confidential to the parties . . . Our client reserves the right to make any disclosure he wishes.'

For a few hours I thought this blunt dismissal might provoke a breach. I would not have been sorry if it had. Rightly or wrongly, I had never doubted that a jury would find for me. But by the time I trooped into Court 11 with my wife, Caroline, to hear the *Mail on Sunday*'s apology read out before Mr Justice Potter, I was glad that it was all over. The statement took less than two minutes to read but the case had taken 18 months of my life. Much of it I found fascinating, but there are more productive ways of spending one's time. A libel action is totally devouring. It had brought out obsessive aspects of my character which must have sorely tested my family and friends. As for my professional reputation, I realised at the start that no one comes out of a libel court smelling of roses. I knew I hadn't but I had shown that I was not prepared to be defamed at whim.

6

The Bite of the Flea

*Sir, there is no settling the point of precendency between
a louse and a flea.*

Samuel Johnson

When Tom Driberg was voted off Labour's National Executive
in 1974 he said his only consolation was that he would never
have to set foot in Blackpool again. I knew just what he meant.
The annual jaunt to that tacky seaside resort for Conservative
or Labour Party Conferences always depressed me. Somehow
I could never come to terms with the 'Pride of the North.' Its
seedy boarding houses, deplorable hotels, tawdry lights and
beastly cafes sum up for me everything that is wrong with the
British seaside. As for the grey, sullen, evil-looking sea, swirling
around the decayed pier, year after year the EEC declared it
so polluted that you needed to be foolhardy as well as thick-
skinned to swim in it.

My dislike of Blackpool was largely to blame for what
followed. Shortly after the 1977 Tory Conference, which was
memorable for almost nothing except sheeting rain, I ran into
Sir Edward du Cann, then plain Mister, with whom I had been
on friendly terms for several years. As chairman of the 1922
Committee he was a key figure in the party, the architect of
the Milk Street mafia, the group of right wing Tories, who
first promoted Mrs Thatcher's candidacy for leadership. He
also had very considerable political talents though he was
denied the highest offices.

Not everyone approved of du Cann, he was dubbed 'oilcan'

99

because of his exceptionally smooth manner, and his city connections during the fringe banking crisis made him vulnerable. But I liked him; he was clever, loved a gossip, was funny, and often discreetly informative. He also had few illusions about himself — a saving grace in any politician. 'My dear boy, how can I mislead you?' was his usual greeting to me.

So when I saw him that day in a television studio I hailed him cheerily and said how delighted I was not to have to go back to Blackpool for another year. He agreed, perhaps, I thought, a touch too readily, for I remonstrated: 'What have you got to complain about, Edward, living it up at the Imperial (then Blackpool's only good hotel)? It's all right for you — I had to moulder in an establishment which would disgrace a doss-house.' But du Cann was insistent. He'd had a perfectly miserable time, he said, made worse by a persistent flea which had bitten him 34 times, concentrating on his right buttock while he was asleep.

At this tale of woe, my journalistic ears pricked up. Had anyone else been bitten, I asked? 'Yes,' he replied, Denis Thatcher, in the next door room. 'What about Mrs Thatcher?' I inquired, anxious about the health of the Leaderene? When told she had escaped unscathed, I cursed under my breath at this missed opportunity. But even without the lady, it was not a bad story. The Imperial, after all, was no ordinary hotel. Just inside its front entrance, it had a plaque which proudly announced its distinguished history: 'The Imperial was built in 1867 and for over 100 years it has satisfied the demands of discriminating guests. From Charles Dickens in 1869 to the visits of Royalty and political leaders in our time, it has been a haven for relaxation and enjoyment. A hospital for wounded officers in 1918, requisitioned again in 1939, The Imperial has always returned to its prime purpose of welcoming and cosseting its guests. Prince of Wales Group of Hotels is proud to continue the great tradition.'

The Observer's gossip column known as Pendennis, was in

the hands at that time of Geoffrey Wansell, a street-wise character who beside being one of my mates on the paper, was an excellent journalist and knew a good story when he saw one. He was delighted when I told him the tale of the flea. After checking the facts carefully with the Imperial's management, he included it in his column the following weekend under the headline, Political Flea Circus: 'The great flea epidemic sweeping the country has claimed at least two political victims. At the Conservative Party Conference last month in Blackpool, Mrs Margaret Thatcher's unassuming husband, Denis, was bitten in bed at the Imperial Hotel by one of the fleas much encouraged this year by our damp and mild autumn. The flea left the Tory leader alone. The Imperial Hotel took every precaution against the invaders even to the length of buying new beds for the Thatchers' suite. Another prominent member of the party, however, was also bitten in his bed at Blackpool and was so incensed that he has written to the hotel where he stayed.'

Three days later an unwelcome missive arrived from Prince of Wales Hotels Ltd, owners of the Imperial Hotel: a writ demanding an apology and substantial damages for what they said was a grossly insulting and disgraceful allegation that Blackpool's finest hotel was infested with fleas. The statement of claim soon followed. It alleged that the natural and ordinary meaning of the words was that: (i) 'the Imperial Hotel at Blackpool was infested with fleas and that guests were exposed to the risk of being bitten by fleas; (ii) that the Imperial Hotel was unhygienic and not fit to be regarded as a luxury hotel and that the Plaintiffs were not fit to run the same'. The statement concluded: 'The words complained of were calculated to disparage the Plaintiffs in the way of their said business and by reason of the premises the Plaintiffs have been seriously damaged in their credit and reputation.'

This writ threw *The Observer*'s managers, who were then in one of their frequent financial crises, into a terrible state of gloom. They soon made it clear that they looked to me, as the source of this story, to get them out of what looked like a very expensive hole.

My first line of defence was to suggest to *The Observer*'s resident lawyer Alec Grant, a mild but obstinate character, that the Imperial was making altogether too much of a fuss. Pendennis hadn't said that the hotel was riddled by fleas, merely that two prominent politicians had been bitten while staying there. Why couldn't we mount a defence on the lines that the Tories had actually brought the flea into the Imperial and that the hotel itself was blameless? After all, I argued, how could Blackpool's finest be responsible for the personal habits and cleanliness of all its guests, particularly Tories? Alec Grant, a former Labour councillor, thought about this, sucked on his pipe, said he liked it, but finally dismissed my plea as too ingenious by half.

There was nothing for it, he asserted, but to go back to my original source. When I nervously did so, Edward du Cann, to his eternal credit, not only stuck by his story but offered to go into the witness box as well and if necessary to expose his injured buttock to the jury. He also confirmed that he had written a letter to the Imperial after his visit complaining of having been bitten. As a result of this the hotel had called in Rentokill to fumigate his room, had bought two new beds for the Thatchers' room and had even called in the Health Inspector to check that all was now well.

The tale du Cann told our lawyers was a sad one. He had spent three nights at the Imperial. He was first aware of being bitten on Tuesday night but it wasn't bad and he thought no more about it. He was bitten again on the Wednesday night and by Thursday morning was very much aware of an assailant. His wife later counted the bites and reached the total of 34 before giving up. Asked by our lawyers what had bitten him, he replied it was definitely fleas: 'They are the only things that bite like that. I came up in great lumps which itched like hell.'

In view of all this first hand evidence, I thought we weren't too badly placed to justify the Pendennis story and I urged our lawyers to stand tall and talk tough. But then came a major blow. Denis Thatcher, on mature reflection, decided that he hadn't after all been bitten by a flea but rather by a sea midge. So whichever beast took lumps out of du Cann, concluded our learned and very expensive counsel, was probably not the same beast as had attacked the leader's beloved husband. The logic was undeniable if expensive.

The Observer's management took a very serious view of this development. Distinguished entomologists were consulted and the precise characteristics and differences between the two species of insect were meticulously logged. While fleas bit, the entomologists agreed, sea midges did not, or at least did not inflict anything like the same degree of bloody damage. Moreover, in view of the fact that both the du Canns' and Thatchers' rooms were quite a long way from the beach and were on the second floor, our experts concluded that it was unlikely that a sea midge could have been the guilty party. But Denis Thatcher's statement was unequivocal. He had not been 'bitten by fleas' nor did 'any member of the Imperial Hotel's staff' suggest he ever had been. Mr Thatcher did acknowledge that he had been attacked and had been in some discomfort from 'a swollen hand' adding that members of the hotel staff 'were most caring, thoughtful and efficient' in dealing with his bites.

The Observer's lawyers, in the light of Denis Thatcher's change of heart, began to take a dim view about the action warning that it could be very expensive if it got to court. The flea was certainly was taking a lot of everyone's time. The original story was written on the 13th November, 1977. Six months later Mr Desmond Browne, counsel for the Imperial Hotel, was filing 'a request for further and better particulars' of *The Observer*'s defence. This is one of the arcane processes that libel cases go through which delight the lawyers but so weary all the participants that less than five per cent of libel actions ever reach a court hearing. This particular request for 'better particulars' was a gem of its kind and is perhaps worth quoting in full, if only to show how tedious a libel action can become.

IN THE HIGH COURT OF JUSTICE, QUEEN'S BENCH DIVISION

PRINCE OF WALES HOTELS LIMITED PLAINTIFFS AND THE OBSERVER LIMITED DEFENDANTS

Under paragraph 4(a): Particulars (4):
Of the allegation that on two successive nights Mr du Cann was bitten in bed at the Imperial Hotel, stating that the dates of the two nights and the number of Mr du Cann's room.
Under Paragraph 4(a): Particulars 4(a):
Stating the characteristics of the bites on Mr du Cann which it is alleged were those bites caused by fleas.
Under Paragraph 4(a) : Particulars (5):
Of the alleged complaint by Mr du Cann, stating whether the same was oral or in writing; if oral, stating when and where the same was made and to whom on behalf of the Plaintiffs; if in writing, identifying the relevant documents.
Under Paragraph 4(a) ; Particulars (7):
Of the allegation that whilst a guest at the Imperial Hotel Mr Thatcher was also bitten by an insect, stating:

(1) the date on which it is alleged that Mr Thatcher was bitten.
(2) the whereabouts of Mr Thatcher at the time that he was bitten.
(3) the number of bites that it is alleged that Mr Thatcher

received, and the parts of the body on which he was bitten, and

(4) the species of insect which it is alleged bit Mr Thatcher.
Desmond Browne
Served the 25th day of April 1978 by Messrs. Fremont & Co., of 5 Fitzhardinge Street, London W1. Solicitors for the Plaintiffs.

By an odd coincidence which may or may not have helped our cause, I was soon to meet the Imperial Hotel's counsel not across a court room but in other more intimate circumstances. That summer, I was invited by old friends to stay with them in their villa in Corfu. Who should be there, to my surprise, but Desmond Browne. That night under the influence of the island's strong sun and wine, I couldn't resist a little gentle teasing about the case.

'You realise Desmond,' I said, 'your clients are going to be the laughing stock of Whitehall if this flea ever gets to court. I warn you we'll be calling Mrs Thatcher as our star witness. Just think of the cross-examination we'll put her through: "Where were you on the night in question, when your husband is alleged to have been bitten by this sea midge?" ' Desmond Browne was not amused. 'You know it's totally improper for me to discuss this with you.' Of course I knew but I couldn't resist the opportunity of pointing out all the disadvantages of pursuing such a hilarious action.

Whether the teasing worked I don't know, but a month later I learnt that the lawyers had agreed to settle the case with mutual assurances of good will and esteem on all sides. No apologies, no payment of costs, no court case — just plain and simple common sense.

Fleas may be irritating but so, I fear, are political journalists. The more I reflected on the settlement, the more I regretted that *The Observer*'s loyal readers should be denied all knowledge of how Pendennis had honourably fought his corner in the matter of the flea and the Tory Party.

When I talked to *The Observer*'s house lawyer, however, and suggested that I was thinking of writing a short article about the happy end to the flea case, the answer was an emphatic 'No'. That seemed to put paid to the idea, but on the dubious grounds that lawyers often say 'No' when they mean 'Yes', I persuaded the editor that we should take senior counsel's advice. Counsel was even more emphatic that any further article about the flea was out of the question. It might, he warned in the most ominous tones, bring the distinct threat of reviving the whole action; it was also, he added disapprovingly, totally against legal etiquette.

Somehow, I am not quite sure how, I persuaded Donald Trelford in one of his bravest editorial decisions to ignore the lawyers and allow me to put pen to paper. The following weekend *The Observer* carried a small piece announcing the happy end of 'the libel case of the century'.

Three days later another letter arrived from the Imperial Hotel. Groaning I opened it. Mercifully this time it was not a writ. The manager of the hotel had merely written to say how much he had enjoyed *The Observer*'s flea story. Would I and my wife like to come and spend a weekend at the hotel's expense? I wrote back to decline this kind offer but I couldn't resist sending a copy of the Imperial's letter to 'my learned friends' with my scribbled comment in the margin: 'Wrong again!'

The tale of the flea was not, however, quite over. Two years later I was at Blackpool yet again, this time for a Liberal Conference. During a debate on some obscure constitutional proposal, I was sitting next to Geoffrey Smith, *The Times*' very proper political columnist. Suddenly in the middle of the interminable proceedings Geoffrey, totally out of character, rolled up his trouser leg and began to scratch vigorously. 'Geoffrey,' I cried, 'what are you doing?' 'I don't know,' he said plaintively, 'I seem to have been bitten.' 'Where are you staying?' I asked. He gave the name of a Blackpool hotel which I fear for obvious reasons, must be nameless.

But the moral is clear. If you have to go to Blackpool — and I don't advise it — be very careful where you stay. For if the fleas don't get you, the sea midges will!

7

The Case of the Three MPs

I was hoping to build up a little pot of gold for my old age.

Reginald Maudling, Chancellor of the Exchequer 1962–64, Home
Secretary 1970–72.

The House of Commons prides itself on being the best club
in London — a club which relies on its members' honour to
protect its good name. A severe dent to that reputation came
in January 1972 when the architect John Poulson, who claimed
to have the biggest architectural practice in Europe, filed his
petition for bankruptcy at Wakefield Crown Court. The
hearing that followed unravelled a web of corruption that
stretched across the country enveloping senior civil servants,
councillors and, most seriously of all, several MPs. It also lured
me into the most expensive libel action of my journalistic
career.

Poulson's 22,000 meticulously documented files, over eight
cubic yards of paper, with their damning evidence of corruption
led to the jailing for four years of an Under Secretary at the
Scottish Office, George Pottinger, and sentences of one to three
years on a dozen other local government, coal board, and
hospital officials. Altogether 21 people were prosecuted out
of some 300 originally targeted by the police as subjects for
investigation.

The Wakefield architect, the spider at the centre of the web,
was given a seven year prison sentence after being described
by the judge as 'an incalculably evil man'. Poulson's method
was a simple one. By spreading his favours among those his

108

unerring eye saw as potentially greedy, he sucked into his clutches politicians, civil servants, local government officials and anyone else who was in a position to help him secure contracts. Once there they were expected to deliver and were mercilessly browbeaten if they did not.

The best flavour of the architect's conduct emerged during his cross-examination by Muir Hunter QC, the counsel for the creditors at the bankruptcy hearing. On being asked what he got for the £155,000 paid to T. Dan Smith, leader of Newcastle-on-Tyne council and head of Poulson's public relations organisation, Poulson replied: 'Phew! It is fantastic, I had no idea it was that big . . . I've no accounts.' What about the £11,508 paid to Albert Roberts MP: 'Oh, good Lord,' sighed Poulson unhelpfully. And the £5,928 paid to John Cordle MP: 'I mean, Cordle was . . . well, I consider, I was conned.'

Later Muir Hunter questioned the architect about a letter he had written in 1967 to Mr Maudling, then not only Shadow Commonwealth Secretary and Deputy Tory Leader but also chairman of one of Poulson's subsidiary companies, asking him to arrange a holiday for an official at the Department of Health.

QC: Is it part of your job to fix up senior civil servants with whom you work with cruises?

POULSON: No.

QC: How many other senior civil servants did you send on cruises?

POULSON: None to the best of my knowledge.

QC: He is the only one, is he? Well, this really is a very singular incident.

POULSON: Well, it isn't; it is because he was going there on his retirement and he couldn't get on. He said there was a waiting list and he couldn't get satisfaction.

QC: Just listen to this letter of February 22, 1967 written by V.M.

POULSON: Miss McLeod, my secretary.

QC: Yes, of course, the secretary girl — addressed to Mr Maudling: 'A personal friend of Mr Poulson's — Mr A.J. Merritt, Principal Regional Officer at the Ministry of Health, Leeds — who has been extremely helpful to the firm in that capacity, is retiring at the end of this year and wishes to take a sea voyage in January/February 1968; would your travel agents be able to do anything?' So had Mr Merritt been extremely helpful to you as Principal Regional Officer at the Ministry of Health?

POULSON: No more than anybody else.

QC: Do you mean Miss McLeod was mistaken in what she wrote?

POULSON: No, not mistaken but it was probably a bit of a boast.

QC: And Mr Maudling was sufficiently impressed with your secretary's letter to send off some directive to his own travel agents, Clarkson Booker All Travel, was he not?

POULSON: Yes . . .

QC: Very well. So you and Mr Maudling, both persons afflicted by the cares of state and business, were occupying yourselves with booking a year in advance a cruise for an elderly civil servant. Is that what you most spent your time on, you and Mr Maudling?

POULSON: No.

QC: Well, what was it for, Mr Poulson?

POULSON: It was absolutely, purely, that this man asked me to help him to get on a cruise, as how would I have known anything about it?

QC: And then, after he went on the cruise, duly refreshed no doubt suntanned, he came back and he worked for you, is that right?

POULSON: Yes.

By the time I came to work at the Commons as a political

correspondent — first for *The Guardian* in 1974, transferring to *The Observer* 18 months later — most of this was history. Poulson and Pottinger were in prison, so were the chairman of the Durham Police Authority, Alderman Andrew Cunningham, T. Dan Smith and a host of smaller fry caught up in Poulson's net. The biggest fish of them all, the former Home Secretary Reginald Maudling, had resigned from the Government in July 1972 protesting his innocence: 'I do not regard this (his relationship with Poulson) as a matter of criticism or for investigation. However, there are matters not relating to me that do require investigation . . . I think I can reasonably claim a respite from the burdens of responsibility and from the glare of publicity which inevitably surrounds a Minister and inexcusably engulfs the private lives even of his family.'

But was it all so innocent? Why, I wondered, had no action ever been taken against Reggie Maudling or any of the other MPs who had so eagerly taken the Poulson shilling? The only reason I could imagine was that it might be politically embarrassing. But for a long time I got nowhere with inquiries. Eventually a chance conversation with Andrew Roth in the press gallery cafeteria pointed me in the right direction. Roth is an interesting character. The author of *Parliamentary Profiles*, he knows more about the business backgrounds of individual MPs than anyone else at Westminster, having specialised in this area for nearly a quarter of a century.

So I pricked up my ears when in a casual discussion about John Cordle, the Tory MP for Bournemouth East, Roth said he had recently been threatened by him with a writ. He added for good measure that Cordle was not only litigious but a nasty character to be watched carefully. 'How can I find out more?' I asked. Roth suggested that one useful avenue to explore might be the Salmon Commission.

In 1975 the then Prime Minister, Harold Wilson, had established a Royal Commission under Lord Salmon to look at the standards of conduct in public life. It was one of two institutional responses to the Poulson scandal; the first being the setting up in October 1973 by Edward Heath of a committee under Lord Redcliffe-Maude which concluded that local government was essentially honest.

The Salmon Commission was less complacent. It recommended the revamping of the Prevention of Corruption Acts giving the police wider access to financial records, and the right to set up detailed inquiries into allegations of corruption. Curiously the Commission said very little about the extent of high-level political corruption. But when I began to talk to sources in Whitehall and at Westminster, I eventually stumbled on someone who was so outraged by the way MPs linked to Poulson had been allowed to get away scot free that he was willing to tell me part of what I wanted to know. It was a sensational story, the sort that journalists dream about.

What had happened, I discovered after months of inquiry, was this: The Salmon Commission had been shown detailed evidence of payments to three MPs, John Cordle, Albert Roberts and Reginald Maudling. The police view of the actions of Roberts and Maudling was that the former was small fry while the latter had behaved corruptly though the evidence needed for prosecution was still incomplete. But the behaviour of John Cordle was so blatant that in the words of Lord Salmon, it made his 'hair stand on end'. A member of the Royal Commission remembers an even more vivid comment by its Chairman. Cordle's conduct, he told his colleagues, was one of the most flagrant cases of corruption he had encountered in all his years on the Bench.

John Cordle was a backbench Tory who combined a public appearance of high moral rectitude with a colourful private life. When the first of his three wives tried to have him committed to prison for contempt he pleaded that as an MP he was outside the Court's jurisdiction. In another of his matrimonial disputes he hired security guards to keep his mother-in-law out of his home. And he complained bitterly when his third wife, a Finn thirty years younger than himself, was snubbed by the wife of the Bishop of Bath and Wells who reportedly refused to sit next to her in church. Yet despite these well-publicised tiffs, Cordle had somehow established a reputation as a stickler for morality.

A prominent churchman and former member of the Church Assembly, Cordle, a smooth, well-dressed country squire, made it no secret that he thought the country was going to the dogs. After hearing that the disgraced former Army Secretary, John Profumo, was to be given an audience with the Queen to honour his work for charity, he thundered: 'It seems to me an affront to the Christian conscience of the nation at a time when the standards in public life need to be maintained.' And in the debate on the Queen's Speech in November 1974, Cordle deplored the fact that there had been a collapse of moral Christian principles in British life, warned that Britain was becoming a sick society and said the courts should be given greater powers to punish the wicked.

The principle evidence against this self-proclaimed defender of public morals, I eventually discovered, was an astonishing letter written by Cordle to Poulson on March 2nd, 1965, reminding the architect that he had an agreement for fees of £500 a year plus commission on contracts and expenses. 'I feel that the expenses cheque so far paid of £150 is somewhat uncomplimentary to myself.'

The letter, found by the police among thousands of files recovered from the architect's office, referred to all the work put in by Cordle in furthering Poulson's interests around the world, citing a speech the MP had made in the Commons on 17th April 1964 about a West African contract that the architect was interested in getting. 'It was largely for the benefit of Construction Promotions,' wrote Cordle, 'that I took part in a debate in the House of Commons on the Gambia and pressed for HMG to award construction contracts to British firms.'

The point of that speech, in which Cordle signally failed to declare his financial interest, was to press the Government to approve a development scheme at Bathurst in the Gambia for which Poulson was a potential contractor: 'The country [the Gambia] is being prevented from enjoying the benefits of the limited generosity which we have shown already,' Cordle told the Commons. 'I believe that it would please the British taxpayer if they knew that such money as was being provided by HMG was finding its way into the pockets of British contractors, who could undertake many of the civil engineering developments, rather than into the pockets of local governments.'

This was a sentiment calculated to appeal to Poulson, the master architect, who through his associated company, Construction Promotions Ltd, was then seeking to break into the lucrative West African market. The letter from Cordle was, however, prima facie evidence, if not of corrupt behaviour, certainly of improper conduct for an MP and a gross breach of Parliamentary privilege. The closeness of the relationship between the Tory MP and his paymaster is shown by another letter written by Cordle to Poulson a month later:

My dear John,

In acknowledging the cheque you gave me this afternoon, I want to thank you again and express my sincere wish to be of continued and positive assistance to you and to Construction Promotion Ltd. I was particularly grateful to you for confirmation of our original discussion at the Dorchester Hotel which dealt with the main points for the service agreement which you are now arranging to be drawn up in my favour.

It was agreed that a retaining fee of £1,000 per annum should be paid to me for five years from 1 January 1965, and that a one per cent commission will be paid on all projects which I am able to introduce and facilitate to your companies. Expenses to be paid as and when they arrive . . .

Over the past 15 months I have done what was asked of me, and to the best of my ability. I shall continue with renewed vigour knowing that I am in your hands and under your watchful eye. My endeavours for you and Construction Promotion will be maintained throughout.

With again many thanks for the cheque.

Kindest regards,

Yours sincerely,

John Cordle

The Director of Public Prosecutions, Sir Norman Skelhorn sought counsel's advice on these letters from two leading QCs, Peter Taylor and John Cobb. Their opinion was unequivocal. Describing Cordle's begging letter to Poulson asking for increased fees on account of his Parliamentary efforts as 'breathtaking', they concluded: 'It would be hard to imagine a clearer admission of improper motive on the part of a Member of Parliament.' As well as the Gambia letter, the Cobb–Taylor opinion listed four other possible criminal charges against Cordle: his failure to declare his interest in this and other Commons debates, approaching Ministers on Poulson's behalf, lobbying the Crown Agents, and seeking to have Poulson appointed as planning consultant to Belfast Council. Despite all this, the two QCs reluctantly concluded in their secret memorandum to the DPP that it would not be possible to bring Cordle to justice because an MP could not be prosecuted for corruption in respect of his parliamentary duties.

This was because the two main acts concerned, the Prevention of Corruption Act 1906 and the Public Bodies Corrupt Practices Act of 1889 did not apply to MPs. In the

1906 Act, MPs were not covered by the term 'agent' while the 1889 Act referred to 'public bodies' which did not embrace Parliament. The legal advice to the Director of Public Prosecution concluded: 'If Mr Cordle had been a servant or Minister of the Crown any one of the above five matters might well have been sufficient to support a charge of corruption but as the law in relation to MPs stands we are of the opinion that such conduct does not amount to indictable corruption, however repugnant it may be.'

Appalled by this immunity enjoyed by MPs which enabled them to get away with actions which would have landed an ordinary citizen in prison, the Royal Commission was sharply divided on whether the law ought to be changed. Lord Salmon, backed by a minority of its members, felt that MPs ought to be brought within the ambit of the criminal law in respect of their Parliamentary duties. But the majority, led by Lord Houghton, former chairman of the Parliamentary Labour Party, argued that Parliament should be left to deal with its black sheep through the rules of privilege. In the end, to maintain a united front, an oddly worded compromise was devised. The Royal Commission in its published report called on Parliament 'to consider bringing corruption, bribery, and attempted bribery of a Member of Parliament within the ambit of the criminal law.' But there was total silence as to what this referred to and it was not followed up by MPs or the Press.

This inability to prosecute Cordle so disturbed Lord Salmon that he privately went to see the Attorney General. He expressed his concern that no action had been taken against Cordle in spite of the fact that his letters to Poulson had been in the hands of the police for more than four years. The Attorney General, Mr Sam Silkin, replied that the Government felt it would be prejudicial to refer one case to the Select Committee on Privileges while police inquiries into the cases of Maudling and the others were still continuing. This view was strongly disputed by Lord Salmon who stressed there was no legal bar to Parliament taking action. Another member of the Royal Commission was so angered by the foot-dragging that he considered pinning a copy of Cordle's 'Gambia letter', together with the legal explanation as to why he could not be prosecuted, on the MP's noticeboard at the Commons.

It was this explosive scandal, not a hint of which had so far become public, that I had stumbled upon thanks to a good deal of luck. But getting it published by *The Observer* was not easy. Draft after draft was pored over by the lawyers and it took more than three months of work before they were satisfied. Even then it was recognised that the story was likely to attract one or more libel writs. The principal difficulty was that though I was confident that the evidence of misconduct against Cordle was water-tight, my information in respect of both Maudling and Roberts was circumstantial and depended almost entirely on what my informants told me had been said to the Royal Commission. As these sources were confidential and indeed had taken a considerable risk in helping me, I knew I wouldn't be able to rely on them if it went to court.

Even with Cordle, right up until the moment of publication I lacked the crucial incriminating document, his letter to John Poulson of March 2nd, 1965, in which he boasted of his efforts on the architect's behalf including speaking in a House of Commons debate. But barely two hours after the first edition went to press I got a call on the internal telephone saying that a packet had been left for me at *The Observer*'s front entrance in St Andrew's Hill, near St Paul's. Inside was a copy of the Cordle letter I had been seeking desperately for months.

The serious nature of the allegations and the evidence I had dictated the shape of the story. On Sunday October 17th, 1976, *The Observer*'s front page was dominated by a huge headline: 'Corruption — 3 MPs Escape Prosecution.' John Cordle defended his action in not disclosing his interest by denying that he had any financial interest to declare: 'My relationship from the outset with Mr Poulson was governed by an agreement drafted by my solicitors and approved by his. I cannot now recall exactly how much Mr Poulson paid me [£5,628] but . . . I was left with no profit or gain after disbursements.'

There was deliberately no mention of Albert Roberts, the only hint of his involvement in the story being the Attorney General's reported view that one of the cases was 'relatively small fry'. It was not possible to treat Maudling in this way because his involvement with Poulson was so widely known. The continuing police inquiries into his conduct had also been cited to me as a crucial factor for the delay in taking any action against Cordle. So in what turned out to be a vain attempt to avoid a writ, the story sought somewhat artificially to distinguish Maudling's case from the other MPs on the grounds that he was still under investigation: 'One such inquiry concerns the Shadow Foreign Secretary Mr Reginald Maudling though it should be stressed that he is not one of the three MPs referred to in this account. Nearly a year ago the Attorney General (Mr Silkin) said in a letter — that no decision had been taken on Mr Maudling's case and that he had given no assurances to anyone that he would not be prosecuted.'

If the story had confined itself to that, we might just have got away without it. But unfortunately at the lawyers' urging, a sentence, 'Mr Maudling is now not expected to be prosecuted,' was added late in the day. That together with a picture caption under a photograph of the former Chancellor: 'No decision yet' were to prove expensive though both were true.

The Observer's story produced the expected crop of writs from Maudling, Cordle and Roberts but also a satisfying political chain reaction. Within 24 hours Lord Salmon called on Parliament to deal with the Parliamentary immunity that made it impossible to prosecute corrupt MPs. The next day, Tuesday, the Attorney General Sam Silkin announced that police inquiries into the Poulson affair would cease, opening the way for Parliamentary action.

Adam Raphael after giving evidence in the Archer trial
(Photo News Service, Old Bailey)

The libel trial of the century – the Archers leaving court
(Daily Mail)

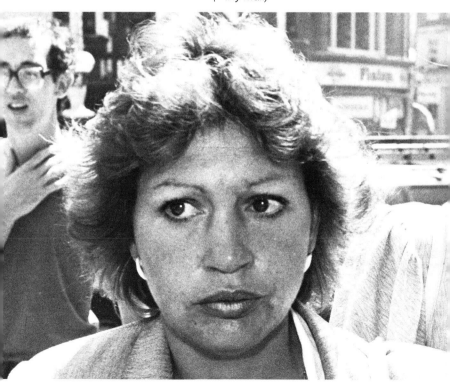

Monica Coghlan
(Press Association)

Mr Justice Caulfield
(Universal Pictorial Press)

Aziz Kurtha
(London Weekend Television)

Stewart Steven, editor of the *Mail on Sunday*
(Press Association)

Lord Kearton, former chairman of Courtaulds
(Observer)

Reginald Maudling
(The Hulton-Deutsch Collection)

John Cordle
(Universal Pictorial Press)

Derek Jameson
(Jane Bown/Observer)

Charlotte Cornwell
(Jane Bown/Observer)

Michael Meacher
(David Harden/Observer)

Richard Ingrams
(Sue Adler/Observer)

The following day, however, the Prime Minister Mr Callaghan did his best to bury the affair. He doubted whether there was much point in the Commons concerning itself with the Salmon Commission's 'rather obscure recommendations' about the need to remove MPs' immunity from prosecution for corruption. The focus, said Mr Callaghan, should be on practice for the future rather than a rerun of the past. As for Mr Cordle and the other MPs referred to by *The Observer* as having escaped prosecution, the Prime Minister added ominously, 'I can see many thorny problems in the way of referring individual cases to the Committee on Privileges.'

Mrs Thatcher for the Opposition appeared to agree that the best thing was to forget the whole unpleasantness, most of which, she said, had been got up by the Press. At this point when I was despairing in the Press Gallery the Liberal Leader David Steel called on the Government to take a lead and attacked the 'billing and cooing' between the two front benches. Mr Denis Skinner, MP for Bolsover then proceeded to put the boot in: 'While it might be important and necessary to preserve the fundamental freedom of speech of MPs, it should not give them licence and freedom to line their pockets at the expense of the ordinary taxpayer . . . millions of people outside this place will regard these statements as nothing short of a cover-up of MPs to safeguard other MPs.'

The ensuing row amid cries of foul and favouritism forced a hasty change of mind. By Prime Minister's question time the next day Mr Callaghan acknowledged that a full Parliamentary inquiry was inevitable. The motion to set up a Select Committee was approved by the Commons eight days later. The ten-member committee was charged with considering whether the conduct of MPs linked to Poulson amounted to 'a contempt of the House'. That, translated into non-Parliamentary terms, meant whether the MPs concerned had properly declared their financial interests when speaking in debate or in correspondence with Ministers. The Select

Committee's second duty was far more difficult. It was asked to consider whether the conduct of the MPs concerned 'was inconsistent with the standards which the House is entitled to expect from its members.'

That unfortunately was the vaguest of formulas. In the 1960s when the Poulson empire was at its height, it was a convention rather than a rule of Parliament that MPs should declare their pecuniary interests. It was not until 1969 after disclosures that Gordon Bagier, Labour MP for Sunderland, had received £500 from a public relations firm working on behalf of the Greek Junta, that the convention of declaring an interest was codified.

The Select Committee on Members' Interests, which was set up in the wake of the Bagier affair, recommended that it was 'contrary to the usage and derogatory to the dignity of the House' that MPs should advocate measures in the Commons for a fee or any other kind of reward. Yet it was another five years before the Commons passed a resolution requiring an MP to disclose 'any relevant pecuniary interest or benefit of whatever nature, whether direct or indirect that he may have had or may be expected to have.'

It was against this somewhat murky background that the Select Committee had been established. It had arguably been set an impossible task. A group of MPs meeting fortnightly over many months is ill-equipped to judge complex questions touching on criminality which involve many witnesses and huge numbers of documents. The complex issues in dispute would have seriously tested the highest court in the land. Moreover the Select Committee was having to pass judgment on actions committed several years ago against standards which were imprecise and changing. And for the three MPs concerned, with their reputations on trial, a gimcrack court without proper rules of evidence was no substitute for a properly conducted Judicial Tribunal.

The public too were ill-served by a Select Committee conducted in secret and which, in the end, divided partly on political lines. The best club in London appeared simply to be protecting its own. Eight months after it was set up, the Select Committee's report was finally published on July 13th, 1977. It stated that none of the actions it had investigated amounted in its view to 'corruption'. But its verdict on John Cordle was that he had committed 'a contempt of the House' by raising a matter for financial reward in the Commons.

'What your Committee find objectionable about Mr Cordle's conduct is that his motive in pressing the interests of the Gambia in the House was to further his own unavowed commercial interests, that is to say, that he was raising a matter in Parliament for reward, and they consider that he abused his membership of Parliament thereby.' The Select Committee also criticised Cordle's failure to disclose his financial interest in the Commons debate on the Gambia, a failure which its report judged was 'inconsistent with the standards of conduct which the House is entitled to expect from its members.'

The verdict on Albert Roberts was less severe. The Committee judged his relationship with Poulson to have been 'inappropriate', noting an incident in which the MP signed a letter on House of Commons notepaper to the Maltese Minister of Works recommending Poulson after it had been dictated over the 'phone by the architect to his secretary who had been specially sent to Roberts' house. The Committee's report said that Roberts' failure to declare his interest on this and other occasions was not in accordance with the standards which Parliament was entitled to expect.

In Maudling's case the Select Committee censured his failure to declare his interest in his frequent interventions in the Commons on Malta where Poulson had huge construction projects at stake. In particular it noted a speech he made on February 28th, 1967, in which the Shadow Minister on Commonwealth Affairs argued for increased British aid: 'In the case of Malta, there is no doubt that further British expenditure there would generate pretty well in entirety further British exports . . .'

The Select Committee concluded that Maudling's considerable financial connection with Poulson should have made him much more careful. Its report quoted a letter written by Maudling to Poulson on April 6th, 1968, after accounts had been sent to him showing he was entitled to director's fees of £11,500 a year and that his wife's theatre trust had received more than £25,000 from Poulson: 'The account Baker sent me set out very graphically the total cost to you of the Maudling family and their interests. It certainly is colossal. I only hope that you think it is worthwhile; never hesitate to tell me if you have doubts.'

The Select Committee, however, reserved its harshest criticism of Maudling for his failure in his letter of resignation as Home Secretary to be frank about his relationship with Poulson. In that letter, Maudling was economical with the truth about his financial ties to Poulson claiming, 'Before I accepted his invitation to become Chairman of an export company, for which post I took no remuneration, he had made a covenant in favour of a charitable appeal which had my support. I do not regard this as a matter either for criticism or investigation.'

The Committee's report took a dim view of this prevarication: 'Had the House been aware both of the close business relationship between Mr Poulson and Mr Maudling and the nature of the financial arrangements between them, it would have considered Mr Maudling's statement to have been lacking in frankness. Your Committee consider that in this respect Mr Maudling's conduct was inconsistent with the standards which the House is entitled to expect from its members.'

The three MPs reacted strongly to these findings. Reggie Maudling said the criticisms of him were 'outrageous' and a breach of natural justice in that its criticisms had not been put to him in advance of publication. Albert Roberts, who had told the committee, 'I may have been a little bit unethical at times,' kept his own counsel. Earlier he had warned me, 'You watch it lad, I'm pristine white.' As for John Cordle after telling the Committee that he sought 'total vindication after trial by the media' he claimed the report had done just that. Its findings, he said, were 'a vindication' of his reputation.

However within days of the report's publication Cordle resigned as Conservative MP for Bournemouth East, complaining that he had been hounded out by the media. This resignation, as it was meant to, took much of the sting out of the Commons debate that followed. Having thrown one of their colleagues to the wolves, Tory MPs were in no mood to take any action against either Maudling or Roberts. Indeed what was remarkable about this Parliamentary occasion was the refusal of two Conservative members of the Select Committee to accept even the guarded conclusions of their own report. No less shameful was the way voting divided on party lines, proving, if proof were necessary, that the Commons is not and never will be a judicial body.

In the end MPs voted narrowly not to endorse but merely 'take note' of the censure of Maudling and Roberts thanks to a solid phalanx of Tory votes, which provoked ironic inquiries from Labour backbenchers whether a three line Whip was on. A motion moved by the Father of the House, Mr George Strauss, MP for Vauxhall, that the two MPs should be suspended for six months was heavily defeated. Perhaps the wisest comment on this tawdry Parliamentary occasion was given by a member of the Select Committee, Mr Emlyn Hooson QC the Liberal MP for Montgomery. He told the Commons that there were grave deficiencies in the Select Committee system of investigation, nearly all of which were to the benefit of those who were being inquired into. There were, he noted, no back-up services provided to the Committee, no independent sources of inquiry, and no means of checking crucial bits of evidence. The same warning was given in vain by the Royal

Commission which noted that MPs were inadequately staffed and equipped for such an inquiry.

No one followed the outcome of the Select Committee's report with greater interest than I did. For by now *The Observer* was deep in writs as a result of my original article. The first two from Cordle and Roberts were not very worrying and eventually were lost in the mists of time. The serious one was from Maudling who needed money. The day after my article in *The Observer* appeared, Maudling, whom I knew distantly, wrote to me personally saying he took grave offence to what had been written about his involvement with Poulson.

'Your references to me in your piece on Sunday were grossly unfair. It may be that they are also defamatory, and on this I am taking legal advice. You made it clear that I was not one of the three MPs referred to in your headline. This I appreciate, though I must tell you that I have been rung by journalists who read the story in broad terms and did not notice your qualifications. You went on to further remarks about me which are by your own admission wholly irrelevant to your main story and you said that "Mr Maudling is not now expected to be prosecuted." Taken with the caption attached to my photograph, "No decision yet", the effect on the reader is quite clearly to suggest that Mr Silkin had been considering evidence placed before him for the purpose of deciding whether I should be prosecuted, that at one time such a prosecution had been expected, and that it is still not ruled out. This is a gross distortion of the truth.'

Two days later *The Observer* received a stiff letter from Maudling's solicitors, Allen and Overy, saying they regarded *The Observer*'s story as 'a most serious libel'; this was rapidly followed by a writ. Maudling was also suing both Granada TV and the *Daily Mirror*. The Granada action followed its 1974 World in Action programme, 'Business in Gozo', which detailed the part Maudling had played as a front bench Tory spokesman in securing a spectacularly large hospital contract for Poulson on an undeveloped, rather barren island just off Malta.

In the programme Maudling had denied that he had played any part in the Gozo contract, claiming to its reporter Ray Fitzwalter that it had been awarded to Poulson before he had become involved. But a few days later the *Daily Mail* obtained a copy of a letter that Maudling had written to Malta's Minister of Works, Dr Caruana, recommending Poulson for the job. Confronted with this letter, Maudling puffed out his cheeks in the considerable splendour of the President's suite at the George V Hotel in Paris and confessed his memory had been at fault: 'Oh, my goodness, what else is it possible that I've forgotten?' he sighed. 'When is all this Poulson business going to end? I keep hearing of people being interviewed by the police but they never come to see me.'

The *Daily Mirror*'s article had been published two days after mine in *The Observer*, covering much the same ground, but it went further, alleging that Maudling would indeed have been prosecuted for corruption if he had not been an MP. Unfortunately, *The Observer*'s legal advisers decided early on to fight the case on the meaning of the words in the article and not to seek to justify the actual charge that Maudling had been investigated by the police and had been lucky to escape prosecution.

This decision, which meant that we were first in the legal firing line, had been partly dictated by the way the story had been written. With hindsight, I realise I was wrong to have sought to create an artificial distinction between Maudling and the other MPs who, I had written, had escaped prosecution for corruption on the grounds of their parliamentary privilege. The story as published after endless tinkering by the lawyers was thus ironically far more difficult to defend. As often happens, the very efforts that had been made to avoid a writ, had in the event made things much worse.

Mr Maudling was almost certainly getting identical advice

from his counsel David Hirst QC. Though the Granada TV programme had predated *The Observer*'s article by more than two years, the former Home Secretary had deliberately soft-pedalled this action in favour of accelerating his suit against us. The more serious *Daily Mirror* action had also been put on the back-burner. Opportunities for a plaintiff to delay are almost endless in a libel action. Unfortunately for *The Observer*, a defendant's room for manoeuvre is more circumscribed. At the beginning of 1978 we were warned that the case would probably come on either in the spring or early summer. In early January therefore our solicitor, David Natali at Herbert Smith, arranged a conference with Robert Alexander QC, who already was one of the top libel practitioners at the bar.

In the intervening months I had got hold of a considerable amount of evidence with the help of both Granada and the *Daily Mirror* which showed that if anything *The Observer*'s article had understated the serious position Mr Maudling had been in. Not only had he been thoroughly investigated, he should in the opinion of the police have been prosecuted. One of the senior policeman leading the inquiries into his conduct told me, 'I see no difference between Reginald Maudling and George Pottinger. If George was guilty, so was Reggie. He escaped because there was a political fix.' A Department of Trade Inspector, A.S. Ford, had compiled a report in early 1975 which cited five potential criminal offences committed by Maudling ranging from perjury to conspiracy to defraud. But weeks after his report was sent to the Director of Public Prosecutions, Mr Ford was removed from the inquiry and sent into exile in the provinces.

I had also acquired from Ray Fitzwalter of Granada, whose book *Web of Corruption* published in 1981 after Maudling's death contains the fullest account of these events, the actual legal opinion that had gone to the DPP. Written by John Cobb QC and Peter Taylor QC, it described Maudling's conduct as 'reprehensible' and suggested that if he had been a civil servant there would have been prima facie evidence of corruption.

'There is abundant evidence,' the Cobb–Taylor legal opinion stated, 'that Mr Maudling was doing his utmost to advance the interests of Poulson, to recommend him to Maltese Ministers, and to use his name to add weight to the recommendations; and to secure the payment to Poulson of fees. There is evidence that on several occasions Mr Maudling spoke in debate in the House of Commons recommending the British government to give substantial financial support to the Maltese Government . . . so far as can be discovered Mr Maudling never declared an interest.'

'What then is the position,' the QCs asked, 'if an MP receives a sum of money knowing its purpose to be to secure for reward his influence, his vote or, as the case may be, in relation to some proceedings in Parliament or in some other way, in connection with his "status" as a Member of Parliament? As the law now stands he commits no crime although he undoubtedly commits a breach of Parliamentary privilege. Indeed it may very well be that it is because the criminal law regarding corruption does not ordinarily "reach" MPs . . . that the rules of Parliamentary privilege are so strict.'

Cobb's conclusion, summarised to his colleagues, is that a prosecution of Maudling should be proceeded with only if there was 'a one hundred per cent, copper-bottomed guarantee of winning'. That is a much severer test than is normally applied to criminal prosecutions but the authorities clearly felt they had to tread carefully when faced with a former Home Secretary. The result, as *The Observer*'s story had accurately reported, was that the DPP decided to drop the case. With all this supporting evidence I was confident that we had a very good chance of winning Maudling's action. But the lawyers took a gloomier view.

At the January conference Robert Alexander was emphatic that it would be counterproductive to plead justification. First it would be difficult to ride two horses in court, namely that *The Observer*'s article was either not defamatory or if it was, it was true. Secondly if one did seek to justify, and the plea failed, there was a serious risk of inflating the damages awarded by a jury. There was also the further difficulty, Alexander pointed out, that if *The Observer* sought to justify, I would be pressed in the witness box to disclose my sources. This I would have to refuse to do and that could tell against me.

These conclusions, which I didn't enjoy hearing, virtually put the seal on *The Observer*'s willingness to fight. If the risks of fighting the action head-on were seen as too great, an expensive argument in court about the meaning of the article was no more attractive. At the end of the conference it was agreed that our solicitors should sound out Maudling's with an offer of a statement in open court, *The Observer* paying his costs if necessary.

It quickly became apparent, however, that the former Home Secretary, who was always chronically short of money, had something rather more substantial in mind. Mr Maudling, it turned out, wasn't too fussed about the terms of any statement in open court but wanted £30,000 in settlement of the action.

With the case now fixed for early summer, another conference was arranged with Robert Alexander in mid-April. His advice was again unequivocal. *The Observer* was at risk of going down to the tune of £30,000 to £50,000 before a jury and he therefore urged a pre-trial settlement on the best terms that we could achieve. Though I knew it was too late, I argued very strongly that it would be disastrous for both my reputation and *The Observer*'s to settle in this way when the article about Maudling had been substantially correct and when both Granada and the *Daily Mirror* were still fighting him strongly. Alexander appeared to be a bit taken back by this layman's counter-attack and suggested that *The Observer* might like to take a second opinion.

Two days later we had another conference with Anthony

Lincoln QC, another very distinguished libel practitioner. His advice initially sounded more hopeful. He believed that if the case were being dealt with by a judge alone, he would be fairly confident that the judge, 'looking at the case technically and logically' would find for *The Observer*. But then came the rub. Before a jury, he said, the issue was more of a lottery. Much would depend on the nature of the judge's direction and whether this was understood by the jury.

Lincoln was also gloomier about the possibility of exemplary damages being awarded against the paper. Overall there was no doubting his view that *The Observer* should settle if at all possible. At this point my resistance to the legal experts collapsed and the discussion turned to the terms of a possible settlement. It was agreed that the paper should offer Maudling £10,000 and if necessary make a payment into court of a similar figure.

Within 24 hours the details of a settlement were thrashed out with Maudling's solicitors. *The Observer* paid Maudling £12,500 in damages and in addition contributed £5,000 towards his costs. A bland statement in open court was also read out claiming that *The Observer* had never intended to suggest that Mr Maudling had escaped prosecution for corruption because of his Parliamentary immunity. It was, as the lawyers, say 'a commercial settlement'. The risks of going to court and losing were too great for the paper to take on. That I could understand but it made it no easier for me to swallow.

A few days later Reggie Maudling rang the editor, Donald Trelford to say how pleased he was this disagreement with *The Observer* was now over and that he had always been a great admirer of the paper. Maudling fared less well against the *Daily Mirror* and Granada. Those two actions were still outstanding when his death in February 1979 after a brief illness brought them to a conclusion. Both Granada and the *Daily Mirror* were confident that they would have won in the High Court.

Looking back on the case I recognise that I made some

serious errors. But what still rankles is the fact that what I wrote about Reginald Maudling was almost 100 per cent accurate. He had been investigated by the police for corruption, a prosecution had been considered and if he hadn't been an MP and a former Chancellor of the Exchequer and Home Secretary, he might well have had to face a judge and jury. As it was he collected a useful tax-free bonus from *The Observer*. It was a salutary lesson for me that it is not so much what you say that matters in a libel action but who you say it about.

8

Starvation Wages

Alas! How deeply painful is all payment,
They hate a murderer much less than a claimant.

Byron, Don Juan

The Guardian has always had a tradition of eccentric motoring correspondents. The chief qualification for the job was, if not a positive dislike of motor cars, a distinct ambivalence about their social merits. My predecessor in the job, J.R.L. Anderson, a noted writer and scholar, was less interested in testing the latest model built in Dagenham than in retracing the voyages of the Vikings in alarmingly unseaworthy small boats.

So when I was appointed the paper's motoring correspondent shortly after arriving at *The Guardian* in 1966 as a raw recruit from the *Bath Evening Chronicle*, I accepted the honour for what it was. I did not realise that it would eventually lead me into an horrendously time-consuming libel action.

The late 1960s were a time of big profits, lavish expensive accounts and unlimited optimism in the car industry. Even the ailing British Motor Corporation, shortly to become British Leyland, was selling every car it could churn out while German, Japanese, French and Italian importers were beginning to import their latest models into an apparently insatiable British market. With times so lucrative a big chunk of the marketing effort was directed at the two dozen or so motoring correspondents who wrote for national newspapers and leading motoring magazines. We were wined, dined, flattered and generally spoilt. Understandably we were not very popular with

131

our fellow reporters. 'The *reductio ad absurdum* of all journalism', Bernard Levin's unkind description of our breed, had more than a grain of truth in it.

In those days of lavish advertising accounts, the manufacturers thought nothing of launching their latest model by chartering a plane and flying the assembled motoring corps to somewhere exotic like Outer Patagonia where we were entertained with belly dancers and lots of alcohol. As a way of trying out a new car this was not ideal, as the Patagonian roads were invariably straight for mile upon mile as well as being dry for three hundred and sixty four days of the year — making comparisons with British conditions peculiarly difficult.

The effort and expense from the manufacturer's point of view, however, was well worthwhile in terms of the amount of space that the papers felt obliged to give the launch announcement in order to justify their reporters having been away for so long. The manufacturers also took a cynical view of that well-known quatrain: 'You cannot hope to bribe or twist, Thank God, the British journalist. Seeing what the man unbribed will do, there's simply no occasion to.' To lubricate publicity wheels that just might need a spot more oiling, they also brought along gifts for the assembled motoring corps, usually small items such as attaché cases, rugs, and ties but sometimes reaching the heights of tape recorders, tyres, and rally jackets.

Occasionally the ethical limits were stretched further. One foreign manufacturer — sadly just before my time — laid on a lavish trip replete with champagne and caviare. When the weary hacks finally made it to their hotel bedroom, they found an envelope containing a considerable quantity of Deutschmarks together with a girl's name and telephone number. Few, it was reported, objected to the money; rather there was chagrin that the girls were as ugly as sin!

There was also a distinct, if discreet link between the amount of advertising a paper got and the way the manufacturer's products were reviewed. One of my fellow correspondents who worked for a tabloid daily was telephoned at home before breakfast one morning by his irate boss. The editor who was renowned for the delicacy of his language launched into a diatribe on the lines of: 'The *Daily X*, the *Daily Y* and the *Daily Z* have got full-page ads for this bleeding car. Why the bleeding hell haven't we?'

After 18 months or so of this decadence, I was asked to write a piece in *Punch* telling all. By then the thrill of driving Lamborghinis, Astons, Rolls-Royces and other exotica had begun to fade. So under the title 'Confessions of a Car Tester', I listed all the bribes I had been offered and, even more regrettably, had accepted. This was on the dubious rationale which struck me as convincing at the time that any car manufacturer worth his salt knew that trying to bribe *The Guardian*'s motoring correspondent was a waste of time and money.

Shortly after my article had appeared in *Punch*'s autumn number to coincide with the Earls Court Motor Show, I was called in to see *The Guardian*'s editor, Alastair Hetherington, a kindly but puritanical Scot, much given to hill walking and other unworldly pleasures. He had in front of him the *Punch* article which clearly he didn't find funny and asked with a trace of steel in his voice: 'Do you not realise that the paper has a house rule?' 'No,' I replied nervously, 'what is it?' The answer was brief: a *Guardian* man could only accept gifts that could be consumed within 24 hours.

As tyres, tape-recorders and the like clearly fell outside this sensible guideline, the next question from the Editor was inevitable: 'I think you've been doing this motoring job long enough, don't you?' The upshot of this exchange was that I was relieved of writing about the Earls Court Motor Show and sent to Washington as one of the paper's few foreign correspondents. For a motoring correspondent in disgrace, it was a very fair sentence.

It also had a happy consequence for it was on my new beat that I met a South African, Caroline Ellis, the daughter of a former Editor of the *Rand Daily Mail*. I had been asked to cover the launch of Apollo 10, the trial mission just before men landed on the moon. I had first watched the blast-off at Cape Canaveral in Florida before travelling up to Houston, Texas, where Lyndon Johnson had insisted, to the inconvenience of all, that Mission Control should be sited. Caroline, who was known as 'Moon', was also in Houston as a BBC researcher and I quickly realised on meeting her that she knew all about such essential but mind-boggling technicalities as trajectories and space capsules.

My reports for *The Guardian* had up until that point concentrated almost exclusively on the more basic features of the Apollo mission, such as the astronauts' bowel movements and how they were keeping fit in space. Having failed 'O' level science, I found my 2nd class history degree no help in making any sense of the technical jargon coming out of mission control. Anyone reading my copy could see I needed help. Caroline was it and by the time astronaut Neil Armstrong had actually landed on the moon, I had nervously taken an even larger step. We were married by a judge in the Federal District Court House in Washington unromantically clutching our VD clearance certificates — a necessary formality in the District of Columbia even in those pre-AIDS days.

All this is by way of being a preamble to explain how I stumbled onto the one story that I remain genuinely proud of having written. Partly because I had married a South African, I was a keen observer during my years in Washington as the pressure increased on big American companies like Polaroid and IBM to justify their continued operations in the Republic. A Congressional Committee led by a black Congressman, Charles Diggs, began holding a series of hearings on Capitol Hill into the wages and conditions of African workers employed by American firms which, with my new-found interest I attended as often as I could.

This spotlight of publicity, I soon realised, achieved results. Under the pressure of public opinion leading American firms began to change their employment practices in South Africa, taking the hard-headed view that this was the only way they could remain there without jeopardising other parts of their world-wide business. Polaroid, badgered by two of its black employees to stop selling its cameras and film to the South African government which was using them for the hated pass-books, sent out a delegation to investigate. When the audit group reported back that 'South Africa alone articulates a policy contrary to everything we stand for', Polaroid, whose South African profits amounted to only one per cent of its total revenues, publicly announced that it would give a third of its South African profits for black education and put up its wages in the Republic by more than 20 per cent. Big business is very much a matter of dog watching dog and the example set by the most prestigious companies was soon followed by less well-known firms, spurred on by codes of conduct published by church groups.

At the end of 1973, with my time in Washington coming to an end, *The Guardian* wanted me to return to London. But as I had a lot of holiday due, Caroline and I decided to take our year-old son Thomas to visit her family in Capetown. It was my first trip to South Africa and, heavily influenced by my American experience, I thought I should spend at least some of my time looking at the employment practices of British companies in the Republic. British investment there was four times the size of American, and of much greater significance to the British economy. An excellent book, *The South African Connection* by Ruth First, Jonathan Steele and Christabel Gurney (Temple Smith 1972), spelled out the importance of British commercial links. What I hadn't appreciated until I arrived in Capetown was the size and difficulty of the investigation I had so lightheartedly undertaken as a part-time holiday enterprise.

Before I left Washington, I went to see the South African Ambassador Pik Botha, later to become South Africa's Foreign Minister. Not surprisingly neither he nor the head of the South African information service, Eschel Rhoodie, who I met in Pretoria, were prepared to give any help. But Rhoodie, who was to be driven from office in the scandal over misuse of government information funds, said something in passing which led me to suspect that I was on the right track: 'There are a number of British companies in this country with prominent reputations in the world who are paying their workers less than they should,' he told me. I got no more assistance from the British Embassy in Capetown. The Labour Attaché, whose job it was to monitor the employment practices of British companies in the Republic, appeared to be not only ignorant but also remarkably complacent.

Without the help of South African journalists such as Stanley Uys, Donald Woods, Tony Heard, and many others still in the country who had better remain anonymous, I wouldn't have got anywhere. But thanks to their generous hospitality and invaluable contacts, I was put in touch with black trade unionists, student activists, academic researchers and church leaders who, if they didn't know the answers, were able to tell me how to go about finding them. From my initial contacts in Pretoria, it was obvious that the vast majority of British companies operating in the Republic were no better, and in a few cases considerably worse, employers than their South African counterparts.

Talking to researchers at the South African Institute of Race Relations, I learnt that the simplest way of judging whether British companies were behaving properly was to find out whether they were paying all their workers above the poverty datum line. This, the PDL, was the theoretical minimum wage needed for a family to survive in reasonably good health. It was not a high standard, for a PDL was calculated on the basis that it was the minimum needed for a family to avoid malnutrition. It did not allow a penny for amusement, for sport, for medicine, for education, for saving, for hire purchase, for holidays, for odd bus rides, for newspapers, tobacco, sweets, hobbies, gifts, pocket money or comfort or luxury of any kind. Nor did it provide for replacements of blankets, furniture, or crockery. It was not, in fact, a humane standard of living. According to Professor E.L. Batson of the University of Capetown: 'It thus admirably fulfils its purpose of stating the lowest minimum upon which subsistence and health can theoretically be achieved.'

I soon discovered from white trade unionists that many British companies operating in South Africa, if not the majority, were paying substantial numbers of Africans below even this minimum standard. But how could I prove it? My time in South Africa was limited, there were many hundreds of British companies operating in the Republic, getting accurate wage information from their frightened work forces was difficult, and the companies themselves were unlikely to co-operate.

After a tentative start, I decided on a mixed approach. I thought I could get partial if not complete wage information on a dozen or so of the companies with reputations as the worst payers by direct contact with their workers, if necessary by standing outside factory gates to get pay slips. To back up this limited sample, I also wrote to 100 of the biggest British companies with a detailed questionnaire on their wages and conditions of their African employees. Finally by putting the word around black union activists that I was sympathetic to their cause, I believed I could get a good deal of raw information though it would need careful checking.

I was lucky in the timing of my visit. A wave of labour unrest was sweeping the country, caused by high inflation and desperately low wages. The whole issue of African employment rights was coming to the forefront. As a result I was helped by almost everyone I asked. After six weeks I had amassed enough information to confront some of the companies.

The answers were revealing. The Personnel Director of Illovo Sugar Estates, a subsidiary of Tate and Lyle, which admitted to paying its 3,000 contract workers from the Transkei about 55p a day told me, 'This is not magnificent but you have to remember these Bantu are mostly illiterate. And they are unproductive at first — we have to build them up. At home they just lie around and have a good time.'

Some British companies were paying wages which were low even by South African standards. The Company Secretary of White's Portland Cement, a subsidiary of Associated Portland Cement, after admitting that hundreds of its African workers were being paid just over £3 a week at its Lichtenberg plant said, 'This is just an unfortunate time for you to raise this matter. We are having negotiations with the wages board and wages will shortly be reviewed.'

A process control engineer, Brian Harvey, who had emigrated from Britain to work for Whites at Lichtenberg, told me he was shocked when he saw how the company treated its African employees. Four Africans — one of whom spoke nine languages — worked under him mending boilers. They earned less than 9p an hour, a total wage of about £4 a week. He said the Africans lived eight to a hut with only the crudest facilities, in concrete compounds surrounded by 9ft fences topped with barbed wire. Their food, about which they complained bitterly, consisted chiefly of mealie-meal, with scraps of meat twice a week. 'They treat the Bantu like machines — in fact machines are better looked after,' said Mr Harvey. 'They're getting their profits and they just couldn't give a damn how the Bantu live.'

During a visit to Natal, I was taken to a wattle plantation near Durban owned by Slater Walker's Natal Tanning Extract. Workers there, I discovered, were being paid as little as 24p a day. A Zulu worker told me: 'My child is dying but I cannot buy milk. I must earn more money.' The farm manager dismissed the child's malnutrition sores as 'fleabites' and said that any milk left over after feeding his dogs was 'given to the Bantu'. The Managing Director of Natal Tanning denied that wages and conditions of his workers were bad, saying that rations and accommodation provided were more than adequate to prevent malnutrition: 'I can assure you that our ration scale is superior to the firms around us. We believe that these totally illiterate labourers on our farms live humane and reasonably happy lives.'

However on the nearby Newlands Estate near Pietermaritzburg, I was shown a hut 10ft by 15ft where seven women workers had to live, sleep, and eat. The only washing facility was a cold tap 30 yards away. Many of the timber workers were in rags and said they could not afford to buy clothes. No sick leave was given to the vast majority of the workers who, if unable to work because of bad weather, were paid nothing. One 50-year-old man, who had hurt his foot while loading a lorry, said he had not been paid for nearly three months. 'My children are getting very sick,' he told me through an interpreter. 'They are sleeping on the floor and dying. I can't do anything except pray to God.' The Industrial Director of Slater Walker SA, Mr W. Hirst, declined to discuss the company's wage scales. 'We do not believe in the concept of cheap labour,' he said, 'but we do not propose telling anyone about our wages structure. It would create an embarrassing precedent for us. This is not a matter for the press at all.'

The wages of unskilled migrant workers employed by companies such as Natal Tanning, White's, and Illovo, though shockingly low, were not untypical of many enterprises in their sector. The excuse always offered for appalling wages was that workers preferred to be paid in kind with free food and accommodation, but the true value of these extras could be gauged from the fact that workers who lived with their wives outside the compound often received as little as £1 a week extra.

Even less excusable were the many instances I found of British industrial companies employing unskilled or semi-skilled workers yet still paying them below poverty line wages. At British Leyland's factory in Capetown, I was told by union activists that some cleaners and assembly workers were getting less than £5 a week. The company's personnel manager, Mr Peter Noble, declined to discuss the matter with a characteristic comment: 'This is the Republic of South Africa whether you like it or not,' he said. 'I personally am anti-press. I have had too much trouble with you lot buggering up labour relations.'

By now I realised that I had got hold of a potentially explosive story. The South African special branch, the Bureau of State Security (BOSS), which I had been aware had been watching me for some time, was also hot on my tail. Shortly after the visit to the Slater Walker wattle plantation, my notebooks were stolen from my Durban hotel room. Fortunately I had taken the precaution of duplicating most of the information, but it was a warning sign that it was time for me to leave South Africa.

I arrived back in Britain at the beginning of March 1973 certain that I had an extraordinary story to tell. But it took some argument on my part to convince *The Guardian* that it was worth publishing. The first reaction of the then Foreign Editor was that it was 'a bit dull' but that it might make a leader page piece. In the end more by luck than anything else, it became the main story on the front page on March 12th because the French election results which had been planned to be the splash on the Monday morning, traditionally a slow news day, had been delayed.

Running across three columns, *The Guardian*'s headline was 'British Firms Pay Africans Starvation Rate' over my article which named a number of blue chip British companies including Metal Box, General Electric, Reed, Rowntree Mackintosh, Chloride, and Associated British Foods as having paid below the poverty datum line. The copy reported that only three British companies — Shell, ICI, and Unilever — out of more than 100 operating in South Africa appeared to be paying all their workers above minimum subsistence rates.

The Chairman of the United Kingdom South Africa Trade Association, Mr W.E. (Billy) Luke, was quoted as saying he agreed there were grounds for concern. 'There are some British firms I am not proud of. But we can't tell our members what their morals should be. I would very much like to see wages increased,' he said. Mr Luke should have known the problems at first hand. A leader page article inside the paper pointed out that one of his associated companies in South Africa, Natal Thread, was paying some of its workers half the minimum needed to sustain an African family.

Other companies such as Metal Box and Dunlop, despite their claims to the contrary, were described as paying substantial numbers of their workers below the poverty line. Both the front page and the inside article were illustrated by pictures I had taken of starving workers on the Boscome Estate wattle farm in Natal owned by Slater Walker. The pictures were more powerful than all the thousands of words for they showed the reality of the consequences of sub-poverty wages.

Alastair Hetherington from the start had been a firm supporter of mine but neither he nor I, nor indeed anyone else on *The Guardian* quite realised the seriousness of the libel risks we were running. When I came into the office that Monday they quickly became apparent. More than a dozen people had telephoned or were waiting to speak to me. Most of them appeared to be lawyers, representing companies named in our report as paying starvation wages to their African workers.

The next few weeks were a blur of writs and threats of legal action from the cream of British industry, many of whose boardrooms appeared to be genuinely shocked by what they were told they were doing in South Africa. Lord Kearton of Courtaulds, in particular, took exception to the charge that his subsidiary, South African Fabrics, was paying its unskilled workers in Durban just over £8 a week including bonuses which was 25 per cent below the PDL for the area.

When I had challenged the Managing Director of SA Fabrics, Mr Peter Holden, about these wages he had replied, 'The African is a trainable chap but he has no interest whatsoever in what he is doing. Consequently productivity is very low. We tried paying bonuses similar to England but it didn't work. If these chaps earn too much, they just take a holiday.'

Kearton, who prided himself on his reputation as a caring left wing industrialist, treated the article as a smear on his personal reputation. He complained that I had published totally false figures, claiming the conversation with the Managing Director of SA Fabrics had never taken place. Faced by this blunt denial and the imminent threat of legal proceedings, I was persuaded that *The Guardian* had no alternative except to publish a partial retraction. Reluctantly I wrote in the next day's paper, 'The details of wages paid by British companies in South Africa are still not known because most firms believe it would not be in their interests to release them. An exception is Courtaulds, which yesterday made a full disclosure to *The Guardian* of the wages of its employees at South African Fabrics. This showed that earnings of all adult employees, though not basic rates of pay, are now above the poverty datum line for Durban. Holidays and fringe benefits are also well above the clothing industry's average.'

No sooner had this been published on March 16th than I received a summons from Lord Kearton demanding that I come and see him in his office. I found the Courtaulds' chairman still extremely angry, threatening to sue us for millions to right the wrong he claimed I had done him. Much of the meeting was taken up by a curious confrontation which he staged on the telephone between myself and the Managing Director of his South African subsidiary, Peter Holden. With Kearton listening in, an impish look in his eyes, not much was proved either way. Holden insisted that he had never spoken to me. I told him he was the man who had confirmed to me that wages rates at SA Fabrics were below the PDL. It was a dialogue of the deaf.

Alastair Hetherington had been exceptionally steadfast in his support but as more and more threats of legal action as well as total denials flooded into the office his confidence in me understandably began to be shaken. *The Guardian*'s management were also worried. Though specific cases were hard to pin down, the advertising department later discovered that the growth in display advertising, which had been increasing steadily over the previous three years, suddenly flattened out. With my sources 8,000 miles away and the only evidence to support my story one rather scruffy notebook filled with my illegible writing which most people assume is some arcane form of shorthand, it was not surprising I felt under pressure.

Wilson Rowntree, a subsidiary of the chocolate making Quaker firm Rowntree Mackintosh, was the next to deny flatly the wage rates I had attributed to it. *The Guardian* felt obliged to publish a long letter from Rowntree's Chairman, Sir Donald Barron who gave details of Rowntree's wage rates and claimed that it had been unfairly vilified. This letter clearly impressed the editor who knew Barron personally. As a result, despite my vehement opposition, a further retraction was published in a leader written the next day saying *The Guardian*'s original report should have made clear that Wilson Rowntree were paying all its workers above subsistence levels.

Twenty-four hours later I learnt after an urgent round of calls to South Africa that Rowntree had only been able to make this claim because it had increased its basic rates of pay by 30 per cent on the very day of publication of my article. I was furious and let fly with a bitter private memo to Alastair. Unusually harsh words were exchanged between the editor and myself, almost the only time we ever fell out. 'You are the most arrogant man I have ever dealt with,' Alastair said in exasperation after I accused him most unfairly of bending too easily to pressure. Overwrought and utterly depressed, I thought of resigning but fortunately a wiser head in the shape of my uncle Jim Rose, who I have always consulted in moments of crisis, persuaded me it would merely damage the campaign *The Guardian* was waging.

The next development, despite my protests that all the facts in the article could be proved, was yet another apology to buy off Courtaulds: 'Some companies mentioned by *The Guardian* as paying below the poverty datum line mounted a vigorous defence. Courtaulds is one company in particular that feels it has been unfairly criticised. Lord Kearton, the chairman, points out with justice that his company has one of the better records of British firms in South Africa for training and fringe benefits, and takes its responsibilities very seriously. Earnings of its employees at South African Fabrics have always been above the poverty datum line. The report that basic wages were below subsistence levels was based on telephone conversations with the managing director of SA Fabrics who was away from the factory at the time and who now says he was misunderstood.'

The Chairman of Tate and Lyle, Sir John Lyle was also angered by *The Guardian*'s report. Choosing the oblique response of a letter to *The Times*, he claimed that poverty datum lines were not applicable to agricultural workers and that in any case wage were fixed by the South African Sugar Association. The next day *The Times* published a letter from me pointing out that Tate and Lyle's South African subsidiary had made a profit of more than £500,000 the previous year and that Tate and Lyle should set an example to the sugar industry which was paying some of the lowest wages in South Africa.

Apart from these angry company denials, there were some more positive developments. The day after the story broke, a leading article in *The Times* generously showed that dog does not always eat dog: '*The Guardian* is to be congratulated for bringing into prominence the fact that well-known firms whose head offices or holding companies are in London are among the worst employers in South Africa. There can be no excuse for them.' The influential Afrikaans newspaper, *Die Burger*, a supporter of the Vorster government, suggested the wages furore could be 'the beginning of a comprehensive campaign for the improvement of African conditions.' In the Commons more than 100 Labour MPs called for a debate and the Prime Minister Mr Callaghan responded by saying he would consider whether an official inquiry was needed.

Not every reaction was so welcoming. The *Transvaler*, leading organ of the Nationalist Party, bitterly attacked *The Guardian* and claimed its report was part of a conspiracy to smear South Africa. The Managing Director of GEC's South African subsidiary, Mr Frank Lester, told the *Cape Times*: 'I would have thought the people of Britain had enough of their own problems without worrying what we pay our workers.'

Most press and public comment, however, was overwhelmingly supportive. The *Rand Daily Mail*, South Africa's leading morning newspaper commented scathingly: 'When an overseas company accused of paying starvation wages to its African employees in South Africa says it didn't know, we find such a confession almost as disturbing as the initial accusation. For such companies have no business not knowing. Their countries are levelling strong moral accusations at us; therefore the companies themselves have a moral obligation to check on how they stand in relations to these accusations . . . But perhaps it is unfair to single out Mr Slater [chairman of Slater Walker]. His ignorance of how his South African companies treat their black workers is typical of many overseas enterprises operating here — particularly British enterprises.'

Sensing the overwhelming tide of public opinion, several leading industrial companies, among them Hoover, Reed International, and British Leyland, announced immediate inquiries into their South African labour practices and promised they would in future pay all their black workers above the relevant poverty datum line. Chloride said it was prepared to take a drop in profits to improve the wages of its South African workforce. Other financiers beat their breasts in public. 'I personally as well as fellow members of my board and I am sure my shareholders would not be able to sleep at night if we were not satisfied that the employment conditions were satisfactory,' said Mr Jim Slater, the chairman of Slater Walker.

These public statements were followed by a spate of extraordinary wage increases. Tootal put up its lowest basic rates at its South African subsidiary Natal Threads by 147 per cent in three rises in March, April, and June 1973. Slater Walker announced increases in April of 100 per cent for its lowest paid African workers together with a package of housing, educational and medical reforms. Courtaulds also introduced a new wage structure in April, incorporating family allowances representing an increase of up to 100 per cent for some workers. Other British parent companies which put up basic wages in this period between 40–60 per cent included Rio Tinto Zinc, Tate and Lyle, Associated Portland Cement, Barclays Bank, Armitage Shanks, Pilkington Bros, and Metal Box. Increases of 20–40 per cent were made by Consolidated Goldfields, ICI, British Leyland, and Cape Asbestos.

By March 1974 Mr W.E. Luke, chairman of the United Kingdom South Africa Trade Association, was boasting that wages of Africans employed by British companies had increased by an average of 50 per cent over the past year. 'Not fast enough for *The Guardian* but fast enough for most other people,' he said.

The spur for these dramatic wage rises was the decision by the Commons Select Committee on Trade and Industry on April 4th, 1973 to mount 'an investigation into the wages and conditions of African workers employed by British firms in South Africa.' Chaired by William Rodgers MP, the Select

Committee inquiry heard oral evidence from more than 30 major British companies and written evidence from a further 100 companies with controlling interests in over 650 businesses in the Republic employing more than 200,000 Africans.

Some company chairmen went out their way to deny in their evidence to the Select Committee that adverse publicity and the fact of a Commons inquiry had been responsible for their wage increases. British Leyland claimed that recent strikes in Durban had been its catalyst for action. RTZ claimed that its wages were already on a steady accelerating upward path. Associated Portland Cement said its wages were determined by the size and timing of the Government controlled cement price. But others, among them GEC, Tootal, Great Universal Stores, and Johnson Matthey admitted that they had responded to public pressure.

Lord Kearton, who gave a virtuoso performance before the Select Committee, armed with a wealth of detail and an impressive account of improvements to relate, said that Courtaulds had used the recent climate to 'bring home forcefully to our South African friends and colleagues that there is room for a faster rate of improvement'. The tide of publicity, he explained, had helped his company to accelerate along the path on which it was already going. 'We try to push things along, not because we are saints, but because we think we owe it to ourselves.'

Other witnesses made a less favourable impression. Johnson Matthey's Managing Director, Mr H.R. Brooker, when asked whether he was worried that his lowest paid black workers were being paid less in cash per month than the company's own estimated cost of upkeep for a single man replied: 'It does not disturb me. I am not disturbed by all sorts of things that happen in the world and which I accept as a matter of observation.' Lord Stokes of British Leyland also had an uncomfortable time. After saying that his company felt obliged to accept 'custom and practice in South Africa', he objected bitterly when asked whether, if he had been in the cotton industry in the early 19th century, he would have accepted slavery as inevitable.

Mr W.E. Luke of the United Kingdom South Africa Trade Association (UKSATA), told the committee that it would be unwise to have black African unions. Blacks, he said, 'lacked the mental capacity' to do many skilled industrial jobs and there was a tendency for the African if you paid him more money to put in less time. 'I think,' he said, 'if you want to understand this problem, it can only be done if you have a knowledge on the ground of South Africa and see the black people there, the hordes of them; that is what you are dealing with.'

The Chairman of Consolidated Goldfields, Mr Donald McCall, claimed it would be a mistake to press ahead with African advancement too quickly. 'The tribal Africans have really only been in contact with the Europeans perhaps during this century. Let us not try and jump too far in seventy or eighty years what has taken us, say, a thousand years to achieve.' The Committee's chairman Mr Rodgers responded acidly, 'I am grateful for that revealing statement but it does not entirely answer the question I put to you.'

One of the last witnesses, Sir Reay Geddes, chairman of Dunlop, questioned why his subsidiary company in South Africa was paying below subsistence level wages, insisted that the matter was one for local management to decide. Asked when his main board in Britain had learnt of the low wages being paid, he replied to the astonishment of the committee that they had known since the first Dunlop factory was opened in the Republic nearly 40 years ago.

Almost a year to the day after my story was published in *The Guardian*, the Trade and Industry Select Committee finally published its report. Pulling no punches, it named 63 leading British companies as having admitted in their own evidence to paying below the poverty datum line and recommended that in future all British owned firms should pay minimum wages not less than 50 per cent above this subsistence level.

To ensure that this code of conduct was followed, the Committee recommended that the Department of Trade and Industry should play a supervisory role monitoring the wages and conditions of Africans employed by British companies in an annual published survey. 'Too many British firms normally look little further than the balance sheets of their South African subsidiaries,' it concluded. A *Guardian* editorial noted that a number of companies were so ashamed of their evidence that they had asked permission to withdraw it. The principal conclusions of the report were backed by the Government and later an EEC Code of Conduct was adopted by the Common Market countries. But by then I was deep in a libel action.

Despite the Select Committee's report, which to a large extent substantiated my original story in *The Guardian*, we were far from being out of the legal thicket. Rowntree Mackintosh, Metal Box and others had withdrawn from the fray but Courtaulds and its indefatigable Chairman, Lord Kearton, were still going strong. It was largely my own fault. During the Committee hearings I had established a working though uneasy relationship with Courtaulds' Chairman. He was an extraordinary character. To master his brief before giving evidence before the Committee, he got up at 4.30 every morning for two months. By the time he appeared before it, he knew every wage rate and bonus in the company and as a result gave a bravura performance. During this period I was twice asked to lunch by Kearton at Courtaulds' Hanover Square headquarters. These were distinctly odd occasions. Though most of the members of his board were also present, neither they nor indeed I were allowed to say anything. Our role, it was made crystal clear, was to listen to the Chairman's extensive monologue about his South African operations and how Courtaulds' wages and conditions were the best in the dark continent.

Given Lord Kearton's intense degree of personal commitment and fury with my original story, I should have been on notice to be very careful. But in a further story written by me which *The Guardian* published on December 10th, 1973, I quoted officials of the Trade Union Congress of South Africa (TUCSA) as alleging that South African Fabrics, a Courtaulds subsidiary, was one of five British companies who had refused to recognise the union representing African textile workers.

In itself this was not a very interesting charge, nor was it even original as my story was a follow-up of a similar piece which had appeared a few days earlier in *The Observer*, written by Andrew Wilson. But to Lord Kearton it was a red rag. Four days later, without warning, another writ arrived from Courtaulds and this time it was for real. The accompanying Statement of Claim said that the article had gravely damaged the company's reputation and was part of a reckless and malicious campaign being waged by *The Guardian* against it. To adduce this last point, Courtaulds had harked back to its complaint about the original article of March 12th and the two retractions we had published under duress. What I had foolishly done was to revive the original action with a vengeance.

At the first meeting to discuss Courtaulds' writ, *The Guardian*'s counsel, Peter Bowsher, took a relatively optimistic view. He thought that Courtaulds had made a mistake in alleging malice in addition to libel. By opening up the question of its wage rates prior to March 12th, 1973, Courtaulds might be forced during the discovery process into some embarrassing admissions. The charge of malice, he felt, was particularly odd in view of Lord Kearton's remark in a BBC interview on April 4th about the setting up of the Select Committee: 'Well I think it is a triumph for Mr Hetherington, the Editor of *The Guardian* and for his reporter Mr Raphael.' But Bowsher pointed out that our case was not helped by the fact that we were not in a position at present to prove that South African

Fabrics had been approached for recognition by the union and had refused.

Frantic telephone calls to South Africa and interviews with witnesses produced only a confused story. Mrs Harriet Bolton, secretary of the mixed race Textile Workers Union, and an official of TUCSA confirmed that as far as she was concerned South African Fabrics was 'uncooperative'. Mr Halton Cheadle, national organiser of the union, said that he was told by Mr Bruce, a senior manager of South African Fabrics, that he recognised 'neither me nor the union I was representing'. But both Cheadle and Bolton conceded that they had not applied for formal recognition of the union because they felt the ground had not been sufficiently prepared. To that extent my story had been wrong.

Peter Bowsher's view became gloomier after a stormy meeting in the Middle Temple the following month with a team of Courtaulds' lawyers led by Thomas Bingham QC who made clear that Lord Kearton would settle for nothing less than a statement and apology in open court. An opinion written by Bowsher four days later described *The Guardian*'s prospects as 'not very bright'. He pointed out that two of the key potential witnesses in the case had been placed under banning orders and thus probably would not be able to give evidence for the defence. The one ray of hope, he pointed out, was that the plaintiffs had created difficulties for themselves by claiming malice. Overall he believed an out of court settlement could be achieved. If not, he reckoned libel damages might be of the order of £20,000 plus costs.

That summer was spent in the interminable processes of libel actions as the plaintiffs and the defence probed for each other's weak spots. As more and more details were revealed under pressure of court orders, the mood of *The Guardian*'s solicitors, Lovell White and King, became distinctly bullish. Geoffrey Grimes, one of its leading partners, who handled our legal problems, concluded that though there may have been no formal approach by the union to SA Fabrics, its generally obstructive attitude towards the union would not enlist sympathy from a jury.

Moreover Courtaulds had been forced to admit that its claim that it had always paid its workers above the poverty datum line was false. In its 'Further and Better Particulars of the Statement of Claim' it admitted: 'It is not alleged that the second Plaintiffs (South African Fabrics) had always paid all their Bantu workers above the poverty datum line during this period.' That admission was particularly damaging because it showed that the two retractions which Courtaulds had forced *The Guardian* to publish after my original story in March 1973 were inaccurate and that we had been misled.

The same also applied to letters written by Lord Kearton to his shareholders at the same time attacking *The Guardian*'s statements about SA Fabrics as 'untrue', ending with the blistering comment: 'It seems odd to me that such widely circulated allegations can be made against a company like ourselves on no foundation and with no checking but I suppose it is the price we pay for a free press.'

At a further meeting with Counsel that Autumn, Peter Bowsher said he was encouraged that Courtaulds had been forced to concede it was wrong about the wages paid to its African workers. He believed that Lord Kearton's letter to shareholders was defamatory of the newspaper, the Editor and its reporter and that it might be helpful to launch a counter-action against Courtaulds. He now felt that the paper's chances of winning the main action on union recognition were fairly good. The case was not open and shut but the chances of winning on justification were quite reasonable, he concluded.

The outcome of this conference was that it was agreed that I should write a personal letter to Lord Kearton pointing out the difficulties in which Courtaulds latest admissions on wages had put him and asking to remedy the attacks he had made against me to shareholders. The phrasing was deliberately silky:

'Since it is so clear that your understanding of the matters has been mistaken, I ask you to consider whether you may not possibly also have been in error about other matters which have formed the basis of criticisms which you have levelled against me and which gravely reflect upon my professional standing and reputation as a journalist. I hope that you will recognise that you have done something of an injustice to me personally and I would be grateful if you would turn your mind to putting matters right.'

This letter appeared to have its desired effect of making Courtaulds think twice because from this point on the libel action appeared slowly to go to sleep. Events also conspired to restore the odd personal relationship I had with Lord Kearton. That autumn I was invited by the Cambridge Union to propose a motion urging the cutting of all trade and sporting links with South Africa. That was a view which the World Council of Churches among others supported. But it was one that I had never shared. So I replied I would be glad to take part if I could speak *against* the motion.

When I arrived I found that I was speaking in support of the Chairman of Courtaulds. Quite what Lord Kearton thought of his seconder, I don't know. But soon after we had won the debate handsomely, he once again invited me to lunch. Little was said about the libel action until the very end when Kearton mentioned it with some embarrassment. He said he had had nothing to do with it and it was being handled by Courtaulds' director in charge of legal affairs. I said I regretted it had gone on for so long but that *The Guardian* felt it had gone as far as it could when it had offered to correct any misinterpretation about union recognition. In view of the difficulty even now of establishing the precise position, neither I nor my colleagues felt that an apology in open court was called for. As we parted Lord Kearton said he would have a word with Mr Wright, his legal director.

The final stage took place in the summer of 1975 shortly

before a further meeting with our counsel when we learnt that Courtaulds had amended its statement of claim and dropped its allegation of malice. That meant we were entitled to that part of our costs, then totalling more than £4,000, which related to malicious falsehood. But Peter Bowsher advised that rather than seek to strike out the rest of the action and recover that part of our costs, it was sensible to let sleeping dogs lie. Shortly afterwards negotiations began between solicitors on either side on an acceptable statement in open court, both sides agreeing to pay their own costs.

On August 1st *The Guardian* published a brief statement of the settlement in the High Court. Mr Christopher Bathurst for the plaintiffs said that Courtaulds had brought the proceedings because it was not true to say that South African Fabrics had refused to recognise the union representing African Textile Workers. 'The defendants now acknowledge that SA Fabrics received no approach for recognition. Although the parties remained at issue as to the character of the contacts between SA Fabrics and local union officials, the defendants admitted with regret that their article was likely to mislead readers on this important point.'

Courtaulds, for its part, recognised that its allegation of malice against *The Guardian* in respect of earlier articles could not be substantiated and regretted it had been made. Mr Peter Bowsher, counsel for the defendants, said *The Guardian* regretted that the article should have been misleading. They accepted the spirit in which the serious allegation of malice had now been withdrawn. Under the terms of the settlement,' no damages have been paid to Courtaulds or its subsidiary and each side is paying its own costs.'

So ended a time-consuming and expensive episode. *The Guardian*'s total bill amounted to nearly £6,500 but that did not include the considerable expenses in wear and tear and of executive time not to mention many peace-making lunches at Hanover Square. All in all for a two paragraph follow-up to another paper's story, it was a worrying and unnecessary affair. As to my original story, my South African friends say there was a small upwards blip in the wage scales about 1973–1974. But beyond that it is hard to claim permanent results. The British code and the EEC codes of conduct did undoubtedly have some effect on British and other European companies operating in South Africa in making them behave better towards their African workers. Starvation wages are not the cause — only the result of apartheid. For all that, I continue to believe that foreign investment is a wiser route than total sanctions for those who seek a peaceful solution of the South African tragedy.

9

A Trio of Losers

Few attacks either of ridicule or invective make much noise but with the help of those that they provoke.

Dr Johnson

Derek Jameson, dubbed Sid Yobbo by *Private Eye* but more widely known to Radio 2 listeners as the genial compere of the Morning Show, rues the day he instructed his learned friends to sue for libel. Charlotte Cornwell, star of the Royal Shakespeare Company and the National Theatre will go down in legal history as 'the actress with the big bum'. Michael Meacher, Labour MP for Oldham West and front bench spokesman on employment, was landed with legal bills for £130,000 after being advised to sue *The Observer*. All three cases are frightening examples of how treacherous the law of libel can be for private individuals, and why the only sane response, if you are ridiculed by the media, is to go and have a stiff drink and forget about it.

Derek Jameson's troubles began with an off-the-cuff light-hearted answer on the BBC's popular radio magazine programme Today, in March 1980. He was explaining why he had just fired his fellow editor of the *Daily Star*, Peter Grimsditch. 'Grimbles' was the victim, he said, of a bout of internecine bloodletting that Fleet Street engages in from time to time. 'One of us had to go and you can guess who that was,' said the editor-in-chief of Express Newspapers. This flippant remark was heard by a BBC scriptwriter John Langdon, who reckoned the editorial axe wielder was a suitable victim for a sketch. It was broadcast a few days later on the BBC's satirical radio programme Week Ending: 'This week we burrow into the no-bars world of Fleet Street, to pay tribute to an editor who sees reality with half an eye, humour with half a wit, and circulation figures with half an aspirin. Yes the *Daily Star*'s editor of the month and our man of the week is Derek Jameson.'

After a few rousing bars from Elgar's King of the Barbarians the skit went on: 'In Derek Jameson we have the archetypal East End boy made bad, narrowly surviving a term of active service on the *Mirror* he retired from newspaper work to become Editor of the *Daily Express*. He arrived uncluttered with taste or talent and took to his new role like a duck to orange sauce, displaying an editorial policy characteristically simple — all the nudes fit to print and all the news printed to fit. But it's as a craftsman we remember him best; the writer who thinks from the wrist, the author who is to journalism what lockjaw is to conversation and the creative force who's made the *Express* what it is today — the thinking man's bin-liner.

There was a good deal more of the same humour: 'Never lost for clichés, Derek Jameson is always ready to speak his mind, however small. But tonight we honour him for his promotion to the lofty obscurity of the *Daily Star*. We salute him as an editor with the common touch, who regards nudity as only skin deep, and who still believes that erudite is a glue.' Then came the finale after some more rousing music: 'So join us now as we congratulate this man of a few syllables as he approaches his new labour of lust and starts the ball rolling in the paper that put the media in mediocrity. Derek Jameson, the nitty-gritty titivation (sic) tout from Trafalgar House is our Man of the Week!'

Bad news doesn't take long to travel in Fleet Street. When Jameson heard about Week Ending's sketch from a colleague he was irritated. When he got hold of the script he was furious. As his autobiography *Touched by Angels* makes clear, Jameson is proud of his achievement in clambering to the top from the poorest of poor backgrounds. The illegitimate son of a washerwoman and a Kosher butcher, he has made the most of his talents. The broadcast touched on a sensitive spot. Satire it may have been but it wasn't at all funny to its victim. Looking back on the affair, Jameson recognises that he should have taken the sound advice of his old East End mum: 'Find out who wrote it and go and punch him on the nose. The worst that can happen is you'll be fined 50 quid.'

Instead Jameson went to law. 'Don't let them get away with it, go for them,' urged the Chairman of Express Newspapers, Lord Matthews. On the advice of the *Express*'s legal manager, Jameson approached Peter Carter-Ruck, a leading solicitor with a flamboyant reputation for winning large settlements from newspapers. 'You can't go wrong with him, old man, the best in the business,' Jameson was told. The *Express*' Editor thought why not? After all, the papers he had edited had had to pay out more than a few bob in the past after receiving threatening letters from Peter Carter-Ruck written on his elegant pale yellow notepaper.

His new legal adviser was bullish about the case. According to Jameson, the message he received as the mounds of documents began to pile up was: 'Don't worry. I know the BBC. They'll settle out of court.' But the BBC was reluctant to do so. The Corporation took the view that if it gave in on such a case it would mark the end of satirical sketches. To Jameson's statement of claim alleging that the broadcast was defamatory and professionally damaging, the BBC therefore responded with a defence of fair comment. Right from the start it should have been clear, if not to Jameson at least to his solicitor, that this was going to be a difficult case to win. Not only did it turn on the meaning of the words — the BBC denied that the broadcast was defamatory — but the issues in dispute ranged over Jameson's whole career as a tabloid journalist.

It was also soon apparent that the BBC was prepared to go to great lengths to prove that Week Ending's satire had been well founded. Derek Jameson had made his name in the 1970s as the Northern Editor of the *Daily Mirror* with the brief of stopping the onward march of *The Sun* owned by the Australian tycoon Rupert Murdoch. His tactics had been, as he admits unashamedly, to out-Murdoch Rupert by copying *The Sun*'s formula of naked girls and provocative features. This reputation as a brash merchant of tabloid sex followed him to the *Express*' new downmarket tabloid. 'The *Daily Star* will be all tits, bums, QPR and roll your own fags,' Jameson was quoted as saying in *The Observer*'s gossip column. The new editor-in-chief of Express Newspapers angrily denounced the quote as a fabrication but it stuck like the Sid Yobbo nickname pinned on him by *Private Eye*. Justified or not — and Jameson is a much cleverer man than he lets on — there was no shortage of damaging material for the BBC to mine.

Twelve years as editor of tabloid newspapers was enough to give any lawyer material to construct a case that here indeed was a 'titillation tout'. Sensing the way the wind was blowing, Jameson sought in 1981 to get out of the case on reasonable terms. He had just been fired by the *Express* and knew that whoever was going to pick up the bill for his action, it wouldn't be Lord Matthews who had initially urged him on.

On October 14th, 1980, Jameson wrote to his solicitor Peter Carter-Ruck: 'Thank you for your kind letter of the 12th. I enclose a cheque for £2,392.73 as requested. It scares me to be £2,900 down before the first shot is fired across the bows — especially now Lord Matthews is no longer underwriting me. But I guess all will be well in the end.'

Jameson was persuaded by Carter-Ruck that it would be throwing money away to go for an early settlement. With the costs of the action already mounting, he was asked: 'Why should you pay £5,000 to be insulted?' 'Too true,' thought

Jameson, who was then jobless. 'Leave it to Peter, he's the expert.'

It was a refrain that was to be constantly repeated. According to Jameson, he was never told by his solicitor that it was a high risk case. By 1982 Jameson's own costs, quite apart from the BBC's, were £8,000; a year later they were £10,000. By the time of the trial four years after the Week Ending broadcast, they were £14,000. Every time Jameson voiced concern he was reassured by Carter-Ruck that the BBC would settle, even possibly on the very steps of the court.

The BBC, however, sensing that it for once had a plaintiff on the run, contented itself with paying a nominal £10 into court. Jameson could have accepted this offer and had most of his expenses met by the BBC but once again Peter Carter-Ruck advised him against settlement. On October 13th, 1983, the solicitor wrote to Jameson saying that he was holding out for at least £1,000 in damages and a letter of apology: 'I still take the view that if this action did go to trial you could be awarded between £25,000 and £50,000 in damages. It is in my opinion a very serious libel.'

When the trial finally opened at the Royal Courts of Justice in the Strand on February 13th, 1984, Jameson, unemployed and apparently unemployable, had a sinking feeling as he watched a high-powered procession of BBC executives and their lawyers sail past him into the Queen's Bench Division. The feeling turned into near despair as he was battered for nearly six days in the witness box by the BBC's counsel, John Wilmers QC. The theme repeated over and over again was that Jameson's long career in editing popular tabloid papers meant that he was tarred with the same lurid brush. Much of the most damaging material came from his own cuttings book which the defence had acquired under the discovery process of a libel action. Confronted by this evidence which included the 'Sid Yobbo' gibe and thousands of pictures of ladies in various states of undress published under his editorship, Jameson denied that he was notorious as the editor of 'tit and bum' papers. 'I don't think you can defend publishing nudes journalistically — it will not win you the Pulitzer Prize — but it does sell copies of newspapers,' he told the jury.

Jameson sought to prove his credentials as a serious journalist by pointing out that after he had moved to edit the *Daily Express* it had a strait-laced policy of not publishing nudes. Mr Wilmers asked why a holiday feature about Spain in the *Daily Express* had been illustrated by a girl wearing a skimpy bikini. 'Sexual titillation, Mr Jameson?' Retorted the plaintiff: 'What should I have put in there? A picture of General Franco?'

It was a nice crack but for the most part Jameson was on the defensive. He was grilled at length about his reasons for buying Soraya Kashoggi's story for £75,000. The former Leicester shop girl tore up the cheque because she was suing her ex-husband, the tycoon Adnan Kashoggi, for a great deal more money than that. But the story of her cavortings with Winston Churchill, MP for Davyhulme, featured heavily in the *Daily Star* on February 5th, 1980. The front page headline provided all the reader needed to know: 'The Faster you Go, the More I'll Take Off . . . In no time at all Winston was doing 100 mph.' Reading from the *Daily Star*'s exclusive 'Soraya's Own Story', Mr Wilmers demanded, 'Isn't that sexually titillating?' Replied Jameson: 'I don't think so, those stories are not reeking of sex.' Well how would he define it? After a long pause, Jameson said thoughtfully, 'Rabelaisian.'

Jameson also found himself in difficult waters over his decision to buy the story of Joyce McKinney, an American model who caused a sensation in 1978 by skipping the country while awaiting trial for kidnapping a Mormon missionary. She had apparently kept the missionary in chains as a means of forcing him to have sex with her. The *Daily Express* found the model hiding in Atlanta, Georgia and promptly cast Joyce, albeit accompanied by a large photograph of her dressed in a nun's habit, as a naive frustrated small-town American girl who had taken to bondage simply as a way of persuading her sexually repressed Mormon boyfriend to make love.

Alas, as Jameson ruefully admitted, it was not quite the whole story. Two days later the *Daily Mirror* published the unexpurgated version revealing that Miss McKinney was no innocent Southern belle. Rather she had made about $50,000 by posing for pornographic pictures. 'We were out-McKinneyed,' confessed Mr Jameson to the court. Nothing abashed he pointed out that the BBC itself had not been uninterested in the bondage saga, running a two-part McKinney special on the Tonight programme. 'There you are,' said Jameson in triumph to his persecutor Mr John Wilmers QC, 'two nights running on BBC television. Joyce McKinney talking about bondage, handcuffs, sex, massage, pictures reproduced of her in kinky gear. To take me to task over the *Daily Express* story is pure hypocrisy.'

John Wilmers finally ended Jameson's ordeal of cross-examination after six days, one day longer than the time the plaintiff had been told the entire case would last. 'By that time I was ready to confess all rather than spend another minute under the interrogation of this master advocate,' wrote Jameson. 'I remember thinking to myself: If that's how they treat the innocent party, God help the defendants.'

The verdict turned on this prolonged cross-examination. Though Jameson had given a good performance, the impression left with the jury of the sleazy world of tabloid journalism was very damaging. When David Eady QC came to sum up for the plaintiff, he accused the BBC of using all its resources to try and destroy a small man. 'The BBC's time and vast resources,' he said, 'have been turned on Derek Jameson in a vast military operation to leave no stone unturned to find anything they can to discredit him.'

John Wilmers in his final speech for the BBC pointed out that editors of papers like the *Daily Express* might expect people they attack to have fairly thick skins and be able to take criticism. 'One is entitled to say what is good for the goose is good for the gander.' He went on: 'Why shouldn't the scriptwriter be allowed to express a strong opinion? We are all entitled, in a free country, to express our views.'

The judge, Mr Justice Comyn, in his summing up was brief: 'You have been asked to look at Mr Jameson as an editor — but is he not also a man?' Had the sketch gone too far in 'poking fun'? Should not the plaintiff, as the BBC had suggested, be 'the last man to complain'? The jury took a long time to decide these issues. The lawyers on both sides with the assent of the judge had agreed a list of five detailed questions to guide them in their verdict. There was also a set of accompanying 'guidelines for the jury', the flavour of which can only be demonstrated by quoting the last in full: 'If any of the imputations: (i) are both factual and defamatory or (ii) are comment but could be made by an honest person on the facts; or (iii) are comment which an honest person could make but malice has been proved against the BBC — what damages do you award to the Plaintiff?'

After wrestling for five hours with these and other conundrums, the jury returned, asking for a dictionary. When this was refused the foreman asked the judge to define the word 'imputation'. Following consultation with the two QCs the judge ruled that 'imputation' meant 'meaning'. The jury digested this for another two hours before finally coming back with its verdict: 'The broadcast though defamatory was fair comment.'

Outside the court Derek Jameson told the throng of reporters that the £75,000 costs he would now have to bear would wipe out his life-time savings. 'I brought this case,' he said, 'to show that honesty, integrity, decency and fair play do exist in Fleet Street. I hoped that I had demonstrated those virtues. Clearly the jury has decided otherwise and I can only accept their verdict.'

There was an extraordinary sequel to the case. Two weeks after the verdict, Jameson, interviewed by *The Guardian*, was asked whether he had been surprised by the verdict. 'Yes,' he replied, 'all through the lawyers told me what a splendid case I had. They were talking about a gross libel and exemplary damages.' So was his legal advice unsound? 'It would be churlish to quibble,' said Jameson magnanimously.

One person who was disturbed to read these remarks was Jameson's counsel, David Eady QC, who had warned his client in a written opinion delivered to Carter-Ruck six months before the trial that he ought to settle the case. The opinion, dated September 20th, 1983, could not have been clearer. David Eady wrote:

> This must be regarded as a 'high risk' piece of litigation which is likely to turn upon the jury's reaction to the personalities involved rather than upon any close legal analysis of the pleaded issues. Accordingly the recent payment into Court needs to be considered seriously, not because £10 represents a realistic figure (either for compensation or vindication) but rather because it does present one means of avoiding the considerable financial exposure now confronting the Client.
>
> The trial is bound to take some time . . . even if successful there will be a very substantial solicitor/own client bill (irrecoverable from the Defendants), a large part of which has yet to be incurred. I should be very surprised if a jury were to make a large award in this case, and the reality is therefore (assuming a win for Mr Jameson) that he will be out of pocket to a greater extent than if the £10 were taken out within the permitted period.
>
> I would hardly add that, if he loses (and therefore becomes responsible for the totality of the BBC's taxed costs, including trial), the prospect for the Client is bleak indeed. An analysis of the figures involved can be provided no doubt

by my Instructing Solicitor but clearly in deciding what course to take (on the payment in) the Client will have in mind that he is in effect gambling with many thousands of pounds.

I have little doubt that the BBC regard their chances of success as being higher than 50 per cent but certainly so far as Mr Jameson is concerned it would in my view be prudent to approach the case on the footing that he has no more than an evens chance of winning. Moreover, I would consider the prospect of his recovering a sufficient sum of damages to cover the solicitor/own client costs in respect of a trial to be remote.

The opinion concluded as ominously as it had begun: 'It seems to me that the ordinary listener to the radio programme would see the satire as being directed towards the Plaintiff's brand of journalism and perhaps also his personal style, rather than against his intellectual capacity or his technical competence. Thus the jury too may dismiss these points on the footing that they represent a personal reaction to the attack and an over-sensitive interpretation of its message.'

Not surprisingly in view of this unambiguous warning, David Eady could not understand how Jameson could fairly claim that he had been urged on by his lawyers. He therefore wrote to Peter Carter-Ruck on March 19th asking what on earth had happened. If it really was the case that Jameson believed what he had been quoted as saying in *The Guardian* there appeared to be only one explanation.

Though couched in polite language, this was a very tough letter. Barristers are not allowed to communicate directly with lay clients; they have to do so through solicitors who are trusted to pass on to the client the advice which counsel gives. For David Eady to break such a rule the circumstances would have to be wholly exceptional. But the implication that Jameson had been kept in ignorance of his counsel's advice could obviously not be ignored.

However, two weeks later on April 2nd, Carter-Ruck wrote to David Eady to reassure him that Jameson had been shown the opinion: 'The client is fully aware of the situation and of your advice, which he has seen.' Derek Jameson is clear that he was not shown his counsel's opinion by his solicitor either before or after the trial. But he remembers that when he went to see Carter-Ruck a few days after the case, he was told: 'Look here, Derek, you mustn't go round saying all your lawyers said you had a strong case. David Eady is most upset. He never thought so.'

Jameson was dumbfounded. 'What do you mean?' he asked. Carter-Ruck tried to calm the waters. He explained that counsel had indeed submitted an opinion saying it was a high risk case but subsequently he had changed his mind. 'So why wasn't I shown this opinion?' Jameson asked. 'I thought it would be bad for your morale, Derek,' replied the solicitor.

A month later Peter Carter-Ruck, a former council member of the Law Society, defended his conduct to his professional body. In a letter on June 12th to the Law Society's Secretary General, he said that he had acted 'entirely as I considered to be in the best interests of the client.' He pointed out that had he advised Derek Jameson to settle on derisory terms, he would have been entitled 'to my full fees'. Instead because of the case's outcome and the considerable financial crisis faced by his client, 'I made a substantial reduction in my fees which I would not otherwise have done.' On the merits of the case, Carter-Ruck wrote that counsel had failed to advise on the merits of the case for more than two years and only then suggested that it was 'high risk'. But the veteran solicitor claimed that David Eady had not at that point heard the broadcast and that he had then changed his mind about the chances of winning after listening to a tape.

Derek Jameson did not realise just how damning the missing counsel's opinion was until his new solicitor eventually obtained a copy five years later. As he says in his autobiography *Touched by Angels* (Ebury Press) if he had seen counsel's opinion he would never have approved the risk of a trial. 'Had I known, there was no way I would have gone ahead,' he said. Understandably Jameson blames Carter-Ruck for 'deliberately withholding' David Eady's opinion from him. 'What puzzles me to this day,' he says, 'is whether Carter-Ruck charged me for the opinion he thought was too strong for my stomach. I cannot find it in his final account.'

No better explanation emerged why the counsel's opinion was not shown to the plaintiff when Peter Carter-Ruck publicly responded to Jameson's charge in his autobiography that he had been led up the garden path. Claiming that Jameson had been a bad witness who had lost a sound case, he said that 'nothing had been deliberately withheld from him.' The solicitor said that he had worked on the case for three and a half years with David Eady and was most concerned when the QC decided it was 'a high risk' case. Carter-Ruck gave no reason why he failed to show the counsel's opinion to his client beyond saying: 'I have always done what I consider right in the clients' interests, and the hundreds of appreciative letters I have received are the real indication of the services I have rendered.'

The claim that Jameson was a poor witness is not shared by other observers of the trial. Equally Carter-Ruck's statement that counsel changed his mind about the merits of the case is unsupported by any written evidence. Whatever the explanation for all of this, it is surely a disgrace that his own counsel's opinion should be withheld from a client. The Jameson libel trial raises an important question mark over the wisdom of isolating barristers from those whom they represent. If David Eady had been allowed to communicate directly with Jameson and tell him that it was folly to continue, the case might never have come to trial.

Carter-Ruck's final account which Jameson had to pay in full came to £41,342.50. For Jameson it was a horribly expensive lesson that the law of libel is not for the ordinary citizen.

Luckily for 'Sid Yobbo', there was a happy ending. The BBC, recognising that he was crushed, generously did not press for their £35,000 costs and took him under their wing. Within a very few months he was transformed into a radio and television personality. Jameson has now signed a contract for Rupert Murdoch's satellite channel Sky Television to present a five day a week chat show at £250,000 a year. The former £1.37 a week messenger is an East End boy made triumphantly good. By chance and his native wit he is wiser but not poorer. As for Peter Carter-Ruck, he remains one of London's most fashionable libel solicitors.

THE ACTRESS'S BIG BUM

Derek Jameson's experience of a libel action may be a horror story but the case of the actress Miss Charlotte Cornwell is arguably worse. After five years, three libel trials, one Appeal Court hearing and two awards of damages and costs in her favour, she ended up £70,000 out of pocket and had to sell her house. As for her reputation, despite her libel wins she is now more widely known for having been criticised for the size of her bottom than the serious Shakespearean actress which she is.

Miss Cornwell's problems began when she agreed to take the part of an ageing rock star Shelley Maze in a modern rock drama called No Excuses, made for commercial television. She had already played the role on stage to critical acclaim. But the television series was less successful. Its ribald language proved too much for the moguls of Thames Television who decided that it should be put on late at night rather than in a prime time slot in the early evening as originally scheduled. This decision angered Miss Cornwell who denounced it in an interview with *The Guardian* as a Pavlovian starch-collar response by 'men in Burton suits who don't know a good piece of television from a piece of cod fillet'.

Among those who read this interview was Nina Myskow, the *Sunday People*'s television critic, otherwise known as the 'Bitch of the Box' in recognition of her vitriolic style. Each week Miss Myskow devoted part of her column to an attack on some television personality under the heading 'Wally of the Week'. Having watched Charlotte Cornwell in the first two episodes of No Excuses, she thought she would make an excellent 'Wally'. There were only 179 words in her review that week in May 1983, but they were clearly designed to wound:

Actress Charlotte Cornwell made a proper pratt of herself in Central's crude new catastrophe, No Excuses. And then she prattled about it pompously in public. This repellent rubbish about a clapped-out rock singer is without doubt the worst I have ever clapped eyes on. It bears no relation to rock and roll today — all concerned must have been living down a sewer for the last decade — or indeed to human beings.

As a middle-aged star all Miss Cornwell has going for her is her age. She can't sing, her bum is too big and she has the sort of stage presence that jams lavatories. Worst she belongs to that arrogant and deluded school of acting which believes that if you leave off your make-up (how brave, how real) and SHOUT A LOT, it's great acting. It's ART. For a start, dear, you look just as ugly with make-up, so forget that. And as for ART? in the short sharp words of the series, there is just one reply. It rhymes.

As soon as she read this review, Miss Cornwell consulted the well known show business solicitor Oscar Beuselinck who dispatched a letter to the *Sunday People* pointing out: 'Our client is of normal weight and appearance' and demanding an apology. None was forthcoming so a writ for libel was issued.

The *Sunday People* decided to fight on the grounds that though tough, the review fell within the bounds of acceptable television criticism.

Two-and-a-half years later Miss Cornwell's action for libel was heard by the High Court. Her counsel, Andrew Bateson QC, described the review as a malicious and vulgar personal attack: 'Nothing that consists of vilification, vituperation, and vindictive abuse is fair comment. When one comes to reviews — and this is recognised by most reviewers — they may be very rude about performances and very rude about the play . . . But this piece which has been written is an attack on her personally, not on her as an actress. It was made in the most intemperate and abusively unpleasant terms.'

Miss Cornwell told the court she was appalled when she read the review in the *Sunday People*: 'I was shocked, and I felt sick. I felt humiliated.' After the article appeared, she said, she was out of work for more than a year. The actor Ian McKellen, a National Theatre colleague, said she was a serious actress, one of the top dozen in her age group in the country. The review in the *Sunday People* was not criticism but a personal attack designed to damage. It could well have affected her employment prospects, he said.

The judge, who found theatrical jokes hard to resist then intervened: 'You would not take the size of someone's bottom from the *Sunday People* presumably. If it was important to the part you would have to look at it yourself?'

For the *Sunday People* Michael Beloff QC pleaded that Miss Myskow's article, though couched in strong terms, was honest comment on a matter of public interest. After describing No Excuses as 'a desert of darkness punctuated by oases of sheer nastiness' Mr Beloff said the case was as much a trial of Miss Myskow's abilities as a journalist as Miss Cornwell's attributes as an actress: 'If you do form such a contrary view, you are, in effect, saying that Miss Myskow is not fit to practice the profession of journalism at all.'

At the end of the five-day trial, the jury of eleven men and one woman found for the actress and awarded her £10,000 damages, considerably more than the £5 that the *Sunday People* had paid into court. She was therefore entitled to her costs, estimated to be £30,000. The judge, Mr Justice Michael Davies, who confessed to the court that he was an avid theatre-goer and a personal admirer of Miss Cornwell's stagecraft, refused the *Sunday People*'s plea that the damages should not be immediately handed over with the comment: 'If I had tried the case without a jury, I would certainly have awarded Miss Cornwell a substantial sum.'

This judgment did not meet with universal favour. In particular, it roused Auberon Waugh in his *Spectator* column to a high pitch of fury: 'Christmas and New Year, while I pondered the suggestion that I should succeed Emma Soames as editor of the *Literary Review*, were made hideous for me by the spectacle of Miss Charlotte Cornwell's big bum . . . If Mr Justice Michael Davies' asinine instructions to the jury pass into law as a result of this silly, vain woman's complaints about her bottom, any disparaging comment can be made the subject of a libel action and any single libel action like this one, awarding £10,000 plus £30,000 costs could easily prove to be enough to close down the *Literary Review* — as well, I dare say, as *Books and Bookmen*, the *New Review* and most other publications in the field.'

Charlotte Cornwell's triumph was short lived. The *Sunday People* immediately appealed on the grounds that the judge had misdirected the jury on damages. The judge had also, it claimed, allowed inadmissible evidence by Ian McKellen. In his summing up the judge had said: 'Well of course you are not bound by Mr McKellen's view but there it is, and the more impressive you thought him as a witness, the more attention you will give, no doubt, to what he said.' So through no fault of her own, Miss Cornwell was faced by the possibility that if she lost in the Appeal Court, she would have to pay the costs of not only the appeal but also the costs of the first trial as well having to face the hazards of another trial in the High Court.

Two years later, in February 1987, the appeal was finally heard by the Court of Appeal. After a three-day hearing Lord Justices Parker, Slade, and Mustill set aside the £10,000 award and ordered a retrial. The Appeal Court concluded that while the article attacking Miss Cornwell was 'grossly offensive', the trial judge Mr Justice Michael Davies had misdirected the jury and the verdict could not stand. In particular the Appeal Judges declared that Ian McKellen should not have been allowed to give evidence about what he thought the article meant.

The Appeal Judges upheld the defence's submission that the trial judge had failed to direct the jury to disregard all Mr McKellen's evidence apart from that which concerned Miss Cornwell's reputation at the time of publication. Worse, he had actually invited jurors to pay high regard to those parts of McKellen's evidence which were the most prejudicial. They also found that the judge had allowed evidence of reviews of plays which were staged after the libel action had begun and had further failed to direct the jury fully on the issue of damages.

The net result of these judicial errors was that Charlotte Cornwell was now faced by financial ruin. She had to return the £10,000 damages awarded to her as well as pay the £36,000 costs of the appeal. And hanging over her in addition were the estimated £60,000 costs of the first trial which the Court of Appeal left to be decided by the judge at the retrial. Burdened by this avalanche of debt, she was forced to sell her house leaving an uncertain future for herself and her five-year-old daughter.

So when the retrial started ten months later in December 1987 much was at stake; not just a damaged reputation but upwards of £100,000 in legal costs. Amazingly there now occurred yet another legal cock-up. On the second day of the retrial the case suddenly ground to a total halt when Miss Cornwell, who was understandably under considerable emotional strain, answered an indiscreet question from her counsel, Andrew Bateson QC, a little too directly. Asked whether she owned the garden flat where she lived, she replied: 'No, I have had to sell it to cover the costs of this litigation.' Mr Justice Mars-Jones, declaring this answer to be grossly prejudicial, said the case could not continue before the jury. This meant that Miss Cornwall was a further £6,000 in the red, having to pay the costs of the abortive two-day action.

It also meant going back to the beginning again with a third trial before a new jury. The questions were similar to those asked at the first trial two years earlier but the atmosphere in court, with such huge costs at stake, was bitter and the cross-examination far tougher. At one point Miss Cornwell was being questioned by counsel for the *Sunday People*, Mr Gareth Williams, who suggested that the comment in the review that 'she has the sort of stage presence that jams lavatories' referred to the well-known phenomenon in rock concerts that when a supporting band was playing many of the audience took the opportunity to go to the lavatory.

Miss Cornwell disagreed bitterly, tears coming to her eyes: 'Having been referred to as something that lives down a sewer, the only things that I know that live down sewers are filth and vermin. Having been referred to as filth and vermin, it seems to make sense to me that then to refer to jamming lavatories is again a reference — yes, people going to the lavatories and what they do when get to the lavatory . . .'

Nina Myskow was also given a tough going over by the plaintiff's counsel, Andrew Bateson QC, who wanted to know why she was obsessed in her television criticism with the male anatomy. She explained: 'There are very few variations on the word "wally". You can have "wally", you can have "welly" and you can have "willy". And obviously in journalistic terms, to vary it, you use what you can when you can. When you are faced with a situation like that, it is very obvious — and I apologise for that — but I would do it. And if you think it is vulgar, then indeed it is vulgar. But it is a bit of fun . . .'

After a week's such 'toing and froing' it was only fitting that Mr Justice Mars-Jones' summing up was interrupted by a pigeon which had decided to roost above his head. When the judge refused to continue until it had been removed, the full majesty of the law was brought into play in an attempt to catch the bird. To no avail. For the remainder of the case it continued to swoop over the heads of judge and jury. It was, commented Richard Ingrams, one of many interested spectators in Court 13, an appropriate finale to one of the most bizarre cases in legal history.

The judge in this third trial once again found for Miss Cornwall awarding her £11,500 in damages. But at the end of the day she was more than £70,000 down because the costs of the first trial were split and she had to pay all the costs of the appeal and the abortive two day retrial, as well as a proportion of the *Sunday People*'s costs.

Miss Cornwell's solicitor, Mr Oscar Beuselinck is understandably bitter on her behalf, pointing out that it was absurd that she should have to pay the costs of an appeal caused by judicial error. 'Surely,' he said, 'there should be a fund, possibly the legal aid fund, for meeting costs of this nature.' Mr Beuselinck said it was stupid for Appeal Court judges to be asked to deal with libel cases in which frequently they had no practical experience. One of the appellant judges in the case, he explained, had admitted he knew nothing about libel. 'Indeed, he asked what is libel, and it had to be explained to him by Leading Counsel, at Miss Cornwell's expense.'

Finally Mr Beuselinck pointed out that procedures in libel cases, particularly in relation to what is admissible or not, need to be streamlined. In Miss Cornwell's retrial the judge dismissed the first jury because of her inadvertent remark that she had had to sell her house. Yet the week before in the High Court the boxing promoter Mickey Duff was cross-examined with no interference from the judge as to his finances. 'Admissibility of evidence plainly varies from judge to judge and it is most unfortunate that leading QCs, appearing as experts, find the law so obscure that they have to argue its meaning and admissibility, sometimes for hours, and on occasion to the Court of Appeal.'

Despite everything Miss Cornwell is not sorry that she went ahead and sued. But she is angry about the way she has been treated by the courts. 'If we live in a society that tolerates this sort of Press,' she says, 'then there must be ways of putting these evils wrong without bankrupting the individuals concerned.'

THE FARMER'S SON

For a politician the High Court is a particularly dangerous place. Michael Meacher found that out the hard way in his action against *The Observer*. By the time it reached Court 14 of the Royal Courts of Justice in the Strand I had rejoined the paper and thus was a committed spectator. But as the trial ground away day after day I could not help but feel sorry for Labour's front bench spokesman on employment. Why on earth had he put his political and personal reputation at stake for a throwaway gibe about his social origins?

The class war libel began with a lunch in the Autumn of 1983 at the Gay Hussar, the well-known Hungarian restaurant in Soho much frequented by Labour politicians and their acolytes. The host was Anthony Howard, then Deputy Editor of *The Observer*. His guest was Michael Meacher, at the time strongly challenging Roy Hattersley for the Deputy Leadership of the Labour Party. Howard, whose relations with Hattersley have for years been extremely close, questioned the challenger about his background over mounds of roast goose and sauerkraut. The result was an item in *The Observer*'s Pendennis gossip column which appeared on the day of the leadership election, October 2nd: 'I do hope that Michael Meacher and his supporters are not going to start any more "working class stock" nonsense as a last ditch attempt to win support. It's nonsense. Mr Meacher's father was not a "farmworker" or agricultural labourer, as is often claimed. It is true that he worked on a farm — but he trained as an accountant and went to work on a farm owned by his brother. Which is not quite the same thing.'

This story passed without trouble at the time. But a year later Alan Watkins, *The Observer*'s political columnist, returned to it when he devoted his weekly column to an attack on Labour's front bench spokesman on health. The catalyst was a circular from Michael Meacher asking all Labour chairmen of health authorities to report to him on the political affiliations of their colleagues. Not surprisingly this piece of what the judge was later to call 'Big Brother' politics had attracted a considerable amount of unfavourable comment which had caught Watkins' eye. In the course of an amiable perambulation around the 'Stalinist' proclivities of the Labour Party, he had this to say about Meacher's social antecedents: 'Mr Meacher likes to claim he is the son of an agricultural labourer, though I understand that his father was an accountant who retired to work on the family farm because the life suited him better.' The column went on to be mildly dismissive about the quarrel Meacher's health circular had provoked with the chairman of Islington's health authority chairman, recalling Dr Johnson's immortal words: 'Sir, there is no settling the point of precedency between a louse and a flea.'

Mild stuff one might think and at the time the Watkins attack appeared to have caused little offence. Three months later, however, *The Observer* received a letter from Seifert Sedley Williams, a firm of London solicitors specialising in left wing causes, alleging that Meacher had been grievously defamed.

As Anthony Howard, the paper's Deputy Editor, was four years later to tell the High Court, he was 'totally bewildered' by this threatening letter. That very week *The Observer* had received an article which Meacher had submitted for publication, hardly the action of a man who felt he had been libelled.

A further lunch at the Gay Hussar now took place which produced a peace formula. The basis was a correction to be 'woven' into the Watkins column. This was duly printed though at Watkins' insistence it was tacked on to the end of the article: 'In my column on 18 November last I suggested that Mr Michael Meacher MP liked to claim that he was "the son of an agricultural labourer". I am now satisfied that Mr Meacher has never made any such claim — and I am happy to set the record straight.'

Unfortunately Meacher was not satisfied with this correction which he felt was not in the form to which he had agreed. What some might have thought was a passing slight, he had taken very seriously. Actively encouraged by his solicitor Sarah Burton of Seifert Sedley, he now decided he wanted a fuller apology in addition to damages, a demand which *The Observer* was not prepared to meet. The libel action therefore dragged on through 1985. As the costs began to mount, however, Meacher became increasingly anxious that he was plunging into an expensive morass. He wrote to his solicitors towards the end of 1985 saying that he wanted to get out on reasonable terms and was prepared to settle for nominal damages of £250–£500 and his costs. The question of an apology was not mentioned.

At the beginning of 1986 The Observer paid £255 into court, which would have allowed the plaintiff to get out on the terms he had specified. But, according to Meacher, Seifert Sedley failed to tell him of this crucial step. Two months after *The Observer*'s payment into court, an offer which had to be taken up within 21 days otherwise it lapsed, Meacher wrote again to his solicitors saying that he wanted to settle the action if at all possible. Earlier there was another apparent lapse in communication — this time by *The Observer*'s solicitors, Herbert Smith. When Seifert Sedley wrote indicating that Meacher was anxious to settle on modest terms without specifying that he was demanding an apology, this letter was not passed on to *The Observer*. The net result was that each side thought the other obdurate and positions became more and more entrenched.

Two years later, with the trial finally approaching, Michael Meacher had his first meeting with his counsel Gordon Bishop. With the costs on both sides already well over five figures, Meacher was told that if the jury found against him he might be £100,000 poorer. But he was reassured by his counsel that he had a very good — at least 75 per cent — chance of winning and that if he did, damages could be as high as £50,000. As they left the chambers, Meacher's solicitor Sarah Burton turned to him encouragingly: 'That's the most optimistic I have ever heard him — you can't walk away from it now Michael.'

Meacher says he was always led to believe that *The Observer* would cave in. Even the night before the case was due to be heard Sarah Burton was telling him, 'I have a very strong feeling this will be settled in the morning.' What Meacher and his solicitor did not appreciate was that by then iron had entered into *The Observer*'s soul. Having been forced to do a great deal of research the paper's legal advisers were convinced that it could beat off any action. This view was confirmed by *The Observer*'s counsel Richard Hartley QC, who advised the paper that it had a very good chance of justifying what it had written.

The scene was thus set for a head-on confrontation when the trial of Meacher versus Trelford and others opened in the High Court on May 16th, 1988. As an exercise in the English passion for the minutiae of class, it had its fascination but it should have been obvious to the plaintiff's legal advisers, if not to Meacher, that as the basis of a full scale libel trial, there was a grave danger it would be treated as a bit of a joke. For Meacher, who was about to remarry, the case turned into an extended nightmare. At one point he thought he might have to defer his honeymoon because the trial lasted three times as long as his lawyers had estimated.

The case opened promisingly for the plaintiff. In his dark suit, his greying hair swept back, Meacher seemed, as one reporter noted, like an aggrieved schoolmaster who had discovered his favourite pupil writing something rude about Sir in his exercise book. According to his counsel Gordon Bishop *The Observer* had portrayed his client's conduct as 'shabby, mean, unpleasant, and despicable'. Meacher in his evidence said he had been 'stunned' by the claim in the Watkins column that he had lied about his father's origins. He was particularly saddened that it had appeared in *The Observer* which he believed was a good paper. During a three-day cross-examination, he insisted that he had never claimed his father had been a farm labourer, he had merely 'acquiesced' in such a description by profile writers. It wasn't strictly accurate but approximately true and 'I saw no reason to take exception to it.'

Mr Hartley pressed him: 'Didn't it help your chances when you were trying to become Deputy Leader of the Labour Party to have humble origins?' 'No,' replied Meacher. 'I don't think you get anywhere in the Labour Party because your father is a horny handed son of toil.'

Meacher's insistence that his background had nevertheless been relatively humble with 'an outside lav and a bath in the kitchen' received a considerable boost from a surprise witness. On the sixth day of the trial, a retired Church of England canon turned up in court. Mr Wilfred Badger Wilkinson, white-haired, collar fraying, who appeared to have come straight out of Central Casting, said he was only in court by chance because he had read reports that the one-time boy server in his church had been accused of exaggerating the poverty of his childhood.

'I said to my wife that is not true,' declared the former canon in ringing tones. 'They had a real struggle that family.' For good measure, the canon spoke of his admiration of his former pupil: 'I have hardly ever thought so highly of a boy as I thought of Michael as I watched him grow up. He was a tremendous boy. He was so real, he was so sincere and honest and he had such guts. He really was first class. That is why I am here today.'

After the canon's evidence, the mood in *The Observer* camp grew distinctly sombre. But its spirits were lifted by a characteristically rumbustious performance from Alan Watkins, described by one commentator as 'a portly Welsh gentleman with a sword-sharp wit'. Watkins, one of the last of the old Fleet Street hands, a denizen of the Garrick Club and a lover of fine claret, insisted that his article had not been designed to wound. Its mood was one of 'reminiscence, good humour, even jocularity'.

Meacher's counsel, Gordon Bishop, found the columnist difficult to handle under cross-examination. When he sought to analyse the column's literary style, Watkins responded sharply: 'No doubt if I had you by my side when I was writing my articles they would be much better.' Counsel reminded him severely this was a serious matter. 'I doubt that,' Watkins replied. 'I think you are here because you are into something you wish you had got out of.' Later when Meacher's counsel incautiously suggested to Watkins that 'you then had the article typed up', he was again reproved for his poor grammar: 'Typed *up*, Mr Bishop? Typed . . . typed!' There was another passage at arms when Gordon Bishop asked Watkins if he read his local Islington paper. 'I don't read it,' said Watkins. 'You deliberately don't read it,' said Mr Bishop incredulity straining from every pore. 'I don't read it. I don't know how you deliberately don't read something,' riposted Watkins.

Gordon Bishop should have known that he had met his literary match. Earlier he had the temerity to question Watkins about the origins of the Samuel Johnson quote: 'Sir, there is no settling the precendency between a louse and a flea.' In return he received a lecture on the louse Samuel Derrick, an Irishman, and the flea Christopher Smart, who was often incarcerated in a lunatic asylum but 'a poet for all that'. When Watkins offered to go on at even greater length his offer was declined.

Instead Gordon Bishop sought to pin him down on the matter in hand. 'Would you agree that a louse means a mean, unpleasant person?' Mr Watkins neatly avoided the question: 'A louse is a louse. It's an insect.' 'It's used about people?' asked Mr Bishop hopefully. 'I would never use it,' said Watkins, adding unhelpfully, 'People don't say "he is a flea".' Mr Bishop felt on safe ground: 'A louse is used as a hostile term. A flea isn't.' Watkins sensing problems, decided to end the argument: 'I don't think this gets us very far,' he said, usurping the role of the judge. It was a flamboyant but very effective performance.

The Secretary of State for Health Kenneth Clarke was now wheeled on to give evidence for *The Observer*. He told the court that he was responsible for the appointment of health authority chairmen in 1984 when Michael Meacher sent each one a questionnaire asking for the political views of their colleagues. He agreed helpfully that *The Observer* had correctly quoted him as calling the questionnaire 'a shabby political episode'.

A series of journalists then occupied the witness box giving evidence for *The Observer*. Anthony Howard, the paper's Deputy Editor, put the blame squarely on Meacher's solicitor, Sarah Burton, for the way this 'miserable affair' had escalated. She was, he said pointedly, 'the architect of this action'. A *Sunday Mirror* journalist John Knight recalled an interview he had had with Meacher in August 1983. He said when he asked Meacher about his background, he had answered simply, 'My father was a farm worker, we had an outside loo, bath in the kitchen, that sort of thing.' Robert Taylor, former

Labour correspondent of *The Observer*, remembered a similar interview he had had with Meacher. He said he felt that the response Mr Meacher had given to his question about his origins struck him now, in retrospect, as being less than the truth.

At this stage of the trial, I felt that the jury could go either way. But there now occurred an extraordinary event which was almost certainly very damaging to Meacher's cause. During his evidence in chief the previous week while Meacher was being questioned about his antecedents his counsel had incautiously referred to his proof of evidence. This is normally a private document in which witnesses set out the evidence that they will give when called. But the reference to it in open court now made it disclosable, a point that was seized on by *The Observer*'s counsel Richard Hartley ably backed by his junior Stephen Nathan.

The Meacher camp resisted as hard as they could but the judge ruled against them. As a result Meacher was summoned back to the witness box for a lengthy grilling about the document whose contents were made available to *The Observer*. He was immediately on the defensive denying that its contents were 'devastating' to his case because it contained the sentence: 'I have always described my father as a farmworker.' Mr Meacher said the only reason he was reluctant for the statement to come into court was 'because you had me in this witness box for three and a half days.' The plaintiff told his chief tormentor, Richard Hartley: 'I thought if this came before the court it could easily take another day or more. I was absolutely desperate that my marriage and honeymoon were not wrecked by the libel trial hanging over it.'

Wrecked they almost certainly were. The court was in recess for the nuptials but when Michael Meacher returned from his brief honeymoon his case was rapidly concluded with a summing up by Mr Justice Hazan which left no doubt as to what he thought about the action. In two simple words — not much. He described Meacher's action in sending out questionnaires to regional health authority chairmen asking them to report on the political views of their colleagues as 'decidedly un-English'. This action, the judge said, had been bound 'to create something of a furore and to arouse a considerable amount of criticism'.

Mr Justice Hazan said the jury might think that Alan Watkins had 'laid about Mr Meacher with considerable vigour'. But Britain, he noted, was a country with a tradition of trenchant criticism of politicians and political decisions, and a free press was the bulwark of democracy. To ram home the point, he reminded the jury of President Truman's famous caution: 'If you can't stand the heat, keep out of the kitchen.' In deciding on the balance of probabilities whether the article was defamatory the jury should take into account what they might think was 'a deafening silence' that followed publication of the article.

After this summing up, there was little doubt about the result. But there was one last poignant twist. As the Meacher legal team walked back into court through the swing doors of Court 14 to hear the jury's verdict, Gordon Bishop turned to Sarah Burton and asked: 'What was the payment in?' It was only then, according to Michael Meacher, that he learnt *The Observer* had paid money into court and, as was later explained to him, that he could have had a settlement on the terms he wanted. After the jury had found for *The Observer*. Anthony Howard wrote in the paper: 'I remain totally convinced that if the matter could only have been left to Mr Meacher and myself to resolve, this whole high farce High Court action would never have taken place.'

That is certainly a view shared by Meacher. At the time of writing he is suing Seifert Sedley for failing in their duty to him. Seifert Sedley, for their part, deny that they failed to tell their client of the payment in and say that he was in full agreement that the action should continue. As for *The Observer* its new solicitors Turner Kenneth Brown are negotiating with its previous solicitors, Herbert Smith over alleged failures in communication which the paper believes unnecessarily prolonged the action. *The Observer* was able to recoup its agreed costs from Meacher amounting to £80,000 but that still left it about £40,000 out of pocket in irrecoverable costs. For Michael Meacher the case has been both a political and a financial disaster. He says now that if anyone had told him at the outset that the case would get to court, he would have laughed in disbelief.

10

Private Eye

That sort of vicious slander
Arouses all my dander —
But a little bit of gossip
does me good.

Ogden Nash

One of the most astonishing publishing successes of the post-war years has been that of *Private Eye*. Starting a quarter of a century ago as little more than a schoolboy rag which had to be given away, it now sells as many as 250,000 copies every fortnight with an annual turnover of £3 million, yielding in good years profits high enough to maintain a company villa in the Dordogne and to pay its directors £40,000 a year.

Its mixture of jokes, satire, malicious gossip and investigative journalism, particularly of complicated City fraud, appears to have a growing appeal. Success, however, has brought its problems. *Private Eye* is now known to be worth suing and there is no shortage of litigants.

In its halcyon years in the early 1960s, the magazine enjoyed a remarkable immunity from libel actions given its self-confessed reputation as a satirical sheet which was none too careful about checking its facts. Apart from an early brush with Randolph Churchill whom it accused of writing a tendentious biography of his father, and a £5,000 award to Lord Russell of Liverpool for dubbing him 'Lord Liver of Cesspool', the magazine was not taken seriously enough to be a target for many writs. But there was more to its remarkable immunity than that.

Private Eye's success in dodging the attentions of the libel lawyers was in large part due to its ability to create around itself a ring of defences which only a very rich, determined, and even reckless plaintiff was likely to breach. Those few that did found the path to justice less than smooth. Patrick Marnham, who worked for *Private Eye* in the 1960s, told how the trick was worked in his revealing book *The Private Eye Story* (André Deutsch 1982).

The prerequisite was to have no journalistic pride. The game was to print unsubstantiated gossip and, if it turned out to be false and provoked threats of a writ, then retract it with the minimum of apology and the maximum of ridicule. This policy of 'apologise and don't give a damn' is not open to ordinary publications but for *Private Eye* it was crucial to its survival. Many of those who were attacked in its pages, even some of those who were objects of a persistent vendetta, settled for an apology and minuscule damages when they could, if they had persisted, probably have bankrupted Lord Gnome's organ.

The second crucial defence was to sow the impression that those who sued *Private Eye* were ridiculous, pompous humourless fools, who were enemies of the Press. The veteran ex-Editor of *Picture Post* who later became Professor of Journalism at Cardiff University, Tom Hopkinson, told how the trick worked. *Private Eye* he noted, had managed to convey the impression that to sue was 'degrading and absurd, though it is not either absurd or degrading but on the contrary courageous and idealistic for *Private Eye* to be sued'. As libel actions are essentially about restoring reputation, what point is there in suing if the only result is further ridicule?

One particularly ingenious weapon in this defence was The Curse of Gnome, invented by Auberon Waugh. Any disaster happening to anyone who had been rash enough to take legal action against *Private Eye* was charted with merciless glee in successive issues. Just how successful these simple anti-litigant devices proved is shown by the mixed fortunes of my predecessor as Political Correspondent of *The Observer*, Nora Beloff, when she decided to sue the *Eye*.

On February 17, 1971, Miss Beloff wrote a note to *The Observer*'s Editor David Astor proposing that she should write a profile of Reginald Maudling as a potential Tory leader. It was a sensitive moment. Maudling, then Home Secretary, was under attack by *Private Eye* for his business relationship with a convicted swindler, Jerome Hoffman, President of the grandly titled Real Estate Fund of America.

Nora Beloff suggested, on the basis of a conversation with the Leader of the Commons, William Whitelaw, that she should set Maudling's political prospects in their proper context. Not surprisingly the Maudling profile, when it appeared, was not regarded with universal delight, particularly by the business section of the paper which was planning to conduct an inquiry into Maudling's business affairs. Nor was *Private Eye* pleased by Miss Beloff's description of it as that 'fortnightly political comic', a mixture of 'genuine revelations, half-truths, and pure fabrication strung together by damaging insinuations'.

Newspaper offices are hives of intrigue so the next stage was predictable. Someone on *The Observer* leaked the Beloff memorandum to the *Eye* which printed it with glee to the accompaniment of a few additional digs of its own about the venality of political lobby correspondents. In the same issue Auberon Waugh wrote a satirical piece in his political column called HP Sauce about 'the delicious 78-years-old Nora Ballsoff' adding, 'Miss Bailiff, sister of the later Sir Alec Douglas Home, was frequently to be seen in bed with Mr Harold Wilson and senior members of the previous administration, though it is thought nothing improper happened.'

This edition of *Private Eye* resulted in two writs, one for breach of copyright in relation to the leaked inter-office memorandum and one for libel in respect of the HP Sauce satire. In both actions, Miss Beloff was supported by *The Observer*, who paid her costs estimated at more than £10,000. Whether she was wise to sue, however, is doubtful. The problem with the copyright case was that newspapers live by disclosure. It smacked therefore of hypocrisy for a journalist to complain when the tables were reversed. The problem with the libel action was similar. Was it really worth turning the full guns of the High Court against a piece of satirical abuse which no one in their right minds could take seriously?

In the event, Nora Beloff lost the copyright case on a technicality, the judge holding that the copyright of her memorandum belonged to *The Observer*. On the libel she fared better, being awarded £3,000 in damages and £2,000 in costs.

The result, though, was a pyrrhic victory for *The Observer*'s Political Correspondent. The *Financial Times*, *The Times* and the *Sunday Times* all commented unfavourably. Bernard Levin wrote in *The Times* criticising the libel action: 'It has made even the wildest fantasies and jokes dangerous, if they are made about somebody with a seemingly undeveloped sense of humour.' He also attacked the copyright action on the grounds that it was a danger to the freedom of the Press. And he concluded: 'Neither action should have been brought. Both should have failed.'

From Nora Beloff's point of view, worse was to follow. *Private Eye* decided to exact cruel revenge. This consisted of setting up a fund to pay its libel costs — 'the Ballsoff fund' — which was publicised month after month alongside a grim photograph of the victim. It raised more than £1,200 from contributors ranging from Tom Stoppard to the Marchioness of Salisbury. It was, arguably, unnecessary. By early 1972 the magazine's circulation had doubled to nearly 100,000 and its staff were beginning to dream of such pleasures as foreign villas, large lunches and proper salaries.

Financial success brought its problems. A number of *Eye*

victims began to bite back and one, Sir James Goldsmith, proved so venomous that the magazine was, in the words of its Editor, Richard Ingrams, 'very nearly finished off'. In its 1975 Christmas edition *Private Eye* published an article on the sensational disappearance of Lord Lucan following the murder of the family's nanny under the title: 'All's Well That Ends Elwes'.

The article had been sparked off by a second death in the Lucan gambling set — the suicide of Dominic Elwes, a portrait painter and playboy member of the *galère* which played for high stakes at the Clermont Club. At Elwes' memorial service at the Jesuit Church of the Immaculate Conception in Farm Street, Mayfair, a strange incident took place when John Aspinall, the professional gambler and a key member of the Clermont set, was punched by Elwes' cousin, Tremayne Rodd.

These funereal fisticuffs caught the attention of Ingrams and he put the *Eye*'s sleuths to work, notably Nigel Dempster, the *Daily Mail*'s gossip columnist. The tale they came up with was a sad one. Elwes had taken an overdose of barbiturates after he was ostracised by his gambling friends to whom he directed a bitter suicide note: 'I curse Mark [Birley, owner of Annabel's night-club] and Jimmy [Goldsmith] from beyond the grave. I hope they are happy now.'

Elwes had fallen foul of Goldsmith and Birley after helping the *Sunday Times* with a magazine article which drew a less than flattering portrait of Lucan and his gambling friends. The feature had been illustrated by a specially commissioned Elwes painting of the Clermont Set in which Jimmy Goldsmith was shown imperiously summoning a waiter. But the article's real sting was the implication that Lucan's friends knew more than they were willing to reveal about his disappearance.

To *Private Eye* this scandalous pot-pourri proved irresistible. Pinning the blame on Goldsmith for Elwes' suicide, it also sought to establish that he was the key conspirator in Lucan's disappearance. In particular it alleged he had been at a lunch held in Eaton Square the day after the murder, at which the matter was discussed. Unfortunately for the *Eye*'s conspiracy theory, Goldsmith was not even present.

But *Private Eye* is nothing if not persistent. Thinking it had a ripe new target in its sights, it determined to pursue Goldsmith by suggesting that he was connected with T. Dan Smith, the North East tycoon then in gaol for corruption. The only link for this was that the two men had once used the same solicitor, Eric Levine. For Jimmy Goldsmith, who had been asked by the Bank of England to try and save the tottering Slater Walker financial empire, this attack was the final straw. In his biography written by Geoffrey Wansell, Goldsmith claims he was a target of a widespread conspiracy aimed at subverting the City. 'If they could crack me, the whole thing went down.'

What happens when you cross a bitterly angry, obsessive multi-millionaire was now to be revealed. An avalanche of 90 separate writs for libel descended on *Private Eye* and its wholesale and retail distributors. The next 18 months witnessed one of the most spectacular and expensive battles in British legal history, involving 10 court hearings and the expenditure of at least £500,000. Goldsmith was on solid ground in that he had clearly been defamed. If he had proceeded in the normal way he could confidently have expected to receive six figure damages.

Calculating, however, that *Private Eye* merely thrived on the publicity generated by libel actions, Goldsmith made the mistake of over-reacting, spraying writs in all directions and seeking to gaol the writers of the offending article by means of a criminal indictment. When Goldsmith was asked at the criminal libel proceedings about the large number of writs he had issued against *Private Eye* he replied that he had previously issued only one against a newspaper. 'You are making up for it now,' commented the *Eye*'s counsel, James Comyn QC. By reviving the archaic proceeding of a criminal prosecution for libel with its threat of imprisonment against Ingrams and his colleagues, Goldsmith appeared vindictive. And by proceeding against many of the *Eye*'s smaller distributors, he seemed to be an enemy of the freedom of the Press.

What Goldsmith did not appreciate was that libel actions are essentially a battle for public opinion. And the methods of a tycoon are not those best suited to win such a contest. At one point he employed 'a highly reputable' firm of private detectives to go through *Private Eye*'s dustbins each night. They took out the contents, photocopied them, and then replaced them — so that they should not be charged with theft. Lunches of *Eye* journalists were electronically bugged by placing a minute listening device on a coat-stand.

The end result of this legal battle was a messy but expensive draw. By the spring of 1977, Goldsmith had bigger fish to fry. He wanted to become the proprietor of a Fleet Street paper and it was clear that his continued vendetta against the *Eye* was a serious obstacle to this ambition. In May therefore he agreed to call off his criminal libel action on condition that *Private Eye* published a full page apology in the *Evening Standard* and agreed to contribute £30,000 towards his legal costs to be paid in instalments over the next ten years. It was a generous gesture. The case is estimated to have cost Goldsmith at least £250,000. But the money was the least of it.

When you are a billionaire, the odd quarter of a million pounds makes little difference. Indeed Goldsmith was later to argue that the whole affair, by depressing Cavenham's share price at the time he was buying back his master British public company, made him even richer. But money apart, the case was a disaster for him.

The widespread hostility it aroused destroyed any hopes he might have had of either a political career or of becoming a British newspaper baron. First *The Observer* and then Express Newspapers, both up for sale, escaped his grasp because of personal opposition to him. Not just journalists but the British establishment appeared to have turned against him. It was a repeat of the experience suffered by his father Frank Goldsmith, 'Monsieur le Major' in the 1914–18 war, and like him, Jimmy Goldsmith decided to turn his back on Britain.

For *Private Eye* too, the case had not been without cost. It estimated its legal expenses at £85,000, a figure challenged by Goldsmith as a serious under-estimate. But again money was perhaps not the most serious part. The wearying months of non-stop litigation had taken their toll, particularly on Richard Ingrams. As Patrick Marnham wrote: 'The drastic side of his character became more evident.' *Private Eye* from now on was more of a high risk business than an undergraduate's pleasure.

'This dreadful feud', as Lord Justice Templeman was to describe Goldsmith versus *Private Eye*, consumed others. A leading city solicitor, Leslie Paisner, was broken by his involvement and shortly afterwards died. The head of public relations company John Addey was virtually destroyed, exposed as a homosexual and labelled in the Court of Appeal as a liar who 'was not to be believed in any particular'. Finally one of Britain's leading investigative journalists, Michael Gillard, was publicly branded a blackmailer. All this happened as a complicated by-play to the main Goldsmith–*Private Eye* fight.

In its attempt to mount a defence against the criminal libel action, the *Eye* had enlisted the help of Gillard, who wrote City stories for it under the pseudonym of 'Slicker'. A freelance journalist, with a formidable reputation for persistence, his work for Granada's World in Action programme, *The Observer* and *Private Eye* was highly regarded. In the course of his inquiries on behalf of *Private Eye*, Michael Gillard, who has the saturnine looks of many of the villains he pursues so effectively, telephoned John Addey, the head of a firm of financial PR consultants, and asked him for information on Goldsmith's solicitor, Eric Levine. Addey, who cultivated financial journalists, said he would ring 'his old mate' Leslie

Paisner, the senior partner of an old established city legal firm.

A week later Addey, in a state of some excitement, attended one of the *Private Eye* lunches, at which the guests are expected to 'sing for their supper'. According to the several of those present, he said he had some damaging information about Levine and was only too happy to pass it on to help the *Eye* in its hour of need. That night Addey repeated those allegations to Gillard over a friendly dinner whereupon another of the *Eye*'s writers, Patrick Marnham, was dispatched to see Leslie Paisner, who, remarkably for a respected city solicitor, said he was only too willing to help. Paisner then recited a list of charges of financial impropriety against Levine and said he had been forced to dismiss him from his firm.

Two days after the *Private Eye* lunch Addey, whose role in this affair does not bear close examination, told Sandy Gilmour, a stockbroker close to Goldsmith, that the *Eye* was investigating Eric Levine and had dug up considerable dirt. Sir James then swung into action. He interviewed Addey and Paisner who repeated their charges against Levine. But within 72 hours both men, in an extraordinary and to this day unexplained volte-face, totally changed their stories and signed affidavits saying they had lied in order to ruin Levine.

These documents, which spelled their professional ruin, were couched in remarkable language. Leslie Paisner confessed that his allegations against Levin 'were lies and without any foundation whatsoever — they were part of a vicious vendetta perpetrated by me. I am deeply ashamed of my conduct.' Addey's affidavit contained a similar grovelling withdrawal but in addition it charged Gillard with having blackmailed him into making allegations against Levine, by threatening to expose him as a homosexual on the edge of bankruptcy.

What led to these ruinous affidavits is unclear. In all that followed no rational answer was ever produced for these two suicidal professional reversals by hard-boiled and experienced City operators. When John Addey was seen by Richard Ingrams later that week in his Albany chambers, he claimed that he had sworn his affidavit because he was terrified of being prosecuted for criminal libel. 'I never realised they were so powerful,' he said. But when Addey was called as a witness in the Goldsmith bid to secure an injunction against *Private Eye* he was nowhere to be found. He had gone to Italy leaving no forwarding address, provoking Mr Justice Donaldson to say that his absence was 'unfortunate'.

Paisner also did not turn up in court to be questioned on his affidavit. But his QC, John Wilmers and his doctor did. The court was told that their client was 'extremely confused and disorientated'. He was too ill to attend the court. He was suffering apparently from acute depression. He kept saying that 'he wanted to end it all'. Paisner never again practised as a lawyer; his health shattered, he died soon afterwards.

The last of the Goldsmith casualties was Michael Gillard. The claim that he was a blackmailer had been retracted by John Addey who had apologised and paid Gillard £5,000 damages in settlement of a libel action. But Sir James Goldsmith, who repeated the allegation against Gillard to four national newspapers editors, persisted in his charge of blackmail. This left Gillard with no honourable way out except to sue.

The case finally came to trial in June 1979. The five-day action was dominated by Goldsmith's towering personality in the witness box. Though he was able to produce no direct evidence of blackmail — Addey was not even called as a witness — Goldsmith succeeded in convincing the jury that he had been the victim of an orchestrated Fleet Street vendetta. His counsel, Lord Rawlinson QC, moreover drew attention to a series of coincidences which cast an unhappy light on the Gillard–Addey 'friendship'. The anonymous letter which had been sent to *Private Eye* detailing Addey's homosexual and financial affairs had been kept by Gillard in his desk for more than a year. During all that time he had not spoken to Addey but had only got in touch on the day *Private Eye* was sued for criminal libel.

When Gillard did finally hand over the document to Addey, it turned out to be only a photocopy, not the original which he said he had kept for only a brief time before destroying it. Sinister perhaps, but all this fell far short of proof of blackmail. Certainly Gillard would never have been convicted of the charge in a criminal court and it is arguable that he should not have lost his libel case without a chance to test the evidence of his only direct accuser, John Addey. But the Court of Appeal upheld the jury's finding and the only consolation that Gillard had was hearing himself described as a victim rather than a criminal.

Lord Justice Templeman said that the jury's verdict meant that Gillard had gone too far in persuading Addey to find evidence derogatory to Levine but it did not mean that he was in fact a blackmailer: 'It means Mr Gillard has fallen victim to this dreadful feud which has caused him as well as many others so much agony and expense — so far as I can see for no good purpose to anyone.'

After the Goldsmith affair, *Private Eye* was never quite the same again. In the mid 1960s libel actions were costing only £5,000 a year but a decade later they swallowed up twenty times that amount and the costs were rising fast. By 1982 the magazine's circulation was nearly 200,000 but libel damages dug so deep into the profits that the Dordogne property, the Villa Disraeli, had to be put up for sale. In that year Desmond Wilcox received £14,000 and costs estimated at £80,000 after *Private Eye* had claimed that he misused his position as a senior BBC executive to plagiarise a book based on a BBC2 series. By the early 1980s libel costs and damages accounted for more than a third of the magazine's turnover of £1.2 million. *Private Eye* appeared to be more than just worth suing — it was becoming something of a milch cow.

The trouble was that success had bred a new set of

commercial rules. Yet the magazine was being run as it always had been by its editor Richard Ingrams on hunch, smell and prejudice. Jane Ellison, a former *Eye* employee, described his method in an article in *The Independent*: 'Ingrams has always believed that he has an instinct for the truth of a story however defamatory and however insubstantial in terms of the facts. If it sounds right, he will print it . . . after a few moments of concentration accompanied by a paroxysm of facial contortion, he would utter the famous reply: "Put it in!" '

More times than not the Ingrams hunch was right. The *Eye* had some notable successes, particularly during Paul Foot's era in the early 1970s on John Poulson, Jeremy Thorpe, and Reginald Maudling. But balanced against this were many ill-judged vendettas and exposures of private lives which did nothing to advance the public interest. It also developed over the years some very rich and serious enemies who were no less ruthless than they were.

In 1982 Robert Maxwell, an old *Eye* target, reviewed Patrick Marnham's book *The Private Eye Story* in *The Listener*: '*Private Eye*'s speciality is fiction, disguised as anonymous special knowledge — and the seamier, the more saleable.' Maxwell added: 'Couple that speciality with a callous regard for the victim's feelings and with prejudices which find expression in queer-bashing, Jew-baiting, and besmirching those who give service to the public and you arrive at a policy of publication without respect to any consideration other than the victim's power to retaliate.'

Tough words from a tough enemy which should have made the *Eye* cautious about what it said about 'Cap'n Bob', as they liked to call him. But in its issue of 12th July, 1985, Richard Ingrams returned to the attack alleging that Maxwell was acting as paymaster for Neil Kinnock's foreign trips to East Africa, Moscow and Central America. The article ended with the words: 'How many more Kinnock freebies will Maxwell have to provide before he is recommended for a peerage?'

These 17 words were to prove expensive. The immediate response was two furious letters of denial, one from Neil Kinnock's Press Secretary, Miss Patricia Hewitt; the other from Robert Maxwell who threatened to sue unless *Private Eye* printed an immediate apology and paid £10,000 to the Mirror's Ethiopia Appeal Fund. Richard Ingrams printed both letters in the next edition but proceeded to rub salt into the wound by describing Maxwell's denial of his paymaster role as 'lame'.

It proved to be one of the most expensive actions that *Private Eye* had ever embarked on. The problem was that for many months the magazine took the view it could prove the truth of the charges it made. But when it came to court neither of the witnesses on which it relied for its story, one a source in the Labour Leader's office, the other in the *Daily Mirror*, was willing to give evidence. With that its defence of justification collapsed and all the jury had to do was to assess the scale of damages.

Five hours later the jury came back with its verdict, £5,000 in compensatory damages, £50,000 in exemplary damages which together with costs estimated at quarter of a million pounds, meant that *Private Eye* was nearly £300,000 out of pocket. After the case Robert Maxwell said he would devote the damages to AIDS research: 'The money from one infected organ will go to help cure another.' A year later *Private Eye* was stunned with an even bigger award when a jury gave the wife of the Yorkshire Ripper, Miss Sonia Sutcliffe a record £600,000 over a false allegation that she had sold her story to the *Daily Mail*.

The Maxwell and Sutcliffe cases, in the view of those close to Lord Gnome's organ, are likely to be among *Private Eye*'s last great battles in the courts. Writs, of course, it will continue to attract, and no doubt there will be a continuing stream of apologies and damages. But the retirement of Richard Ingrams after a quarter of a century as *Private Eye*'s editor in 1986 was a signal that the character of the magazine was changing.

The *Eye*'s founding editor, according to both friend and foe, is an eccentric puritan, part knight in white armour tilting at the famous and the corrupt, part a malicious but often very funny comic. The combination of the two, together with an aggressive delight in litigation, which Ingrams lists as one of his pastimes in *Who's Who*, was the essence of the old *Private Eye*. The new editor, Ian Hislop is a very different and more cautious character, who reportedly believes in checking his facts rather than trusting his sense of smell.

Patrick Marnham in his book boasts (if that is the right word) that *Private Eye* 'prints what other papers will not print'. That may have been true 20 years ago but it is not so now. During Jeffrey Archer's libel action against the *Daily Star* it emerged that the Asian solicitor Aziz Kurtha had first approached Paul Halloran of *Private Eye* with the story that Jeffrey Archer had had a liaison with a prostitute. But *Private Eye*, scenting danger preferred to let the *News of the World* take the lead in trying to confirm the allegation.

What has happened over the past 20 years is that national newspapers have become more like *Private Eye* and *Private Eye* has become more like them. Much of the material and most of the writers are now recycled between the two. Under Richard Ingrams it was always just possible that the *Eye* might decide to commit suicide and go down gloriously in a blaze of libel writs. But the magazine has become too prosperous to afford such a dangerous luxury. Its attacks are now pored over and toned down by libel lawyers in advance of publication just like any Fleet Street tabloid. Ironically *Private Eye*'s epitaph could turn out to be that it finally became part of the media establishment it once professed to despise.

11

Maggie's Militant Tendency

The first thing we do, let's kill the lawyers.

Shakespeare, Henry VI Part II

Libel actions that go wrong can be calamitous not just for individuals but also for institutions. When the BBC's flagship current affairs programme, Panorama, broadcast an investigation into the racist, right wing fringe of the Conservative Party on January 30th, 1984, few would have guessed that the ensuing row would lead to the sacking of the BBC's Director General Alasdair Milne, a revolution in the Corporation's coverage of news and current affairs and an exodus of some its most talented journalists.

The genesis of the Panorma programme, entitled 'Maggie's Militant Tendency', was a political scandal during the 1983 election. The Conservative candidate for Stockton South, Tom Finnegan, who had taken pains to hide his political past, was exposed as a former member of the National Front. This caused considerable embarrassment which I witnessed during an election rally in Stockton when Sir Keith Joseph, the Secretary of State for Education, was obliged to share a platform with Finnegan. Sir Keith, who looked unhappy, ostentatiously refused to shake hands with the candidate — a Tory own goal which resulted in the loss of what should have been a safe Conservative seat.

As a result of this shaming episode the Conservative Party changed its rules to ensure that prospective Parliamentary and local candidates had to disclose their past political associations.

But in the autumn there was a further embarrassment for the Tories. During the party conference, a draft report of a Young Conservative committee of inquiry into extremist infiltration of the party was leaked to the Press.

The product of 18 months' work, the YC report detailed links between the far right of the party and a number of Conservative MPs. The document, though subsequently much criticised, was a serious piece of research. Drawn up by a group which included six Parliamentary candidates, three of them lawyers, it drew on a large number of published and unpublished resources to present a comprehensive picture of the far right's infiltration of the party. But not content with that, it sought also to prove that a group of right wing Tory MPs were allowing themselves to be used as a bridge to disreputable elements of the racist right.

Much of the raw material on which these allegations were based came from *Searchlight*, an anti-fascist magazine edited by Gerry Gable, an expert researcher on political extremism, who worked for a large number of BBC and ITV programmes. The result was instantaneous. Two of the MPs named in the YC report, Neil Hamilton and Gerald Howarth, threatened to sue, forcing the chairman of the YC committee which had produced the report to make a hurried and abject apology to avoid a writ.

These events were noted with interest by a Panorama producer James Hogan and the programme's award-winning political reporter Michael Cockerell. Shortly after the Tory conference they began to look further into the charges with the help of the YC's Chairman Philip Pedley. Early in December Gerry Gable was hired by the programme as a consultant because of his extensive knowledge of extremist groups. The documents in *Searchlight*'s possession covering nearly all the past and present literature of British right wing groups were also regarded by Panorama as invaluable. By the beginning of 1984 the film, which had been carefully researched, was ready for viewing.

The BBC from the start recognised that the film was both controversial and potentially libellous. Cockerell had a considerable reputation as a very sharp political commentator and James Hogan, the producer, was an experienced operator; both realised the programme was touching on some very sensitive areas. It was therefore seen in advance of transmission on January 28th by the Editor of Panorama Peter Ibbotson, the Head of Current Affairs Christopher Capron, the Political Aide to the Director General Margaret Douglas, and the BBC's solicitor Glenn del Medico. This covey of Corporation top brass approved it, with only minor alterations, for showing on January 30th which coincided with the Young Conservative's final report being handed to the Party Chairman Mr John Selwyn Gummer.

The bulk of the Panorama film, like the YC report, centred on three far right groups, Tory Action, Wise, and the Focus Policy Group, which were avowedly anti-semitic and racist. One Tory Action bulletin, or 'Round Robin', dated Autumn 1982, carried this commentary from its northern correspondent about a disappointing Parliamentary by-election result in Moss Side: 'The result was pretty dismal but, there again, with the extraordinary concentration of coons, and the proletariat, life's failures and human seconds, little else could be expected. I went and had a look at some of the coon-infested areas and it was quite appalling. I felt like taking over a loud speaker van and simply going round saying: "Get out of my country." '

Another bulletin from Tory Action attacked the Queen for consorting with foreigners: 'On every occasion the monarch has to be photographed beaming at piccaninny while Prince Philip and Prince Charles caper about in yarmulkes' (the skull caps worn by religious Jews). The author of these words and the man running Tory Action, Panorama disclosed, was a former Conservative parliamentary candidate and Deputy Director of MI6, George Kennedy Young. Particular targets of his pen were Jewish members of the Cabinet like Leon

Brittan and Nigel Lawson. 'It would be too much to expect,' he wrote in one Tory Action bulletin, 'a repeal of the Race Relations Act or the disbandment of the Commission of Racial Equality from a government whose leading members include Lithuanian Leon and Latvian Lawson.'

If Panorama had been content merely to lift these Conservative stones and expose a few ugly if unrepresentative racist slugs beneath, the programme would have performed a very useful public service. The last ten minutes of the programme, however, had the much more ambitious purpose of seeking to link a number of serving Tory MPs to Tory Action. It did so on the grounds that they had either hosted social receptions for it at the House of Commons, were on its 'correspondents' list, or had spoken at its meetings. The programme ended with Professor Paul Wilkinson, a respected Conservative academic expert on extremism, calling for the expulsion from the party of four of the MP's: Neil Hamilton, Gerald Howarth, Harvey Proctor and Warren Hawksley.

If the BBC was not prepared for what followed, it should have been. An avalanche of libel writs descended from the MPs named in the programme. This onslaught was followed up by the Conservative Party Chairman John Selwyn Gummer, who attacked Panorama publicly and warned that 'very serious action' would have to be taken. Two days later the Party Chairman and the Government Chief Whip John Wakeham pressed their complaints at a meeting with the BBC's Director General, submitting a list of 38 specific 'errors'. Neil Hamilton also detailed his complaints. The programme had, he said, made him out to be a member of Tory Action on the basis of no better evidence than that he was on its mailing list, had been present at a rally of the Italian fascist party MSI in the early 1970s and had given a mock Heil Hitler salute while on an official Parliamentary visit to Berlin.

The BBC's reaction to these attacks was robust. Three weeks after its transmission, the Governors unanimously declared their support for the programme with one of its members saying afterwards, 'The BBC cannot become a government mouthpiece. It's the job of Panorama to disturb governments of any colour.' After an internal inquiry, the Director General Alasdair Milne said that the programme was 'very strongly founded'. Within days of this interview, Milne went further, telling the BBC's house paper *Ariel* that Panorama's research was 'rock solid'. A month later the Chairman of the BBC's Governors, Stuart Young asserted, 'The Corporation has nothing to apologise for.'

The BBC's confidence was bolstered by the fact that the names of both Hamilton and Howarth were listed by Tory Action among its 70 'correspondents'. The group claimed not to have members as such but merely contributors and sympathisers even though some of them refused to acknowledge any such link. Tory Action also had a much wider mailing list for its literature but the Panorama team believed the fact that some Tory MPs were listed in the much smaller 'correspondents' list was significant. The Young Conservatives meanwhile issued a press statement deploring the attacks 'orchestrated by Central Office' against Panorama and endorsing the accuracy of the programme.

There were three further meetings between the Tory Chief Whip and the BBC's Director General but the two sides were now too far dug in to permit a compromise. On March 16th the Tory Party Chairman issued a press statement claiming that Panorama had used unacceptable methods and had given a grossly distorted picture and was now disgracefully refusing to apologise.

This salvo was followed up by an article in the *Daily Mail* under the heading, 'Lies, Damned lies and Panorama', which gave generous vent to the Tories' anger. The BBC responded with a press statement pointing out that the *Mail*'s charges were identical to those of the Conservative party: 'The Director General has personally examined the detailed evidence for the programme and remains convinced it was well-founded — since the programme is now the subject of legal proceedings it is not possible for the BBC to present its evidence at this time or to rebut in detail the grossly unfair and untrue allegations made against the Panorama team.'

From this point the wheels of the law began to grind in earnest. But libel actions are not only incredibly laborious, they are also painfully expensive as both sides soon found out as they contemplated the scale of what would be involved in a full eight-week court hearing. The leading plaintiffs were Harvey Proctor, Neil Hamilton and Gerald Howarth, because they had been the object of the most direct attack. Proctor soon dropped out and was obliged to pay his own costs. But Hamilton and Howarth, despite facing the possibility of bankruptcy, proved less easy to shake off.

The first attempt at settlement was made six months after the programme was shown. Talks between solicitors that summer revealed Hamilton and Howarth's bottom line. The two MPs wanted damages of £20,000 each plus their costs and an apology. It was too much for the BBC. Neil Hamilton's case against the BBC, which he summarised in a memorandum, was that Panorama had been gulled by a clever Communist plot into launching the attack on him and the other MPs. He had been damned, he said, with guilt by association. 'I claim that the programme, taken as a whole, conveyed the impression that I am a virulent racist, anti-semite, Nazi and fascist who opposes democracy and believes in incitement to violence and racial hatred to achieve political ends.'

Hamilton also denied four specific charges that Panorma had made against him: that on a parliamentary visit to West Berlin in August 1983 he had goose-stepped in front of his hotel, embarrassing his German hosts; that he had delivered fraternal greetings to a conference of the Italian fascist party, MSI; that he was a member of Tory Action; and finally that at university he had called for the abolition of Parliament and the suppression of the lower classes.

Nearly all this 'information' had come, according to Hamilton, from Gerry Gable and *Searchlight*. 'Although both the BBC and the YCs were willing accomplices,' he later wrote, 'Gable was clearly the master-mind.'

Two years on with Hamilton's action finally nearing a court hearing, there was another attempt at settlement in the summer of 1986. Faced by soaring legal costs and the certain prospect of bankruptcy if they lost, Hamilton and Howarth were by now getting very worried. They had already paid out over £40,000 from their own slender reserves and were being told that the full cost of an eight-week trial could be nearly £1 million. A fellow right-wing Tory MP, Edward Leigh, put out peace feelers on their behalf at a BBC reception; they were taken up by the Assistant Director General Alan Protheroe.

Three meetings were held on the neutral ground of the Institute of Directors where Hamilton had once worked as a Parliamentary liaison officer. A basis of settlement eventually emerged. Hamilton and Howarth dropped their demand for separately identified damages but insisted the BBC should pay their full costs, then amounting to about £100,000 and publish a proper apology. 'We were prepared to let the BBC off the hook,' says Hamilton. 'We would have allowed them to save face.' In other words the BBC would have had to apologise but damages would have been wrapped up in the costs. The BBC's Board of Management, however, was not prepared to accept these terms. The idea of paying £100,000 in costs and damages was unpalatable, but the terms of the 'grovelling apology' were too much. In August Hamilton and Howarth suggested a fourth meeting but the BBC's Assistant Director General refused. Protheroe appeared relieved, making his marked personal distaste for Hamilton and Howarth plain when he told the Panorama team: 'I felt I had to take a bath after I had seen them.'

Negotiations now returned to desultory exchanges between the solicitors on either side. About this time the BBC noticed 'a considerable stiffening of Hamilton's backbone', apparently a result of his having secured financial pledges of support totalling more than £100,000 from a number of supporters including Sir James Goldsmith.

At the end of August the Assistant Director General called a meeting in his office with the Panorama team attended by the new head of Current Affairs, Peter Pagnamenta who had succeeded Christopher Capron, and the BBC's lawyers Tony Jennings and Glenn del Medico. Protheroe opened the meeting by saying 'I am glad we made the programme.' He gave a brief account of why he had broken off the peace talks: 'There was no possibility of an agreement remotely acceptable to the BBC.' He then, however, went though the film looking at its most vulnerable points. The Panorama team, Michael Cockerell, James Hogan and Fred Emery left the meeting convinced that the BBC would not fight.

A month later that conviction hardened to near certainty when at a meeting with Charles Gray QC, the leading counsel retained by the Corporation, he told them that there was at best only a 40 per cent chance of winning 'on a good day with a happy Judge.' The position had not been improved by the way several crucial witnesses had changed their stories. One prospective Tory candidate declined to give a statement after earlier telling the BBC's lawyers that he was a first hand eyewitness to the alleged goose-stepping incident involving Neil Hamilton and Gerald Howarth in Berlin.

Another Tory candidate provided the BBC's lawyers with a detailed account of what had happened in Berlin only to recant in the immediate days before the trial claiming that he had not been an eyewitness. Philip Pedley, the former YC Chairman, had earlier written to the Party Chairman John Selwyn Gummer to complain that witnesses to the Berlin incidents were being pressured to change their evidence. John

Gummer replied obliquely on the 29th February, 1984: 'My job is single-mindedly to protect the interests of the Party. I am not in the business of attacking those who present truthful reports. I am in the business of ensuring truth will out.'

When the pessimistic view of the BBC's counsel was relayed to the BBC's Board of Governors at their meeting at the end of September, the information came as a unpleasant shock. The death of the Chairman Stuart Young, a supporter of the programme, had left a vacuum only partially filled by the Deputy Chairman Joel Barnett. The atmosphere was the worse because Alasdair Milne had failed to keep the other Governors fully informed of the progress of the action and the risks involved.

The feeling at the meeting was summed up by the hostile attitude of one of the Governors, Malcolm McAlpine, a member of the prominent construction family and cousin of the Conservative Party Treasurer Alastair McAlpine. 'Why,' he asked, 'is the BBC fighting these cases?' The question needed an immediate response but the Corporation, faced by a hostile government, with its licence fee under threat and a spate of media attacks, was in no mood to answer it.

Relationships between Milne and the Governors had become sour and suspicious. The Governors no longer trusted the Board of Management and the BBC's senior managers were crippled by this lack of confidence. Joel Barnett, in particular, was angry that he hadn't been kept properly informed. He thought there was no point in prolonging the agony of a case, the outcome of which was now said to be highly uncertain. Perhaps not without significance, Neil Hamilton had contacted McAlpine — one of a number of industrialists he had approached in an effort to secure financial backing for his case — not knowing, he says, that he was a member of the BBC's Board of Governors. He had had a reply from McAlpine saying he obviously couldn't respond to a request for financial support but he would see that the matter was fully discussed by the BBC's Governors.

A week before the case was due to start at the beginning of October, the BBC therefore made a further attempt to settle. Charles Gray proposed to Hamilton's counsel, Richard Hartley QC, that the BBC would pay £20,000 damages, full costs, and also apologise in handsome terms. But at this point Neil Hamilton dug in his heels; he was not prepared to settle unless the BBC also agreed to give identical terms to his colleague Gerald Howarth which it was unwilling to do.

Three days later on October 13th, the case of Hamilton v the BBC opened in the High Court. Richard Hartley's opening speech, delivered at near dictation speed for more than five hours, accused the Panorama team of deliberate lies, political bias and smearing innocent politicians by seeking to establish their guilt by association; in short of using methods of which Dr Goebbels would have been proud. This attack was reported in glaring headlines in all the papers. It was decisive in convincing Joel Barnett that the case had to be settled on whatever terms the BBC could get. On Thursday with the case only in its fourth day, the Governors met again with the Acting Chairman determined to pull the plug. The Panorama team were summoned by Protheroe to be told of the decision: 'We are under orders to settle this case as soon as possible.'

The next day, Friday, the lawyers met and the BBC caved in completely. The Panorama journalists, who felt betrayed at not being allowed to put their case to the court, were forced to sign an abject apology having been advised by the Corporation's chief legal adviser that they would have to find up to £500,000 out of their own pockets if they wished to pursue the case on their own. Even if they had had the money it was not a realistic option. Once the BBC had publicly retracted, the defence was fatally undermined. One member of the Panorama team was told that the BBC had decided to let the case run for a week before settling in order to have the chance of cross-examining Hamilton so that it could be judged how he would stand up to having his evidence publicly challenged. This tactic, as another member of the team remarked bitterly, broke the first rule of libel: 'Never let the plaintiff get into the witness box.'

All that remained was a settling of the bills. In addition to damages of £20,000 apiece to Hamilton and Howarth, the BBC paid Hamilton's and Howarth's costs of £240,737 35p which together with its own legal costs brought the BBC's total bill to nearly £400,000. But for Neil Hamilton and Gerald Howarth, who had lived with the shadow of bankruptcy over them for nearly two and half years, it was not quite the end. Philip Pedley, the former Chairman of the Young Conservatives who was also being sued by Hamilton and Howarth for libel, refused to join in the BBC apology and declined to allow the libel action against him to lapse. The result was that Hamilton had to apply to the High Court to discontinue the action and to pay £1,000 of Pedley's costs. 'I didn't like having to do this,' said Hamilton, 'but the only alternative would have been to carry on with the actions which would have immensely disruptive in terms of time. As Pedley had no money, it would also have been a very expensive frolic on our part.'

'Maggie's Militant Tendency' has gone down in BBC folklore as the film that scuppered not only the Director General but also a whole generation of current affairs television. Panorama became a symbol for all the alleged evils of current affairs television that the new Deputy Director General John Birt was brought in to vanquish. That the programme was flawed, particularly in its over-reliance on guilt by association and the failure to label library footage clearly, cannot be disputed. Yet the myth that it was a poorly researched programme that should never have been broadcast is false. It was a serious programme on a serious subject which given tighter editing and closer management control would have been not only legally safe but fair.

The Young Conservative's exposure of the racist right wing fringe of the party, on which the programme was based, was a service to the public and to the Conservative Party. As a direct result Tory Central Office tightened up its vetting procedures for candidates and became much more vigilant about extremist infiltration. Investigative reporting whether on television or in newspapers inevitably carries risks. If there is a lesson to be drawn from one of the most searing episodes in the Corporation's history, it is that bad management rather than bad journalism let the BBC down. The last word should perhaps go to one of the BBC Governors at the time who now looks back with considerable anger at the ham-fisted way the legal surrender was handled: 'It was sheer incompetence,' he says bitterly. 'The whole thing makes me sick.'

12

Who Wants Reform?

I hope to earn a nice tax free sum to pay for Teresa's coming out. I can't lose. It's a question of how much I get.'

Evelyn Waugh

A target for a century and more of 'hatred, ridicule and contempt', the law of libel continues unreformed, a theatre of the absurd rather than a safeguard of reputations. A casino for the rich, it provides not so much justice as expensively staged moments of drama and occasionally farce. Libel, in brief, is a grotesque lottery into which the ordinary man stumbles at his peril.

The problems of a libel action can be stated quite simply. The law is highly technical and the pleadings so complex that even its skilled practitioners often differ on the most basic questions. The costs of the lawyers involved are so high that they make the fees charged by any other profession appear to be a mere bagatelle. The opportunities for obstruction and delay are such that it takes anything from two to five years to bring a libel action to court. When it eventually does reach the court, the damages left to the whim of a jury are so uncertain that the result is often no sounder than a dodgy fruit machine. A libel action has in fact more in common with a roulette wheel than justice. The net result for both plaintiffs and defendants is that such actions are a nightmare with only the lawyers able to sleep soundly.

The basis of the modern law dates from Fox's Libel Act of

1792, amended by various bits of Victoriana tacked on in the last century, the last significant change having been made nearly 40 years ago. Though there have been various attempts at reform since then, Parliament has always taken the view that there are more urgent matters to hand. The history of libel reform has thus been one of endless procrastination. The Porter Committee, which was set up in the 1930s to recommend reform, did not get its limited changes enacted until the 1952 Defamation Act. The Lord Chancellor's Committee on Defamation under Lord Justice Faulks, which published its report in 1975, has been treated no less cavalierly. Only one of its 20 proposals for libel reform has so far been approved by Parliament.

The result is that instead of the law holding a sensible balance between the protection of an individual's character and the essential freedom of the press to report and comment, we have an archaic, complex, highly technical, delay-ridden process. Even that most conservative body of men the judiciary despair of it. More than a generation ago Lord Diplock commented bleakly, 'I venture to recommend once more the law of defamation as a fit topic for the attention of the Law Commission. It has passed beyond redemption by the courts.'

Today anyone who ventures into the Royal Courts of Justice as either a plaintiff or defendant in a libel action has to be rich, a gambler, or pigheaded — probably all three. The complexity of the law, the arcane pleadings and the procedural opportunities for delay are the 20th-century version of Jarndyce v Jarndyce.

One notorious case known as the 'three little piggies' involved a Police Five warning on television about a confidence trickster who specialised in buying animals at auctions and then disappearing without paying. Unfortunately the con man's name was the same as that of an innocent farmer who sued for libel. A straightforward case, but it eventually ended after the expenditure of several hundreds of thousands of pounds before the Law Lords.

'This is an ordinary simple case of libel,' said Lord Diplock. 'It took fifteen days to try; the summing up lasted for a day; the jury returned 13 special verdicts. The notice of appeal sets out seven separate grounds why the appeal should be allowed and ten more why a new trial should be granted, the latter being split up into over 40 sub-grounds. The respondent's notice contained 15 separate grounds. The costs must be enormous. Lawyers should be ashamed they have allowed the law of defamation to have become bogged in such a mass of technicalities that this should be possible.'

Why has it proved impossible to secure reform? The misbehaviour of the tabloid press is clearly one factor. But there are also very considerable vested interests involved. In few branches of the law are the pickings quite as rich as they are in libel. The senior practitioners, the handful of barristers and solicitors who specialise in this highly technical field of the law, are able to command fees which would be regarded as exorbitant in any other profession. An hour's consultation with a Harley Street heart specialist is unlikely to cost more than £100. But an hour's conference with a libel counsel who will want a junior barrister in attendance accompanied by a solicitor, probably a senior partner who in turn will bring along a junior assistant, will set the client back at least £1,000. By the time of the trial — after two or three such aptly named 'cons' together with solicitors' fees of £140 an hour plus a mountain of paperwork and documents — the meter will be ticking up to five-figure sums.

Once the case is on the 'warned list', which indicates that it is almost at the head of the queue of libel actions waiting for trial, the costs really begin to soar. At present it costs anything from £10,000 to £50,000 to secure the services of a senior libel counsel. In addition to this upfront fee the QC, known as 'a silk', will require what is quaintly known as 'refreshers' of £1,000 a day. So in a three-week case — not exceptional for libel — the total fees for the plaintiff's counsel alone could amount to £65,000. And that is only the beginning. A senior counsel will need to be attended in court by a junior barrister whose brief fee will be set at half the silk's fee plus refreshers also at half the silk's rate. The solicitors too will want their share of the action and will probably ask for another £750 a day to cover the attendance of a senior partner and his assistant. Thus the grand total for plaintiff and defence in such a trial can easily reach £250,000.

It is these astronomical fees as well as the highly complex technical procedures that explain why the costs of many libel actions often exceed by a factor of ten the damages awarded. In the June 1986 libel case pitting *The Spectator*'s 'high life' columnist Taki against a fellow Greek socialite, the five-times-married Mrs Rosemary Marcie-Riviere whom he had accused of being 'a merry widow', *The Spectator* had to pay £15,000 in damages but its bill for costs was more than £150,000. A year earlier the BBC paid Dr Sydney Gee, a Harley Street specialist, £75,000 after he had been accused by That's Life of prescribing a dangerous slimming treatment to patients. The settlement was reached only after 87 days in court; the total costs were estimated at more than £1 million.

Even that was not a record. It took the *Daily Mail* six months — 101 days of hearings — and combined costs of more than £1 million to defeat a libel action in 1981 brought by the Moonies after the paper had accused the sect of brainwashing converts and breaking up families. *The Economist* also decided to call a halt after costs of more than £1 million had been racked up in a libel action in the same year brought against it by the Greek newspaper magnate Mr George Bobalas. The weekly magazine had sought to justify its claim that Mr Bobalas' paper *To Ethnos* (*The Nation*) was 'a Soviet mouthpiece', but after 50 witnesses three million words of evidence and 63 days of hearings, the jury deadlocked.

Few, no doubt, will shed tears at wealthy newspapers or television companies being faced by huge legal bills when libel actions go wrong. The consequences for individuals, however, can be horrendous. The case of the actress, Charlotte Cornwell, who was £70,000 out of pocket and had to sell her house because of judicial errors, is, as I described in an earlier chapter, a frightening example of how arbitrary the stakes can be in libel actions. Nor is hers an isolated case. In 1982 Liz Brewer, a leading party-giver and socialite, won £13,000 damages from a fellow high society entrepreneur, night-club greeter Dai Llewellyn, after she had successfully sued him for describing her as 'a plain and simple hustler'. After the trial it was discovered that a woman juror was in the care of the Court of Protection due to her uncertain state of mental health. This led to an appeal and the verdict being set aside. The case was eventually settled out of court leaving Miss Brewer, through no fault of her own, many thousands of pounds the poorer.

The rugby international J.P.R. Williams was likewise faced with ruin when in 1982 a £20,000 award against the *Daily Telegraph* who had accused him of 'shamateurism' was set aside by the Court of Appeal on the grounds that the trial judge had misdirected the jury. As Williams could not afford the costs of a retrial he was forced to settle, and ended up £30,000 poorer. Why plaintiffs or indeed defendants should be forced to pay for judicial errors is an absurdity understood only by lawyers.

Mr Justice Otton told a jury hearing a libel case that the courts were 'open to all, be he or she ne'er so humble nor so high'. That claim, his Lordship must have known, is hogwash as far as the law of libel is concerned. As there is no legal aid for libel, all but the very rich — and that includes anyone with less than £100,000 to spare — are effectively denied the protection of the law. If reputation is thought to be worth safeguarding by the courts, it is hard to see the logic or justice in such a denial. Hardly surprising then that the names that have cropped up most prominently in libel actions over the past few years are billionaires such as Sir James Goldsmith and Robert Maxwell. After Maxwell sued *Private Eye* in 1986, winning £55,000 damages over allegations that he was angling for a peerage by financing Neil Kinnock's trips abroad, he noted: 'Seeking redress for libel is open only to those who can afford it . . . Those who do not have resources of their own or the backing of their employers have to bear and grin any assassination of their character.'

Sir Peter Hall, though hardly poor, claims to be in this latter category. The *Sunday Times* published a front page article in 1986 which attacked him for using his public position as head of the National Theatre to enrich himself. Sir Peter immediately issued a writ for libel but on being advised that the case would probably last several weeks and cost several hundred thousand pounds was obliged to withdraw. As he later commented bitterly: 'A newspaper can apparently say what it likes about the 99 per cent of the population who are not extremely rich with little fear . . . I cannot sue for a statement I consider untrue and defamatory because I dare not risk losing half a million pounds, which would be disastrous to my family and myself.'

You have, in fact, to be not just very rich but also supremely self-confident to pursue a libel case to the bitter end. The stakes are enormous for the loser has to pay not only his own costs but also those of the other side. As the cheapest three-day libel case with minimal costs is likely to cost at least £50,000, with the average case costing £100,000 and the odd exception costing more than £1 million, the risks are out of all proportion to the remedy sought.

These astronomical costs explain why the vast majority of actions — over 95 per cent — are settled out of court. The risk of losing forces the warring parties into a settlement. The pressure is all the greater because of a tactical option open to the defence of paying into court anything from a ha'penny upwards. This ploy is designed to put the plaintiff on an even dicier spin of a roulette wheel. He can choose to accept the amount offered, which will bring the action to an end with most of the costs being met by the defendants. But if the sum paid into court is rejected as inadequate the risks are vastly increased. Unless the jury awards the plaintiff more than the payment into court, he will be responsible for all the costs from the time the payment into court was made.

The risk of rejecting a payment into court is shown by the case brought by a political aide to the Prime Minister, Derek Howe, who was awarded £2,500 against the *Sunday Times* and £500 against *Time Out* in November 1985 over allegations that he had tried to obstruct an inquiry into a housing association. As the damages against *Time Out* were less than the money paid into court, he ended up nearly £50,000 out of pocket.

The boot is occasionally on the other foot. In the famous case a generation ago of Lieutenant Colonel John Elliott Brooks, who had a taste for smacking the bottoms of young girls, the *Sunday People* was burdened with the costs of the trial after the former Mayor of Kensington and Chelsea was awarded a ha'penny damages by the jury. If the newspaper had paid even a penny into court, it would have had not only a moral but also a financial victory.

The enormous pressures to settle are argued by some lawyers as being in the interest of society as a whole but it leads to a very rough form of justice in which the richer of the parties has all the high cards irrespective of the merits or otherwise of their case.

The other weapon in the hands of a wealthy defendant facing a libel writ is delay. Newspapers, in particular, spin out libel actions for as long as they can in the hope that the plaintiff will either run out of funds or get fed up. The *Daily Express* legal adviser Justin Walford commented, 'If newspapers were honest I suspect they would admit to drawing actions out in the hope that a plaintiff runs up large legal bills, loses heart and settles.' Even without such tactics, it usually takes two years to get an action into court. Until very recently the length of the queue of actions awaiting a jury trial meant that there was at least a year's wait from the moment an action was set down with all the formalities completed until the court hearing.

The Lord Chancellor has sought to deal with these delays by appointing a judge to oversee the lists. A libel case needs to be heard speedily. Not only do witnesses have difficulty in recalling the facts but the injury that gave rise to the action will go unchecked until a trial takes place. But the traditions of the law are hard to change. Characteristically a former Chancery Master R.E. Ball has even argued that delay may be beneficial: 'It is one of the judicial arts to manipulate time in the interests of an eventual accord.'

If huge costs and inordinate delay are a certainty, most other aspects of a libel action, particularly damages, are totally unpredictable. In a criminal trial it would be unthinkable to permit a jury to have the power of sentencing. That is left to the judge and even judges have to follow guidelines which if flouted will result in the sentence being reversed on appeal. Why then in a libel action is a jury given the much more difficult task of assessing the precise amount to compensate a plaintiff for the damage to his reputation?

In a libel trial damages are decided by the jury 'at large' without any guidance whatsoever from the judge or counsel. Nor does the jury have any basis on which to assess damage, because in a libel action the hurt to a plaintiff's reputation or career is assumed without having to be proved. The Court of Appeal, moreover, can only alter a jury's award if both sides of the action agree. Otherwise its power is limited to ordering a retrial, but because of the costs and delay involved in a new trial it will normally not intervene unless it concludes that the size of the jury's award was wholly irrational.

This flawed system is producing increasingly perverse results. An early example came in the Telly Savalas case against the

Daily Mail a decade ago. The American television star of Kojak was awarded £34,000 in June 1976 by a High Court jury over an article in the *Daily Mail* which suggested that during filming in Berlin his nightly carousings left him red-eyed and unable to remember his lines. The article, while no doubt hurtful, did no damage to the actor's career. Indeed Kojak was more popular than ever by the time his libel action was heard which led *The Times* to comment that the damages were 'offensively high'.

This provoked the foreman of the jury into writing to *The Times* with this revealing admission: 'It is no betrayal of the secrets of the jury room to confess that, with the other jurors, I entered the Royal Courts of Justice with not the remotest idea what compensation is paid for anything except perhaps a dented boot and wing; haloes are outside our normal terms of reference. Apparently that is why we were asked. If that is so, the court had the outcome it deserved from the appointed procedure.' The jury foreman claimed that he and his colleagues had done their best in difficult circumstances but noted that in future 'their Lordships would do just as well to use an electronic random number indicating machine'.

If the Savalas jury had been told that in the previous six months the High Court had awarded only £25,000 to a 17-year-old boy who had fractured his spine and been crippled for life during a fight at school and £12,000 to a girl whose leg had had to be amputated after she was struck by a bus, they might have had a better idea of what sum to award. But under the present law a jury is not entitled to be given such information; crazier still, a jury is expressly forbidden to be guided on damages by either judge or counsel. Court ushers tell of occasionally finding notes where the members of a jury have despaired, scrawled individual random figures on a piece of paper and then let the foreman divide the result by twelve. Unfortunately because of the Contempt of Court Act 1981, jurors can no longer be asked the basis on which they reached their verdict let alone their assessment of damages. But what appears to influence them are headline reports of previous verdicts and a growing eagerness to punish the excesses of tabloid newspapers.

It is this system which has gained London its reputation as the libel capital of the world. Nowhere are the damages riper and the law more accommodating to plaintiffs whose reputation may or may not have been traduced. Foreigners who have enjoyed the patronage of the High Court range from the pilot of General Sikorski's plane (£50,000) and President Obote of Uganda (£40,000), to the former Labour Minister of Pakistan (£25,000).

Until recently the record for multiple libel actions was held by Princess Elizabeth Bagaya of Toro. She reaped more than £50,000 from the *Daily Express*, the *Daily Mirror*, the *Daily Mail*, *The Sun* and the *Sunday Telegraph* in the 1970s over allegations of unseemly conduct at Orly Airport related by the unreliable President Amin.

Nor is it just British publications which are at risk. A record £450,000 was awarded by a High Court jury in June 1987 to a retired British naval commander Martin Packard against a Greek newspaper *Eleftherotypia*. The libel was a serious one in that Mr Packard, now a businessman living in Malta, had been accused of leaking information to the Greek Colonels and of being involved in drug smuggling. However, as *Eleftherotypia*'s circulation in Britain amounted to only a handful of copies, and the words complained of were all in Greek, the award was hardly proportional to any damage to Mr Packard's reputation in this country.

Neither the publisher nor the editor contested the cases leaving *Eleftherotypia*'s London correspondent, Yannis Andrikopoulos to fight the action on his own. Mr Packard vindicated his honour but it seems unlikely he will ever be able to recover his costs let alone collect the record sum given to him by the jury. Whether such a case should have ever been heard in Britain is doubtful. The notion that a businessman living in Malta should be able to sue a Greek newspaper for libel in the High Court in London over a publication in a foreign language which has a circulation of less than 50 copies in Britain is to say the least curious. Where Mr Packard's reputation was damaged was in Greece and it is there that he should have taken action – at least in the first instance.

While juries have always tended to be more generous than judges, it is only in the last few years that libel damages have soared into the stratosphere. The award of £100,000 to the footballer Billy Bremner who had been accused by the *Sunday People* of offering bribes to players to fix football matches was regarded in 1982 as a huge sum. But recently another quantum leap in jury largesse has taken place. Whatever the law might say, juries have now apparently decided that their task is not so much to compensate plaintiffs for damage to their reputations as to punish Fleet Street for its excesses. As Tom Wolfe put it in his novel *The Bonfire of the Vanities*, 'In a civil case a Bronx jury is simply a vehicle for redistributing wealth.'

The record £450,000 awarded to Commander Packard against *Eleftherotypia* in June 1987 did not stand for long. A month afterwards a High Court jury topped his award with £500,000 for Jeffrey Archer against the *Daily Star*. Four months later a former Royal Navy lieutenant Narendra Sethia was given £260,000* over allegations that he had stolen a log from *HMS Conqueror*, the nuclear-powered submarine which sank the Argentine cruiser *Belgrano* during the Falklands War. Though Mr Sethia was not named by the *Mail on Sunday*, it was said on his behalf that his friends and colleagues would have understood that the reference to a former naval officer of the *Conqueror* now living in the West Indies pointed to him.

*The Sethia verdict was appealed against and finally settled out of court on undisclosed but lucrative terms. The former Lieutenant went on to collect large settlements from a number of other Fleet Street papers.

The year 1988 opened with a bang in the libel courts. In March a small trade paper, *Stationery Trade News*, was ordered to pay £300,000 (later reduced on appeal) to an envelope distributor it had falsely accused of various swindles. The distributor had been willing to settle for an apology, his costs, and nominal damages of £2,000 but in a fit of misplaced pride the deal was turned down. Four months later a Mayfair firm of solicitors was awarded £310,000 against an Arabic language magazine. In November, the actress Koo Stark won £300,000 over two articles in the *Sunday People* which alleged that she had continued to date Prince Andrew even after her marriage. She then proceeded to pick up a further £400,000 from *The Sun*, *The Mirror* and the *News of the World* for related libels, displacing Princess Elizabeth of Toro as the most successful multiple libel claimant to date.

Nor was it just the famous who collected. The same month the highest ever award against a radio station, £350,000, was made to a Liverpool businessman's wife whose caravan business had been described as 'a swindle' by Liverpool's commercial radio station Radio City. Fiction proved even more expensive for *The Sun* who settled at a record figure of £1 million on the steps of the court with Elton John in December after printing a story alleging that the singer had had a relationship with a rent boy. Then there was the chocolate eclair farrago. Two Northern Ireland barristers were awarded a total of £100,000 damages for a newspaper gossip paragraph which suggested that they had almost come to blows in a cake shop over who should have the right to buy the last eclair. No doubt this libel like all the others was wounding but the amounts of money now being awarded by juries are ludicrously out of proportion to the damage caused.

More than a generation ago, Lord Diplock had this to say in McCarey v Associated Newspapers: 'I do not believe that the law today is more jealous of a man's reputation than of his life and limb. That is the scale of values of the duel . . .

In this court recently we refused by a majority to disturb a verdict of a jury awarding £2,000 to a woman thirty years of age who had, after considerable suffering for many months and two operations in hospital, had a leg amputated below the knee. . . . If £2,000 is not inappropriate compensation for a life-long injury of that character which has its physical effect every day of the plaintiff's future life, and £9,000 is the appropriate award for the injury done to the plaintiff in this case, then I can only say that the scale of values is wrong, and if that is the law, so much the worse for the law. But I do not accept that higher scale of values in defamation cases is sanctioned by the law.'

The most recent guidelines of the Criminal Injuries Compensation Board value rape at £5,000, the loss of an eye at £13,000, and total loss of hearing from assault at £32,000. Given these comparatively modest sums, it is wrong that a fleetingly damaged reputation can be valued in multiples of hundreds of thousands of pounds in the libel courts. It is also offensive that performers who appear for a living on the public stage should be thought to possess reputations which are many times more valuable than those of lesser known members of the public.

One way of restraining the tendency for libel awards to escalate out of control would be to require the plaintiff to prove that his reputation, his career, or his pocket had actually suffered. If proof was unavailable damages could be limited to say £10,000. The notion that a jury should be allowed to award any sum it sees fit in order to punish the defending newspaper is to carry rough justice several steps too far. Moreover the idea that a jury has sufficient knowledge to be able to assess without any guidance whatsoever the appropriate compensation in defamation cases is such an obvious nonsense that it is amazing that it continues to be accepted by the courts. If the Court of Appeal would lay down guidelines for awards, the position could be improved immediately without waiting for Parliamentary action.

The combination of huge awards and costs of libel actions has another damaging and chilling effect. While national newspapers and television companies may be prepared to face the risk of a writ on a story when they believe there is a clear public interest in publication, the same is rarely true of smaller provincial papers or magazines which have to weigh up the danger that they could end up in the bankruptcy court. Truth is a defence to libel but proving the facts in court with witnesses who may be reluctant to appear is often impossible. Thus a small local weekly newspaper will often shy away from an important story, for example one involving pollution by a large manufacturer in its area, because the risks of publication are too great. Nor is this syndrome confined to small papers. The decline of investigative journalism in the British Press as a whole is without doubt linked to the increasing costs and risks of pursuing such stories.

The Observer's libel bill is now more than £1 million a year but that is undoubtedly a good deal less than some of its rivals. Recently the paper had to pay out nearly £50,000 to a bankrupt despite being advised by counsel that it would probably win at trial. The problem was that win or lose, *The Observer* knew that it would never be able to recover its costs. No wonder then that the enthusiasm of newspapers for investigative reporting is strictly limited. With costs and libel damages soaring, the pressure to print only the safe rather than the important is considerable. Paul Foot rightly warned in his column in *UK Press Gazette*: 'These huge damages have the effect inside the newspaper offices of terrifying newspaper lawyers and editors and in the process cutting out of print anything which might appear to be remotely challenging or offensive. This in turn increases the trivia, the crudery and the lies about people who don't sue (like the Royal Family).'

In most Western European countries, a public interest defence is open to newspapers if they can show they published the information in good faith and with reasonable care. The

United States has gone even further. As a result of the landmark *New York Times* versus Sullivan case of 1964, a public figure can win libel damages only if he can prove malice on the part of the journalist or publication. The contrast between what can be published without fear or favour on the two sides of the Atlantic is too sharp for comfort. Whereas in Washington, a crooked politician will know that he stands a high risk of being exposed, in London the use of gagging writs and the prospect of huge libel damages prevents many public interest stories from being pursued let alone published.

If Watergate had happened in Britain, it would almost certainly not have been possible to publish the sort of piecemeal exposure by which the truth was finally teased out. The present libel law undoubtedly serves to deter serious investigative journalism but it can hardly be claimed to have done anything to improve the standards of the British Press. Rather the legal restraints have driven many tabloids into a quest for sexually titillating but libel-proof scandals which cause a good deal of unnecessary grief to private individuals but which are unredeemed by any public interest. Punitive awards by juries may make the public feel good but there is no sign that they make much difference to tabloid newspapers, some of whom appear to regard libel awards as part of their publicity budget. When *The Sun* settled its libel action against Elton John, it announced the £1 million peace formula, 'Sorry Elton,' in front-page banner headlines which led the judge to protest that the court had been used in a sordid newspaper publicity campaign.

Overall it is hard to disagree with the conclusion reached by David Pannick, a barrister and fellow of All Souls, that the present law of libel has ceased to serve any useful purpose: 'The whole nonsense,' he says, 'should be swept away — from grovelling apologies which nobody takes seriously to jury awards of damages which are based on no principle whatsoever.' If the libel law is in desperate need of root and branch reform, what can be done? A proposal advanced more than a generation ago by a joint working party of Justice and the International Press Institute recommended the Court of Appeal should be given the power to vary damages awarded by a jury. That minimal but sensible change could be implemented immediately.

A more comprehensive reform advocated by the Faulks Committee a decade ago has, however, found little support. It recommended that most libel cases should be heard by a judge sitting alone, and that a jury trial should be allowed only where it was held to be in the interests of justice. Where the trial was by jury, the Faulks Committee said its power should be limited to stating whether the damages were to be substantial, moderate, nominal or contemptuous, leaving the judge to fix the actual amount.

This carefully drafted compromise failed to find favour and the debate has now moved on. Perhaps the most promising approach to reform is a proposal advanced by a High Court Judge Mr Justice Leonard Hoffman for a 'fast-track' procedure under which a plaintiff who is libelled would be able to secure a rapid apology in court if he was willing to confine his claim to damages of less than £5,000. The proceedings would be short, decided on affidavit evidence by the judge without a jury and the costs would thus be much reduced though paid, as now, by the losing party.

Similarly the defendant might also request a summary hearing which would normally be granted unless the Court decided that a published apology and payment of £5,000 or less would be an inadequate remedy. The advantages of such a simplification are many says Judge Hoffman: 'What most plaintiffs want is the immediate publication of a correction with or without some modest compensation. What they get is three or four years of anxious and obsessional waiting, followed by a trial which, even if it ends in success, may reopen injuries everyone else had forgotten and stamp them indelibly on the public mind.'

David Mackie, senior litigation partner at Allen and Overy, is strongly in favour of such a simplification: 'The summary procedure will fill what to someone with a wider practice seems the strange void in libel cases between the issue of the writ and the trial. This leads to settlements taking place either shortly after the row starts or only when trial is imminent . . . Pleadings in libel cases tell the parties very little because the informative ones (e.g. particulars of justification in support of such a defence) customarily arrive only by amendment as late as possible. The "holding" defence has a sacred place in libel actions.'

The summary procedure, he notes, also remedies the present destructive balance of advantage in libel cases. 'At the start the defendant holds all the cards because nothing nasty is going to happen to him for eighteen months or so and he will take a tough line knowing that a plaintiff may desperately want a swift correction. The plaintiff is in a poor position knowing that if he does not take whatever is offered at that stage he must risk a lot of time, money and worry and will lose the chance of a swift retraction. There is then a long dormant period and the case re-emerges, this time with the balance reversed. The newspaper defendant knows that the jury will reward the plaintiff for his persistence and the real issue is going to be "how much?". At the end of the case therefore the balance is unfair and so the system works against the encouragement of a just solution.'

The former Chairman of the Bar Council, Robert Alexander QC (now Lord Alexander of Weedon) is another supporter of reform: 'We should find a way of preventing powerful media interests from obstructing a plaintiff from clearing his name by digging in for a long, expensive and gladiatorially conducted defence. . . . To put people of moderate means to the choice of going through the mill of our present system or living with the harm done by a libel is less fair than giving them some opportunity of seeking a reasonably inexpensive remedy.'

The company solicitor of Times Newspapers, Alistair Brett has proposed that an arbitration system should be set up under which libel cases would be determined by a panel of three arbitrators. Damages would be limited to £20,000 except on proof of special damage such as loss of a contract, when the maximum amount would be £50,000. The arbitrator's fees would be underwritten by the defendant newspaper but it would be open to the arbitrators to make the plaintiff pay the costs if the defence was successful. He believes that such a reform would make the libel laws 'infinitely more accessible to those of modest means. The answer to the defamation conundrum is not to waste more public money through legal aid funding of this archaic and enormously expensive gladiatorial ritual but rather to introduce a swift, inexpensive and informal arbitration system to enable plaintiffs to obtain speedy redress without crippling legal costs.'

Mr Geoffrey Bindman, a leading libel solicitor, has suggested going even further. He believes that Section 4 of the Defamation Act of 1952, which provides an escape route for defendants who are prepared to apologise immediately for an 'innocent' libel should be extended to cover all libels, innocent or not. 'The incentive to a defendant to correct a false statement without delay should be as strong as possible,' he argues. 'Libel law has become far too profitable for plaintiffs and some lawyers, and the procedures are far too expensive.' Mr Bindman has proposed a four stage plan of reform: jury trials for defamation should be abolished, the County Court should have jurisdiction over libel cases, legal aid should be available, and a judge should have the power to order the publication of a correction and an apology.

If almost everyone concerned with the law of libel is agreed that reform is long overdue, why is nothing done? The answer is that there are powerful forces, not least in Parliament, which see huge awards for damages in the High Court as the only way of restraining a prurient and licentious press. Many MPs would be sorry to see the opportunity for an occasional but useful tax-free bonus to their incomes taken from their grasp. So long as the media wallow in a slough of unpopularity, libel reform is not going to be high on the list of any politician's priorities. The new Lord Chancellor, Lord Mackay has made it clear that he sees far more important tasks to hand in reforming the structure of the legal profession. In an attempt to force his hand, Times Newspapers have appealed to the European Court claiming that the present libel laws are a restraint on freedom of expression.

The Government has now accepted as part of an overall inquiry into the press and privacy that the law of libel should be reviewed. But there is not much support in Parliament for any reform in this area while the excesses of the tabloids continue. Backbench MPs have signalled their views by the promotion of Privacy and Right of Reply bills which, despite failing on the first legislative attempt, will undoubtedly return to haunt the media. The former Liberal Leader David Steel, who collected substantial damages in 1988 from *The Sun* and the *News of the World*, speaks for many MPs when he says he considers the conduct of the press so gross that he will not support changes in the law of libel until it is buttressed by a statutory Press Commission with draconian powers to suspend publication of an offending newspaper.

The scene is thus set for many more years of wrangling and many more libel millionaires. But who really benefits? Neither the public nor the press. Neither plaintiffs nor defendants. Ogden Nash got it right: 'Professional people have no cares. Whatever happens they get theirs.'

BIBLIOGRAPHY

Black and Gold. Anthony Sampson. Hodder and Stoughton, 1987.

Their Good Names. H. Montgomery Hyde. Hamish Hamilton, 1970.

Defamation (2nd Edition). Duncan and Neil. Butterworths, 1983.

Tycoon. The Life of Sir James Goldsmith. Geoffrey Wansell. Grafton Books, 1986

The Private Eye Story. Patrick Marnham. André Deutsch, 1982.

Malice in Wonderland. Robert Maxwell v Private Eye. Macdonald, 1986.

Archer The Making of a Tory Chief. Paul Foot. Article in the *Daily Mirror*, October 30th, 1986.

Goldenballs by Richard Ingrams. André Deutsch, 1979.

Web of Corruption. Ray Fitzwalter and David Taylor. Granada, 1981.

Libel and Slander. P. F. Carter-Ruck. Faber and Faber, 1972.

Wicked, Wicked Libels. Michael Rubinstein. Routledge and Keegan Paul, 1972.

A Law unto Myself. Sir Neville Faulks. William Kimber, 1978.

Public Scandal Odium and Contempt. David Hooper. Secker and Warburg, 1984.

Corruption and Misconduct in Contemporary British Politics. Alan Doig. Penguin, 1984.

In-For-A-Penny. The Unauthorised Biography of Jeffrey Archer. Jonathan Mantle. Hamish Hamilton, 1988.

Touched By Angels. Derek Jameson. Ebury Press, 1988.

The Libel Case of the Century. Dr A. Adoko. London Truth Publishers, 1989.

People Against the Press. Geoffrey Robertson. Quartet Books, 1983.

Law and the Media. Tom G. Crone. Heineman, 1989.

INDEX

233